A Particular Place

A Particular Place

Urban Restructuring and Religious Ecology in a Southern Exurb

NANCY L. EIESLAND

RUTGERS UNIVERSITY PRESS
New Brunswick, New Jersey, and London

Figure 1.1 Map of Atlanta Metropolitan Area, used by permission of the Atlanta Regional Council, 1999.
Gwinnett Daily Post, "Just one more . . . thing we don't need," published January 29, 1994, in the *Gwinnett Post Tribune*, used by permission.

Library of Congress Cataloging-in-Publication Data

Eiesland, Nancy L., 1964–
A particular place : urban restructuring and religious ecology in a southern exurb / Nancy L. Eiesland.
p. cm.
Includes bibliographical references and index.
ISBN 0-8135-2737-6 (alk. paper). — ISBN 0-8135-2738-4 (pbk. : alk. paper)
1. Dacula (Ga.)—Religious life and customs. 2. Ethnology—Georgia—Dacula. 3. Ethnology—Religious aspects. I. Title.
BL2527.G4E35 2000
306.6′09758′223—dc21 99-15069
CIP

British Cataloging-in-Publication data for this book is available from the British Library

Manufactured in the United States of America

For Terry,
who believed in me and this book

Contents

Tables and Figures

Tables

Figures

Preface

*I write because I am a reader. I want to give others what
writers have given me, a chance to hear the voices of
people I will never meet.*

       —Pat Mora, *Nepantla*

For those who believe that ethnography is a process of both data gathering and theory building, reading is nearly as important as fieldwork. In reading the work of other ethnographers, theorists, historians, and poets, we recognize the complicated tales people tell about their lives and the many social factors that shape their accounts. This recognition, in turn, prompts us to be circumspect in our telling of tales and cautious in articulating theories—aware always that we relate an unfinished story. I am indebted both personally and professionally to the many scholars who have engaged in the disciplined study of religious people and groups and the artful construction narratives.

In this book, I tell a tale of the dramatic changes that have been occurring in Dacula, Georgia—a particular place with a particular history. I argue that the changes in this exurb provide a way of thinking about two important types of restructuring that have been mutually implicated but seldom addressed together: urban restructuring and religious restructuring. In an exurb where the social order of a small town has been disrupted by population inflow, service sector development, and housing expansion, the careful observer can witness how congregations alter themselves, their relations with one another, and—over time—their community. These alterations in the religious ecology (that is, the patterns of relations, status, and interaction among religious organizations within a locality) and their effects on the place are certainly not the only aspects of the change in Dacula. But these changes were important to the local community and reveal some challenges that scholars of religion should explore as we give our accounts of American religious life.

I recognize that my account is that of a disciplined social researcher who sometimes felt as close as kin and at other times as distant as a stranger among the people about whom I write. It is my sincerest hope that the people of Dacula, who have shared their stories with me through the years, will find in this tale, if not all the richness of their own narratives, at least a tangible familiarity, and the humility of one who realizes that the story continues to unfold. They have my deepest appreciation and love for their generosity of spirit and time.

I began my fieldwork in exurbia as a research fellow for Nancy Ammerman's Congregations in Changing Communities Project—which resulted in her book *Congregation and Community* (1997a). The Congregations in Changing Communities Project was funded by the Lilly Endowment through the Institute for the Study of Economic Culture, Boston University. Nancy's flexibility in allowing me to find a research site that served our mutual interests was but one instance of her collaborative research style.

As my dissertation director, Nancy exemplified the foremost qualities of a teacher and mentor: generosity, curiosity, and astuteness. The process of researching and writing sometimes overwhelmed me. I recall one afternoon, in particular, when I had signed up for Nancy's office hours. Nancy began our time together by asking me how she could help. The next moments were clouded by tears, as I related how tired I was of spending nearly every evening in the field, how I wasn't sure I was finding anything interesting in hours of committee meetings, and how most of all I was tired. Nancy passed the Kleenex and listened as I spewed out the complaints of a privileged life. Nancy neither clucked nor cajoled; she listened well and thoroughly and helped me renew my energy for the project. For how she offered me her support and clear thinking, I am deeply grateful.

Other members of my dissertation committee have also contributed significantly to the project and to my ongoing work. They are Steven Tipton, Frank Lechner, Cathryn Johnson, and Pamela Couture.

Steve Tipton has continued to give me sage advice regarding my work as a colleague at Candler School of Theology. I have appreciated his encouragement during the revisions of this book.

R. Stephen Warner has been vital to the transformation of the dissertation into a book. As a reviewer of the manuscript for publication, he gave both detailed and conceptual comments that significantly improved the work. As I was nearing the final draft in fall 1998, I was consulting with Steve at his kitchen table when a sudden Chicago storm blew in. The power went out, but Steve asked if I could still see and wanted to continue our work. I could and we did. Discerning and tenacious, Steve has proven to be both friend and teacher.

Ethnography is time-consuming, and groups that provide funding for the efforts of transcribing interviews, managing data, and generally working in the field are deeply appreciated. I express my deepest gratitude to the Louisville Institute from whom I received a dissertation fellowship. Other funding was provided by the Mellon Southern Studies Fellowship of Emory University, the Fichter Research Fund of the Association for the Sociology of Religion, and the Society for the Scientific Study of Religion.

Emory University, where I began my research as a graduate student and where I have completed the book as a member of the faculty, has generously supported this work in tangible and intangible ways. Colleagues have offered comments on drafts and have provided encouragement as I made revisions. Thomas Frank, in particular, often renewed my energies with words of good will as I worked on revision amidst teaching.

My editors at Rutgers have been both patient and stimulating as the book took somewhat longer than I expected to complete. Martha Heller and David Myers have offered insight and shown thoughtfulness that have been deeply appreciated.

I once assumed (perhaps during the early days of graduate school) that when people spoke about "a community of scholars" they meant a club that required the equivalent of secret handshakes and code words to enter. While some would argue that this is indeed the case, I have discovered that the community of scholars is a much more accessible group; for me this community is shaped by many women and men whose support has been crucial to the completion of this work. They include Penny Edgell Becker, Emily Brooker Langston, Arthur Farnsley, Shoshanah Feher, Gary Laderman, Michael McMullen, Barbara Patterson, Scott Thumma, and Sr. Mary Ann Zimmer. Shoshanah Feher read the entire manuscript and gave vital encouragement and support in the last stages. Other, more senior colleagues made the academic world a more inviting place through their gifts of time and assistance. Elizabeth Bounds, Lynn Davidman, Mary Jo Neitz, Nancy Nason-Clark, Helen Rose Ebaugh, William McKinney, Gail O'Day, Carol Newsom, and Barbara Wheeler provided both practical and professional assistance to me throughout this project.

The students with whom I have had the privilege of working during the last years have also taught me much; and I am deeply grateful for the occasions when we have explored together things that matter. In particular, I am grateful for the community of scholars that formed in a graduate seminar on qualitative methods, who generated such energy—both theoretical and practical—that they helped me return to my work with deeper appreciation for the practices of discovery and narrating. In addition, I would like to mention Derek Olsen, who worked for several years as my research assistant, uncomplainingly copying articles, checking bibliographic sources, and doing countless other scintillating tasks that have supported my research and teaching.

At one point during the fieldwork, a stalwart of one congregation at which I was a regular attender began asking persistently where my "better half" was. My husband Terry had accompanied me to several important events in the congregation's life. His charm put people at ease and allowed them to know more about my life than I sometimes was willing to divulge. All along the way, Terry was ready to assist in ways that improved both the research and writing. It is for these and countless other reasons that I dedicate this book to him.

While many have given me good directions along the way, I am alone responsible for the roads I have taken as I have written this book.

A Particular Place

Chapter 1

Changing Places

Ah, the places these interstates can take you.
—Andrei Codrescu, "Road Scholar"

Urban and Religious Restructuring

"You know," Alfred DeVries said with a jab to my ribs, "I've already got my Ph.D."[1] From previous conversation, I knew that the elderly Georgian farmer with his elbow in my midsection had earned his highest degree from Dacula High School.[2] But I was game. "Really, Alfred, what in?" "Posthole diggin'," he said with an air of satisfaction. Every time Alfred played that gag on me during my several years doing research in his hometown and congregation, Hinton Memorial United Methodist Church, he displayed the same tickled demeanor of a man who knew his place and wanted others to know theirs as well.

Finding your place is no small feat, and perhaps particularly not in the midst of rapid social and religious change. This book is an account of the efforts of particular people to make their places in an exurban locale. Through its particularity, it also raises theoretical issues about the nature of the changes occurring in American religious life. In Dacula (pronounced Dah-cue-la), Georgia, homefolks who once seemed to know their places—in church, in the schools, and in the business district—increasingly found themselves at odds with their familiar territory. Life-long Methodists were affronted by regularly being "hebroned"—the term they gave to door-to-door evangelistic campaigns done by the local megachurch, Hebron Baptist. Taken-for-granted habits of accommodation were disrupted when in the span of a decade, the small town that Alfred described as "a neat-as-you-like little community"—with a few stores by the railroad and folks with Sunday-school manners—became host to a throng of new neighbors lured by comparatively cheap housing prices and the town's bucolic appearance.

The newcomers who sought their place at the edges of the Atlanta metro area often differed considerably from Dacula's earlier generations of residents. Many were suburban-born and bred, now seeking homes in a more distant exurb—a place apart where they could provide their children with what they imagined would be a better way of life. "It's peaceful—some folks would call it blue collar—I guess. I'm not opposed to that. Because it's meant that people are still interested in staying put," said Bethany Alley, who had lived in Dacula for three years and attended Hog Mountain Baptist Church at the time of our conversation in 1994. Like many newcomers to the area, Bethany wanted her children to have access to cultural practices and symbols that communicated stability and safety. Yet she also sought opportunities for them that were traditionally not available in small-town Georgia—like computer camp and soccer teams. In Dacula, newcomers, like Bethany, found a town with sidewalks for riding bikes, teachers who have been around for generations, and Little League games every night of the week. For them, Dacula's attractions were its community feel, its sense of tradition and place, and its proximity to the resources, culture, and opportunities of metropolitan Atlanta. For local residents—new and old—the meaning of community and the uses of tradition became sources of contention, confusion, and, sometimes, deep sociability as oldtimers and newcomers sought out their places in this transforming small town.

Dacula's changing organizational, demographic, and cultural life attracted my interest, in part, because the alterations that were happening here reflected changes happening across the United States as urban regions reached into farmland and small towns. Dacula had no stately downtown that historic preservationists battled to safeguard. Nor did it have the trendy addresses that would draw the country club set. Rather Dacula was a small town that assumed continuity in its communal life, and thus, like many small towns across the nation, it was caught unawares by the fast pace of exurban growth. Whether named "sprawl" or urban deconcentration, development around most city centers has expanded outward, subsuming small towns and altering the lives of residents—new and old.

Additionally, Dacula drew my interest because, like so many small towns, long-time residents perceived that it once, not long ago, had a relatively stable religious establishment. In the South, that establishment was likely to be composed of groups, such as the Methodists and Baptists. In other regions of the United States, the mix of religious groups differed. However, in the past quarter-century the institutional and demographic changes that have curbed the dominance of mainline denominations and promoted the rise of new religious movements and groups has resulted in new notions about religious establishment and status. These new and old religious organizations were finding their way in this exurban reality, and I wanted to see how they were doing.

Dacula's location at the intersection of urban restructuring and religious restructuring made this particular place an especially worthy recipient of sociological attention. By treating these expansive changes from the point of view of distinct social and geographical sites, we see the real contests in contested meanings, the pragmatic ways of relating among religious organizations down the road from one another, and the new forms of behavior that accompany interstates and office parks. This ground-level perspective on urban restructuring can best be gained by examining an exurb where the paint was still drying on the family room walls of homes in new high-density subdivisions, sometimes built less than a stone's throw away from traditional Native American burial grounds. In order to assess the day-to-day societal impact of religious restructuring, we must look at the congregations and other religious groups embedded in their local environments. While the changes of urban and religious restructuring have been happening all around us, Dacula was a particularly good place to observe them at close range.[3]

In 1995, Dacula's population was little more than 3,000. In Gwinnett County as across the United States, exurban settlement has not primarily concentrated in incorporated areas. In 1995, only one in five residents of Gwinnett County lived within the city limits of one of the county's fourteen incorporated municipalities. The growth both expanded and stretched the resources of the county. Gwinnett's population exploded from 72,000 in 1970 to 350,000 in 1990, with a projected population of 541,000 by 2000 (U.S. Bureau of Census 1970 & 1990; *Gwinnett 2000 Land Use Plan* 1992). In the 1980s, the county's population increased more than 100 percent, growing by an average of

Figure 1.1 Map of Atlanta Metropolitan Area

nearly 19,000 people per year. Gwinnett's population increased by an average of 10,167 people per year after 1990. In Dacula, Gwinnett County, and the metro Atlanta area, urban restructuring is well underway.

Restructuring American Cities

The social drama occurring in Dacula in Gwinnett County is repeated across the country and the world as metropolitan areas expand into out-lying regions pulling in more and more small towns in their wakes.[4] Along transportation corridors surrounding cities across the United States, a transformation of social and spatial order has been underway since the nineteenth century. But within the past twenty years, the development of shopping malls, office towers, and sit-down restaurants have expanded metropolitan areas far beyond central business districts and traditional suburbia. The metropolitan fringe now constitutes a broad patchwork of inner suburbs, large suburban edge cities, office parks, retail centers, "captured" small towns, and even low-density rural territory (Teaford 1997). Teaford (1993) writes: "In the 1980s and 1990s a whole new pattern of metropolitan settlement was becoming apparent. It might be called post-urban or post-suburban pattern. In many areas, no longer was there a dominant central city and economically subordinate and dependent communities worthy of the name suburbs. So-called central cities were no longer central to lives of metropolitan residents, and so-called suburbs did not merit the prefix *sub*" (161).

This build-up did not result from any centralized plan—much to the chagrin of city planners. The multicentered metropolis, however, relies on the planned infrastructure established by federally funded interstate highways and federally insured mortgages. Edge cities and exurbs are also the result of numerous cultural, economic, and global factors that have facilitated deconcentrated metropolitan growth. According to Fishman (1987), following World War II, physical development of urban locales was characterized by the "simultaneous decentralization of housing, industry, specialized services, and office jobs" and the emerging interdependence of these deconcentrated areas that possessed "all the economic and technological dynamism of the city" (184). Increasingly former suburbs became centers for information processing, manufacturing, and transportation industries (cf. Tittle and Stafford 1992). Businesses were drawn to the less crowded metropolitan periphery where—developers promised—their operations would be free from traffic congestion and would gain access to an underutilized rural population. Whether they were termed "edge cities," "techno-burbs," "outer cities," or "transformed suburbs," these relatively recent formations changed the patterns of metropolitan life as well as of small towns and rural areas now within the metropolitan orbit.[5]

Small towns, once perceived by long-time residents to be distant physically and culturally from the city, are frequently becoming "exurbs," that is, residential and service centers surrounding edge cities.[6] Formed as development gains momentum, exurbs extend the metropolitan region's housing and economy into previously rural areas and once discrete small towns.[7] Small towns are increasingly seen as historic "subdivisions"—surrounded by massive new high-density housing developments. For rural and small-town residents, this exurban growth is often an ambiguous circumstance. The erosion of agrarian life in the United States has resulted in a generational exodus from rural areas (cf. Abbott 1990; Barlett 1993). As small towns are pulled into metropolises, employment opportunities are created that tend to slow this emigration. Yet with exurbanization come social and cultural tensions as small-town values, traditions, and practices, so coveted by exurban newcomers, are transformed (cf. Fischer 1991). Finally, as these rural areas and small towns are filled, land values and taxes increase, propelling the less affluent young families further and further out (Fishman 1990). The resulting changes in demographics, organizational patterns, and lifestyle in these once small towns signal a broad pattern of urban/rural spatial and social restructuring in the United States (cf. Berger 1971; Berry and Kasarda 1977; Hawley 1981; Lyson 1989).

For places like Gwinnett County where Dacula is located, the reality of urban deconcentration has resulted in the county's and the town's complete incorporation into the Atlanta metropolitan region. Over the last two decades, but most notably since 1985, the landscape of Gwinnett—located in the northeast quadrant of the Atlanta metro area—has changed. Once a relatively quiet county of small towns and pastured areas with town-to-market roads, the county has become a nexus of industry, business, and government activity crisscrossed by busy four- and six-lane thoroughfares. The county has been a mecca for young families, attracted by reasonable housing prices, good schools, and the proximity to Atlanta and the North Georgia Mountains.

Statistical accounts of population inflow and new job creation evidence this growth. Gwinnett County had the distinction during the 1980s of being the fastest growing county in the nation for several successive years.[8] Expected to become the most populous county in the metro Atlanta region by 2001, Gwinnett has been experiencing a steady pattern of development. It had an annual growth rate of 5.8 percent between 1991 and 1996 and is projected to have a growth rate of 7.2 percent annually between 1996 and 2001.[9] Some 75 percent of locals did not live there fifteen years ago.

"Jobs, Jobs, Jobs" has been Gwinnett County's motto for the past two decades. During the 1980s alone, over 100,000 jobs were added, mostly in health and educational services and high-tech manufacturing. The total number of jobs in the county grew at an annual rate of 8.6 percent between 1991 and 1996.[10] In the mid-1990s, the top employer was the Gwinnett County public schools, followed by four high-tech firms. Despite the job growth at big, multinational companies, more than 60 percent of Gwinnett's new jobs in the past decade came from small business generation and expansion. In terms of population and job growth, Gwinnett has caught up to its longstanding rhetoric, dating to the early years of the twentieth century, as one of Georgia's most popular places to live and work.

But the statistics do not really tell the story. Population influx and job growth were not the only causes of change; this change was more than the sum of its parts. Tony Goodwins came up to me after I presented some of my data to his church group at the conclusion of my study. Tony fit my profile of a "newcomer" to a tee. He had moved to the area in the past five years; he commuted to an office park near Interstate 285 which rings metro Atlanta; and his wife worked part-time so that she could have more time with their three-year old son. Tony was distressed, however, with what he thought was my portrayal of newcomers as change agents. "You know even if we hadn't moved to Dacula it was going to change. It was going to happen. We just happen to be here to see it, too."

Newcomers were often sensitive to the claim that their presence brought change that resulted in oldtimers feeling out of place. For the most part, they wanted to fit in and be good neighbors as well. Tony was right. Newcomers were not the only change agents, but their arrival certainly brought significant change in its wake. The complex restructuring occurring as urban deconcentration swept across Gwinnett County did not result from unitary or homogenous processes. Rather it was the result of a complex web of alterations in the social structure and culture, including shifts in the configuration of occupations; new constellations of interests and interest groups; different patterns of income; changed routines of belonging—to name only a few of the transformations involved. Clearly newcomers were arriving with new networks and patterns of interaction as well as their U-Haul trailers and moving boxes, but they moved to this particular place, in part, because they were also attracted to Dacula's way of life. Their coming did bring change, but Dacula had been slowly becoming incorporated into Atlanta before this newest population influx arrived.

As far back as 1958, Vidich and Bensman were identifying the processes by which the small town (and indirectly all segments of American society) are continuously and increasingly drawn into "the central machinery, processes, and dynamics of the total society" (xi). Already in the 1960s when locals began to commute from Dacula to work in inner-tier suburban industrial complexes, Dacula was "captured" by Atlanta's economy. The economic effects of urban deconcentration were restructuring day-to-day life. Later as the first wave of newcomers arrived in the early 1980s—often working in public service jobs, such as the Gwinnett County schools—more alterations in Dacula's economic patterns became apparent. By the time of the rapid influx of newcomers in the late 1980s and 1990s, Dacula was economically far from the insular small town that oldtimers liked to portray. The rapidity of change that accompanied the accelerated demographic inflow, however, caused significant cultural disembedding that sometimes seemed to take both newcomers and oldtimers by storm.[11]

Newcomers did not bring the end of a cozy *gemeindschaftlich* community; I knew this and so did most oldtimers and newcomers.[12] Dacula had been for a long time intimately connected to the economy of Atlanta. But the connection now had new organizational, network, and symbolic reality, as longstanding firms and organizations, such as gas stations, grocery stores, and congregations, now increasingly defined themselves in relation to new or expanded ones that were setting up shop. Understanding Dacula as an ecology of diverse organizations that changed over time and in response to urban restructuring illuminated the evolution and processes of change in this particular place. Thus alterations within the organizational ecology—including the concomitant routines of belonging and divergent social logics—provided a way for locals to measure change and furnished a useful lens for me to examine the ground-level effects of urban restructuring.

With more and different organizations in their environment came expanded choices about how individuals and families would organize their lives through routines of belonging.[13] In deciding where to shop, spend leisure time, and worship, Dacula residents—both oldtimers and newcomers—were mediating changes that were beyond their immediate control; but they were also establishing networks of interaction and developing cultural and social logics. As they made use of these networks and employed cultural and social logics in response to organizational changes in their environment, Dacula residents influenced both the directions change took and how they understood their own precarious positions as newcomers and oldtimers. This reality became particularly clear in the conduct of community conflicts.

Restructuring American Religious Life

Paralleling the restructuring of urban geography has been a restructuring of another kind. The restructuring of American religion has, according to Robert Wuthnow (1988), altered the patterns of organization and belonging in the post–World War II era. Wuthnow's organizational understanding of religious change highlights phenomenal growth in the parachurch sector; social and cultural convergence among denominations and divergence within them; and new voluntarism and the concomitant declining significance of denominational loyalty. Whatever else could be asserted about religious life in contemporary America, it was once again becoming more decentralized and more open to individual choice. The growth of voluntarism and its effects on denominations has been the focus of significant research in the sociology of religion (for example, Roof and McKinney 1987; Warner 1988; Hammond 1992; Roof 1993; Carroll and Roof 1993; Hoge, Johnson, and Luidens 1994).

As Hoge and Roozen (1979) note, this discussion can usefully be framed within national contextual and institutional factors, that is, society-wide social and cultural trends and denominational ethos, polity, and programs, or local contextual and institutional factors, that is, changes in particular places and particular organizations. To date, much of the energy in accounting for religious restructuring has centered on the examination of national contextual and institutional factors. In particular, researchers have spent significant theoretical energy accounting for denominational growth and decline (for example, Roof and McKinney 1987; Coalter, Mulder, and Weeks 1990; Finke and Stark

1992; Iannaccone 1994). Others have helpfully documented the growth of special purpose groups, the independent religious sector, and nascent religious consortiums as vigorous competitors in the national religious institutional marketplace (such as Wuthnow 1988, 1994b; Roozen 1993; Shibley 1996; Watson 1997; Miller 1997; Griffith 1997).

As important as national vantage points are in understanding religious restructuring, they only present half the picture. While these organizational shifts have been occurring at a national level, what has been happening in particular localities? How does (if it does) denominational contraction at the national level result in congregational constriction at the local level? Where are the detailed descriptions of the local effects wrought on congregational life by increasingly complex religious organizational environments? Unfortunately we have comparatively few accounts of the contextual and institutional phenomena in local communities. Roozen, McKinney, and Carroll (1984), Warner (1988), Ammerman (1997a), and Becker (1999) are among the relatively few exceptions to this generalization. They exemplify the truth that particular geographical settings provide vantages for theoretically necessary accounts.

In Roozen, McKinney, and Carroll's *Varieties of Religious Presence*, the authors pay particular attention to the nexus of congregational and contextual factors as they develop a typology of mission orientations among 171 congregations in Hartford, Connecticut. Warner's *New Wine in Old Wineskins* examines at close range the effects of regional, cultural, and institutional trends in the 1960s and 1970s on a single Presbyterian congregation in Mendocino, California, as leaders and congregants responded to new populations, new organizations, and altered community ethos. In *Congregation and Community*, Nancy Ammerman portrays nine communities in which significant change had occurred and relates twenty-three local churches to these changed environments. The national scope of this work allows Ammerman to make generalizations about a range of responses to change exhibited by congregations and the internal dynamics, resource mobilization, and support structures that make those changes possible or not. Ammerman's work, however, does not analyze the interrelations among congregations within particular communities. Becker's *Congregations in Conflict* treats a range of religious organizations (twenty-three congregations) within a single community—

Oak Park, Illinois. However, her emphasis is not primarily on the interrelationships among organizations. Rather she attends to each congregation's type or normative identity as key in accounting for its responses to internal and external conflicts. In these works, the authors either treated congregations primarily in relation to alterations in the community or focused on the dynamics of intraorganizational relations. None considers the interrelationship among congregations responding not only to alterations within the community, but also to realignment among the local religious organizations themselves.

While I explore the changes happening both within the community and in intraorganizational identity construction, I also develop more fully the local institutional dynamics as congregations work out their responses to contextual change within a religious organizational ecology. While national (and even global) institutional and contextual dynamics are at work in the local arena, mapping the changes close at hand is necessary for understanding the overall effects of restructuring in American religion.

My contribution to the discussion of religious restructuring is to explore it within a local territory of lived American religion. Within any physical territory there is a religious ecology that consists of the patterns of relations, status, and interaction among organizations as they are embedded within a specific environment. Religious groups may not relate to those nearby, but they are nonetheless part of an ecology because of their physical proximity and by virtue of common environmental factors, for example, economic, educational, or infrastructural changes. Likewise, any religious organization may participate in an ecology that transcends its local environment. In fact, usually sociologists have focused primarily on transcending connections such as denominational affiliation. My intent is to draw greater attention to how religious groups relate to specific other religious organizations through multiple patterns of structured interaction, processes of status ordering within the community, and the belonging routines among congregants.

Also, individuals engage this local ecology as they make their affiliation choices based not primarily on denominational identity, but rather on specific congregational theology, culture, and programs. Such a choice is further complicated by the divergence of congregations within the same denomination. As Warner (1994) has argued, "congregations within the same denomination are as greatly varied as the localities within which they exist" (71). This results in a *de facto* congregationalism, that is, a structural convergence toward the congregational form as the primary model of organizing religion in the United States. *De facto* congregationalism also eventuates in congregations within the same denomination, often becoming more ideologically homogeneous collectivities that relate more to focal populations in their local environment than to a national denominational headquarters— if such even exist. This being the case, it becomes all the more important for sociologists of religion to explore the new pressures exerted on congregations within their local religious organizational ecology.

In Dacula, new and expanded religious organizations were now an integral part of the local religious ecology. Newly established independent congregations, such as Jubilee Worship Center and Trinity Christian Fellowship, located their ministries in office parks or held Sunday worship in Dacula High School. Advocates from the local branch of the Christian Coalition leafleted cars in congregations' parking lots during election campaigns. In this community, a megachurch with more than three thousand members grew from a small country Baptist church. With a membership larger than the population of Dacula, this locally innovative organizational form altered significantly the interorganizational relations and status values among religious groups in Dacula.

Furthermore, new ties among congregations were possible as new groups emerged. Efforts for interracial services of a predominantly African-American Methodist church and a primarily white United Methodist congregation revealed less theological comity than existed between a newly formed white Baptist and the African American United Methodist congregations. Unburdened by historic sleights and memory, organizations new to the area sometimes were increasing cooperation rather than furthering competition.

Additionally, area newcomers who were potential members of congregations often seemed less concerned about a congregation's denominational affiliation than they were about its programming for children and whether or not they felt welcome and supported. For Todd and Faith Penner, who were newcomers to the Dacula area, being faithful meant putting together patterns of religious belonging that responded to the stresses of their lives; for Marie and Vernon England, lifelong Dacula residents, making faith was about taken-for-granted faithfulness to a single congregation. This distinction is new voluntarism, on the ground, face-to-face with another routine of belonging based on longstanding loyalty.

Religious Organizational Ecology

While much of what was happening in Dacula could be addressed using the metaphor of supply-side religious markets and basic tenets of rational choice models of religious change, I have ultimately found another framework more useful—organizational ecology. After beginning my fieldwork in Dacula, I soon recognized the importance of multiple ties among congregations as they respond to changes in their environment. Sometimes leaders and congregants spoke openly about competition with other congregations that they believed were siphoning off new members—such as the disgust with being "hebroned." That language of competition sent me foraging through recently emergent market competition models for insight (for example, Finke and Stark 1992; Iannaccone 1990, 1991, 1994). However, these market competition models failed to account for much of what I saw on the ground. As the number of religious groups in the locality increased, as the variety of religious organizations multiplied, and as human and financial resources expanded, many congregations saw new opportunities for innovation. Some religious organizations saw these developments as a chance for cooperation and coordination of services for the betterment of the community. These congregations sometimes eschewed the notion that they were the only religious body responsible for the spiritual well-being of their community and engaged in efforts to enhance each other's viability and to share limited resources. Such mutualism and organizational interdependence was largely inexplicable in the market competition models. Likewise, cooperation in a religious ecology was underexplored in congregational studies that often focus on a single congregation that dominates or at least is made to appear (by absence of analysis of other nearby religious groups) to dominate local religious life.

Like many qualitative researchers, I generally build theories from the ground up, working always with theoretical interlocutors but constantly weighing the content-fit of the models (Glaser and Strauss 1967;

Strauss 1978; Strauss and Corbin 1994).[14] Initially I employed several general models as sensitizing devices—which over time developed more patina of process, structure, and even typology. If the model no longer generated insights for interpreting what I observed in my fieldwork, I found it increasingly unhelpful and eventually I discarded it. I ultimately found this to be the case with market competition models. The interorganizational dynamics I observed were simply more nuanced and complex than was captured by this conceptual framework elaborated within the sociology of religion, based primarily on national institutional data (for example, Finke 1989), rather than close-range examination of local religious organizational patterns.[15]

As I read within organizational ecology, I found this model provided more useful sensitizing concepts for inductive research. In the end I also tried to extend the theory beyond its current application. First, I used it to explore a small-scale religious ecology within a particular geographical locality, rather than, for example, nation-states or entire metropolitan regions. Second, I employed qualitative research methods, rather than the usual quantitative ones, for mapping the territory close at hand.[16]

Michael Hannan and John Freeman (1977, 1989) explain the diversity of organizational change by analogy to biological species. Arguing that organizations do not simply adapt to change in the environment as though they are isolated organisms, they assert that organizations respond in ways that highlight their interdependence. Thus Hannan and Freeman emphasize that the unit of analysis in examining organizational change is the population of organizations responding to alterations in their environment. This approach seemed particularly well-suited for understanding the local dynamics I was observing. Thus I sought to account for the ways in which religious restructuring shifted relations within the population of religious organizations at the local level. I looked as often horizontally as vertically when seeking to elucidate changes in a particular congregation's culture, mission, or program.

Organizational ecology perspectives drew my attention to how change happens less through adaptation and more by organizational replacement. Some organizations cannot respond to the requirements of altered environments. They become obsolete and new organizations with a better "fit" come in to fill their place. I saw this happening in

Dacula as well (cf. Ammerman 1997a). Some congregations that had served well under circumstances of small-town life with its stable population simply were unable to reinvent themselves under the new conditions of exurbanization. Watching at close range particular congregations in their death-throes, I asked what were the cultural or theological resources that had become dormant or perhaps extinct within their ecology when these religious organizations failed. Though not especially given to nostalgia for rural life myself, having been reared on a hardscrabble Dakota homestead, I did wonder about the particular ways of making faith that were lost when all that remained of a country church was a fenced-in cemetery surrounded by office parks.

Organizational ecology theories also prompted me to pay attention to the development of divergent types of organizations—specialist and generalist—within the religious ecology. Specialist organizations responded to alterations in the environments by concentrating their resources on tightly focused populations, forms, or identities. Generalist organizations persisted in maintaining a "big tent" by serving a wide variety of populations with diverse expectations within a common organizational structure.[17] These various types of organizations were not necessarily in competition with one another, though rivalry was often fierce. Diversification of religious organizations at the local level contributed to a breakdown of formerly fixed religious organizational relations and status values, and resulted in new patterns of interaction and status.

At the individual level, congregants responded to changes in the organizational environment not only by choosing among the available options, but also by devising multilayered habits of belonging to various religious organizations within the expanded exurban environment (cf. Eiesland and Warner 1998; Roof 1993). These individual networks created customized routines of belonging and informal relations among local religious organizations. These patterns demonstrate the complexity of relationships among religious organizations as individuals develop local ties that may include attendance on Sunday at the local Methodist church, placing the children in day care at The [conservative Baptist] Christian School, and weekly meetings of Christian Entrepreneurs.

Organizations at the local level develop varied responses to such multilayered involvement of their members. Although competition and calls for fiscal and spiritual loyalty is one response, another response is the promotion of cooperative relationships with other organizations, including swapping of resources and information (Brittain and Wholey 1988). In exurbs, as in all locales where significant urban and religious restructuring occurs, religious organizations restructure themselves by adopting, adapting, and developing—as well as competing and closing.

A focus on religious ecology enables the researcher to relate organizational prospects in ways more nuanced than is often employed by the market competition or congregational dominance approaches. In an ecological frame, the focus shifts from individual organizations to the population of organizations and the contexts in which they are embedded. Religious organizations are related to one another and to other organizations within their locale—even though some draw from far beyond the locality in which they are situated. Thus religious organizations often behave in ways that are more relational than autonomous—assisting with community projects, sharing information about distressed locals, or supporting anticrime or pro-life campaigns.

Their interdependence is not simply a matter of competition. The religious ecology is not a ceaseless round of skirmishes of groups, organizations, and individuals, caught in a win-lose arena of combat and death. As Ammerman (1997a) highlights, communities rely on religious organizations not simply to serve their own survival, but to serve some larger purpose—that is, the common good. Some organizations may do this more or less adequately than others; nonetheless, a focus on religious ecology assumes that organizations do actually intend to accomplish something more than their own survival. As a colleague and I have written elsewhere, "The ecological frame . . . assumes that [any] congregation is one among many. Other congregations have their place in the community, their own visions, and their particular constituents, and . . . they influence each other for good or ill. Congregations can consciously cooperate and compete; they can hinder (and help) one another without intending to do so; they affect each other by their very presence . . . " (Eiesland and Warner 1998:40).

Organizational ecology allows us not to ignore struggle and competition and to balance it with appreciation of the particular type of organizations that religious groups are, that is, communities of faith bearing witness within their locality, to one another, and beyond. Students of religion must take religious groups, in part, on their own terms, understanding that religious motives and values undergird aspects of group life and keep them going in the face of possible adversity. Whatever else the groups examined in these pages may claim to be, whatever other ends they may serve, their original and continuing identity is religious. The continuing power of religious belief and commitment provides a basis for enduring solidarity and common moral concern.

Sociologists mine other fields for language to communicate social reality, and religious organizations and other groups, in turn, adopt (sometimes after initially denouncing) the language sociologists of religion legitimate (see for example "culture wars"). Our metaphors provide language for those groups and organizations about which we are theorizing—that is, if we are doing our jobs well. Ecological language is particularly useful in that it allows religious groups at the local level to see themselves more clearly as potentially complementing one another, sometimes sharing resources, often serving diverse populations, and now and then competing for the same pool of people, funds, and status. If, however, religious organizations see themselves as perpetually embattled because of limited goods or as singly responsible for the spiritual well-being of the entire community, they may be less willing to cooperate and be more inclined simply to vie for their share. While competition surely happens, it does not characterize the dynamics among many religious organizations. This is reason enough for developing a fuller ecological framework when discussing the relations among religious organizations.

The Plan of the Book

As Dacula was changing, the area's residents and organizations altered their routines of belonging and of social logics, in response to the demographic, infrastructural, and cultural transformations. In order to understand how locals experienced this change, in chapter 2, I give an account of how urban deconcentration brought Dacula nearer to Atlanta. Evident in this overview is the existence of at least two distinct logics within the community, that is, the orientations of "oldtimers" and "newcomers." The religious ecology of Dacula is described in chapter 3 and responses from within the population of organizations are examined. Chapter 4 explores the organizational challenges posed by relating new neighbors—oldtimers and newcomers—within a single congregation. The case study of Hinton Memorial UMC provides a historical account of internal congregational adaptations and identity construction within a changing religious ecology.

Chapter 5 describes the individual networks of community resources and organizations used by two families within Hinton Memorial UMC. The Englands have spent most of their lives making Dacula a good place, and the Penners came to Dacula hoping this would be a place where they could make a good life. These networks feature both the routines of belonging that characterize these families and the networks of resources available to the congregation and its members as they addressed the restructuring of their community. Further exploring these resources, chapter 6 identifies the responses of several congregations to controversies in Dacula's environs. Debates over the use of a church cemetery, the proposal to expand the county airport, and local sentiment related to the state-wide controversy over changing Georgia's flag (which includes the Confederate Battle flag) demonstrate the cultural and social fissures and alliances in this rapidly changing exurb. The book concludes by summarizing what can be discerned from a careful examination of local changes in a religious organizational ecology arising from urban and religious restructuring. Analogous to the "all politics is local" aphorism, this study maintains that in the end religious change is also always local. Altered religious organizational identities must be examined in terms of relations within a restructured local religious ecology; programmatic strategies of religious organizations must be understood as responsive to local innovations; the influence of religious institutions in shaping culture must be explored in local circumstances. Ultimately, however, the changes in the religious scene are intimately linked to the metropolitan transformations of the past three decades.

Researching a Particular Place

This account of Dacula, Georgia, focuses mainly on the effects of urban restructuring on the area's religious organizations. This case study dwells on religious organizations because the change and conflict in the area has been clearly manifested in the relations of this population of organizations.[18] The area's more than twenty-four religious groups constitute a complex interrelated ecology. When Dacula was a small town, its religious ecology was seen as largely institutionally stable; but with urban restructuring, significant alterations began. This work identifies a range of religious responses to the area's development. It also explores the multiple ties among religious groups as they respond to infrastructural, demographic, and cultural changes. Though the focus is on religious organizations, some attention is also given to related changes in other institutions—particularly family and politics.

The story of the change in a religious ecology within a metropolitan area could be told from many vantage points, using many strategies. The account offered here relies primarily on qualitative research. As an ethnographic study, it was designed to enable the researcher to participate in and observe the life of religious organizations within an exurb (Fetterman 1989). Initial information was gathered from the congregations within the Dacula zip-code area as well as several others that were considered part of the community although they technically lie outside the postal delivery area.[19] This discovery phase enabled me to identify a typology of organizational attempts at adaptation in the religious ecology detailed in chapter 3.

This study design is based on methodological triangulation: participant observation, interviews, and questionnaire data. From May 1992 to December 1995, I regularly engaged in participant observation of the routine activities of several congregations. I recorded my recollections of these events in fieldnotes—a full account of all I could recall—and a field journal—my hunches, feelings, and hopes during the research (cf. Jorgensen 1989). Since completing my regular field research, I have been invited to return for several special events, presentations, and regular services in the community on which I took fieldnotes and have incorporated into this book. I also reported to several community groups regarding my study.

Between May 1992 and December 1994, I focused my attention on Hinton Memorial UMC—which underwent a name change to First United Methodist Church-Dacula. (However, since the name was Hinton Memorial UMC during the greater part of my field research, this is the name I use throughout this work.) During my time at Hinton Memorial I attended trustee meetings, covered-dish suppers, Sunday services, cemetery work days, senior citizen outings, camp meetings, Vacation Bible School programs, and the like. In addition to participant-observation, I developed a history of the congregation, based on archival evidence, published congregational histories, and oral reports of long-time members. I also conducted more than thirty-five interviews with key congregational leaders, present and former ministers, denominational officials, disaffected former members and attendees, as well as current members and attendees, both newcomers and oldtimers. Among my interview subjects were seventeen newcomers and eighteen old-timers. A schedule of interview questions is included in the methodological appendix. A questionnaire was administered to Hinton Memorial UMC attendees in conjunction with the Congregations in Changing Communities project. This survey data provided information regarding the socioeconomic and educational characteristics of congregants, as well as length of residence in the community, number of family members nearby, and length of commute to work.

In addition to my fieldwork at Hinton Memorial, from January 1993 through July 1994, I was a participant-observer in other congregations in the Dacula area, conducting interviews with twenty-five congregants and pastors. Finally, in order to gain knowledge about the community and the effects of exurbanization on the community, I conducted mostly informal interviews with twenty-five city council members, local merchants, educational leaders, developers, and county leaders. I participated in numerous community-wide cultural events, such as Winn House Bluegrass Festival, the Dacula Boosters Picnic, and the Annual Memorial Day Parade. I closely followed newspapers and business journals. Likewise, I made extensive use of the archives of the Gwinnett Historical Society.

In writing this ethnography, I have used the actual place names of the town—Dacula—and the county—Gwinnett County. In revealing the site for the study, it made little sense to rename the congregations whose stories are told here. Thus I have used the names of the congregations. Members of congregations, individuals in the community, and other interviewees have been given pseudonyms and some distinguishing characteristics have been changed in order to conceal their identities. I have attempted throughout to use verbatim the words and turns of phrase of the individuals. The power of giving names is an awesome one, and one I did not undertake lightly. Of course, the responsibility was lightened somewhat by the knowledge that some Dacula residents and congregants at the various churches had already named me. I came to be known by several as "Nancy Sue" though my middle name is Lynn. I took it as a compliment. I was an adopted local.

After many months in the field, the final product of this research is an ethnography that emphasizes descriptive detail and offers an interpretative framework. My fundamental goal was to provide a plausible account of the dual restructuring of Dacula in light of the changes they produced in the religious ecology. My tale is largely a "realist" one with which the subjects may or may not agree (VanMannen 1988). My experiences of this exurban community were not the same as those of the residents. No matter how warmly I was accepted into the community, the congregations and religious organizations, I was always an "outsider" who had not chosen to relocate to Dacula. I had come as a transient researcher.

Yet throughout the months of field research, as I traveled the interstates to Gwinnett County, I was personally affected by the changes. On the forty-minute drive from my home to Dacula, I would often note the changes along the road—a new sporting goods mega-store, a fresh produce market gone out of business, and bulldozers blazing a new connector. The rapidity of change in the built environment was often disorienting. On one Saturday trip, after having attended a meeting the previous Wednesday, I missed a turn that I should have made. To my surprise, in the intervening two days a fast food restaurant had sprung up on the corner. The traffic, too, increased significantly during the time of my research. I often took personally the addition of more and more semis to the already bumper-to-bumper traffic on Highway 316. I also noted the filling in of open spaces. Sometimes I detoured, wheeling through the mud to inspect a newborn subdivision or following the Federal Express truck through an office park, looking for new congregations. As the landscape changed around me, I often marveled to myself, "Ah, the places these interstates can take you."

Chapter 2

"The Way It Looks from Here"

Dacula, Georgia

"I DON'T KNOW, the way it looks from here is that the city's just coming out to meet us," said Tony Slade—a person who had lived in the Dacula area for more than fifteen years and who had kept horses on his twelve-acre farm until a bout with cancer forced him to sell the animals. Of course, Tony's perspective on the changes was not the only one. According to a 1992 Atlanta Regional Commission report, the land on which Tony had kept his thoroughbreds was classified "vacant"—beckoning developers out to the countryside. Whether residents viewed Atlanta as coming uninvited to Dacula or as summoned by the large tracts of undeveloped land depended, to a large degree, on whether they had land to sell. For the vast majority—oldtimers and newcomers—the former view held sway. No one had issued an invitation; but the city kept coming anyway.

Most commentators on urban deconcentration have taken the perspective of center city residents watching as their urban core "sprawls" from suburbs to exurbs, the city moving further and further from what has been seen as the real "heart of the city"—the traditional downtown or central business district.[1] In this chapter, I deliberately alter my perspective, looking not from the center toward the outward moving fringes, but from the periphery where new centers seem to sprout up in the least expected places. This was certainly the perspective of most Dacula residents as urban deconcentration occurred in their locality.

Most Dacula residents would be surprised by any account of Gwin-nett County that placed their story at the center. As one middle-aged mechanic informed me when he pumped my gas at Tanner Ford Hard-ware and country store one day, "We're just a grease spot on the road to progress." For many years, longtime residents have seen their town as the poor cousin of Lawrenceville, Duluth, Norcross, and other towns nearby. At the beginning of my research, I often encountered individuals who urged me to study a place that was really changing—not Dacula, which they asserted, was staying more or less the same. In fact, I heard this statement so often that I asked Todd Penner, a newcomer who was to become a key informant, what he made of the comment. "Denial," he wryly commented, "It ain't just a river in Egypt." Whether or not denial characterized many oldtimers' attitudes during the late 1980s and early 1990s, by the late 1990s, they had to confront the reality that their image of Dacula no longer resembled its actual social and spatial rela-tions. When I returned for a visit in 1997, I spoke with Florrie Reynolds, an eighty-three-year-old resident who had lived in Dacula and envi-rons for most of her adult life. Florrie had been a key informant during the early days of my research, telling me where she thought I could find out more about the history of the area. "It's just kept pilin' up," she said gesturing toward the traffic on Highway 316. "Wouldn't have believed it if I hadn't watched it happening . . . ," she allowed her voice to trail off as she shook her head.

On the face of it, Dacula (population 3,089 in 1994) continues to look much as it has for decades—with the small general store on the main road through town and a few businesses in the old downtown that runs alongside the railroad tracks. According to Hal Tanner, a life-long resident and Dacula city councilman, Dacula had a "slow, lazy-type life and we were against living all jammed up." But Dacula is no longer a country town serving local farmers, rather it is a full-fledged exurb. In the mid-1980s, "it was like somebody picked us up and moved us twenty miles closer to Atlanta," said Bobbi Jo Leander, a long-time resident and insurance salesperson. In fact, though there was no change in the distance to downtown Atlanta (it is still thirty-five miles), the expan-sion of Highway 316, which connects the northeast corner of the county to Interstate 85, was completed in the early 1980s. For a while it made the trip seem shorter. From the perspective of Dacula residents, this expansion—coupled with the growth of the Gwinnett Place Mall Corners, an edge city eight miles away—has been key to the changes that have affected their everyday lives. After these developments in the mid-1980s, the town began to receive the attention of housing and retail developers. Before then, the town's only reported claim to fame was its reputation as a speed trap for unsuspecting Athens-bound University of Georgia Bulldog fans.

A History Worth Telling

Dacula's modest and self-effacing attitude is something of an anomaly in Gwinnett County—which has long been known for its boosterism, a quality that has characterized the Atlanta region since its leaders vowed that Atlanta would rise again. For example, motorists entering Gwinnett County via Interstate 85 are met by a water tank emblazoned with "Gwinnett is Great." Robust self-promoting was evidenced in 1941, with a national radio broadcast called "Salute to Gwinnett County." The program included original songs touting Gwinnett's unique and healthful character and short speeches by the county historian, the superintendent of schools, and the home demonstration agent. Sounding like a present-day Chamber of Commerce official, the historian announced: "If you wish to engage in farming, come to Gwinnett. Atlanta stands at our front door and will buy every product of the farm. If you wish to establish a new industry, come to Gwinnett. Competent and intelligent labor is plentiful. If you wish to build a new home, come to Gwinnett. We are a friendly people. Our homes and our institutions send forth brilliant young men and divinely beautiful young women" (Flanigan 1943:277).

Though situated in Gwinnett County, Dacula residents believed themselves to be far removed from where county boosters were making the news. Historical records indicate that Dacula was incorporated under its present name in 1905. The area has few of the historical markers which have begun to spring up around Gwinnett County.[2] (Gwinnett County proudly heralds its founding in 1818 by Button Gwinnett, son of a Church of England minister, delegate to the Continental Congress, and signer of the Declaration of Independence.) Even the origins of Dacula's name are unclear, although some people suggest that it was devised by Dr. Samuel H. Freeman, the area's first medical doctor, who combined letters from "Atlanta" and "Decatur."[3] Others contend that the name is related to the town's Native American history, though a specific etymology is unknown. The name often provides a useful measure of community bond and familiarity. Pronouncing Dacula to rhyme with "Dracula" is a sure sign of a newcomer or other passerby.

As reported to me, the oral history of the area begins with the Creek and Cherokee who inhabited the region until they were forcibly removed in 1838. According to one history, "Indians left very little permanent physical evidence of their long stay in Gwinnett County. They opened no highways, built no bridges, erected no dwellings, established no schools. . . . The hundred and twenty years since the Indians were removed from this county have effaced all markers and mounds that at one time pointed out the last resting places of these primitive people" (Flanigan 1943:2, 8). The ancestors and advocates of these early residents, however, have protested that though the resettlement campaigns removed their kin, evidence of Native American inhabitation of Gwinnett County is nearly as ubiquitous as strip malls. American Indian mounds and markers, they claim, dot the county's landscape, invisible only to those who cannot distinguish them from natural landmarks. Ironically, development has proven their claims, since digging on new subdivisions and office parks frequently unearths archaeological ruins of the displaced civilization.

North of Dacula are about two hundred Native American rock mounds dating from fifteen hundred to two thousand years ago. Now the site of a subdivision, the rock arrangements—one hundred of which are listed on the National Register of Historic Places—stand at measured distances from one another about four-and-one-half-feet tall and spread about five-feet wide. According to a staff archaeologist with the Georgia Office of Historic Preservation, it is not clear why the mounds were built, though he suspects that there are Cherokee or Creek Indian graves in or near them.

The controversy over the subdivision heightened interest in the area's Native American history. Protests over the development resulted in a fifty-one-day prayer vigil on the property, conducted by Native Americans. Other newcomers and Native Americans organized protests, camp-outs, and pow-wows to raise awareness of Native Americans' local culture. For example, in 1992, a Lakota Indian organized the area's first pow-wow in modern times. Native dancers and observers came from throughout the United States, and Southeast especially, to participate in the demonstrations of crafts and skills, music and dances, and preparation of Native American foods. These festivals have continued annually, usually drawing large crowds of Gwinnett residents and generating significant income for the sponsors.

In 1994, Native Americans, including Dennis Banks—leader of the American Indian Movement and veteran of the siege at Wounded Knee in 1973—assembled near the Dacula mounds as part of a protest designed to urge the development of a one-thousand-acre state park as an alternative to the developer's plans to break ground on the proposed subdivision. After years of controversy and legal battles, some of the mounds were finally purchased with funds from the state and a private company and donated to Gwinnett County as a "dedicated green space." And the Appalachee Farms subdivision, which incorporated some of the rock mounds, was approved by the Gwinnett County Commission, with the proviso that the developer fence in those mounds that contain graves. The tensions within the community regarding the subdivision simmered for years. One Dacula city commissioner said, "We want to be friendly to our neighbors, but these people won't have any reason to care about people outside their walls"; or, according to some Native American protesters, what was under their feet. A small group of Native American activists declared the county's decision to permit the development's construction an act of war and vowed to prevent desecration of the land by force if necessary. But the subdivision was finished on time and residents moved in with little disruption, and homeowners in the walled community now golf near the chain-link fence surrounding the mounds.

Other difficult historical truths are also covered over—metaphorically, if not literally. For example, the basis of Gwinnett County's prosperity during the pre–Civil War era was closely associated with the institution of slavery. The 1820 Census, two years after the county was created, reported that 165 of the area's 689 families were slaveholders, and the average slave-holding family had about two slaves (reported in Flanigan 1943:32). Since Gwinnett County was not suited to large plantations and never developed a full plantation economy, the area was dominated by farmers who prospered, despite the setbacks of the war, well into the twentieth century. The black population in Gwinnett County declined steadily (with the exception of the period 1900–1910) from the end of the Civil War until 1990 when their percentages began to climb slightly.

According to official, recorded history, Dacula began in 1891 as a work camp of pine pole cabins and a commissary for the men laying railroad track. A small post office was also located on the site, and was named Hoke, after a railroad official. Even before the railroad camp was established, the Pleasant Hill Methodist and Hebron Baptist churches were founded. The first real house was built in Dacula in 1891 by J. W. Hamilton, who had become a Confederate hero after the battles of Atlanta.

According to residents, one local African-American family was particularly influential in the area's history. Several generations of Hutchins, as well as of four or five other black families, sharecropped one of the area's few plantations on which the historic Elisha Winn House is located. The plantation was approximately one thousand acres and was home to twenty-two families. Sharecroppers raised cotton and corn and ran a sawmill after the crops were in. Mr. Amos Hutchins, former caretaker of the Elisha Winn House, reported the area's black history: "I was born in 1913 in a small log house near [the Elisha Winn House]. . . . We all went to school right where the Mt. Zion Methodist Church is now. The church started in 1870 and it was right by the school. My grandfather, Lemeul Hutchins, was a member of Mt. Zion. Judge Hutchins from Duluth bought him and his two younger sisters when they were not quite grown. They had just been shipped to Virginia from Africa. He wouldn't talk about that trip but he told us about when he was a slave. They worked on the judge's farm at Findley's Bottoms near what is now Duluth. Judge Hutchins taught my Grandpa to read. After Grandpa was freed, he sharecropped on the old Plott place near Dacula in the late 1800s."

Dr. Samuel L. Hinton, for whom Hinton Memorial UMC was named, also operated a large farm worked by black sharecroppers during the late 1800s. In 1870, Dr. Samuel Freeman, Pleasant Hill Methodist's founder, gave a group of black Methodists a small tract of land on Dacula Road, where Mt. Zion United Methodist Church is now located. Refusing to take Freeman's charity, the Mt. Zion congregation paid him ten cents for the land.

Into the early 1900s, the area's economy was closely tied to cotton. Small cotton farmers who tended fifty to one hundred acres often borrowed money from the Cotton Association in the spring in order to plant, and repaid the loan when the crop was harvested. Usually an official from the Cotton Association was waiting at the gin for payment. Highway 29—which runs through Dacula parallel to the railroad—was a roadside marketplace for the community's cotton farmers. In a 10 November 1985 article in the *Gwinnett Daily News*, entitled, "Jewel Moore is Dacula all the way," long-time resident Moore reminisced about those earlier days. "They would sit there and sell cotton from their baskets. They also sold fertilizer. And they shipped what they didn't sell to Atlanta." However, the town fell on hard times when the boll weevil hit the South around 1918.

Both oldtimers and historians tell how the Great Depression brought hardship and suffering to Dacula, as to much of the South. Farming declined as the primary income source for area residents. The county demonstration agent spelled out the dilemma in a 1941 speech: "If the complex problem which faces agriculture today is to be eventually solved, the individual one-, two-, and three-horse farm will need to find a way to make that farm a self-supporting enterprise, geared to meet market consumption and each farm's own reasonable needs. Many of our agricultural economists say that the family size farm will never be a moneymaker for the operation. Therefore, we should place emphasis on the good life, and less on commercial agriculture" (Flanigan 1943:278).

The emphasis on the good life led many Dacula residents to leave the farm for work in industries. Many worked for manufacturers such as Bona Allen, Inc., a leather goods factory in Buford, which from the late 1800s until the 1940s was one of the largest industries in Georgia. General Shoe Company, which began its operation in Lawrenceville in 1939, employed 370 people; and the Henson Garment Manufacturing, making the popular Red Fox work clothing line, also began production in Lawrenceville in 1939 and took on 135 workers. Manufacturing replaced farming as the means to support family life in Dacula.

In the 1940s and 1950s, GIs returning from the war worked in an increasingly varied array of industrial companies within commuting distance of Dacula.[4] Many local men worked at the General Motors plant in Atlanta. Hal Tanner tells of the employment options then: "I went to work for General Motors corporation when I was eighteen. And never did really like it. But it was in 1948, and there was not any industry in Gwinnett County at all except the General Shoe Corporation in Lawrenceville. Kind of a small factory. Employed like, maybe a few hundred people. Also a fellow out in Buford had a harness factory. That was the only two public works, you might say, in the county. So I went to work for them at eighteen, married when I was nineteen. Began to have children when I was twenty-one, and my Daddy said that anybody that quit a job like that is just sorry. [laughs] So I stayed with it, and retired in 1981." For many men of Hal's generation, a few acres for a garden, a home where they could raise their children, and a stable job was the good life. Unfortunately, the good, high-paying industrial jobs began to evaporate by the early 1970s.[5]

From the 1960s until the mid-1980s, most young Dacula residents left the area, often for inner-tier Atlanta suburbs or elsewhere in the Sunbelt where employment was plentiful.[6] Lula DeVries, Alfred's wife and long-time Dacula resident, recounts her son's work history, which differed dramatically from the life she and her husband lived as Dacula farmers and merchants. "My son—he's an architect—graduated from [Georgia] Tech, then went and served his time overseas during the Vietnam War. And when he came back he worked a year or two with an architect, then he decided to open his own business, and that was in 1975. He started out real small. His office was in Lawrenceville. And before the recession [in the early 1990s] he had a thirty-person firm." For this generation the good life required advanced degrees. Service sector jobs were not located near Dacula; until the late 1980s most high-tech jobs were still located closer to the city center or developed edge crisis. These sons and daughters of Dacula residents moved in order to live in established suburban neighborhoods with small yards and small gardens.[7]

During the late 1970s and early 1980s, Dacula and its surroundings saw a modest first wave of newcomers, like Tony Slade, who moved to the far outer rim of Atlanta in order to have a few acres for keeping a garden or animals. According to my informants, many of these early newcomers, for instance Elaine and Nowell Altoona, worked in the county's expanding school systems. Though newcomers, their association with the highly valued educational system or their desire for a rural estate made them assimilable within the regnant accounts of Dacula's way of life. Their organizational ties were familiar; they moved into homes with acreage; and there were not too many of them.

However, since the late 1980s, many good jobs have become available near Dacula at distribution complexes, high-tech manufacturing centers, office parks, and retail complexes. These jobs brought newcomers in much greater numbers. Young people could now attend college within easy commuting distance of Dacula at Gwinnett Technical Institute and Gwinnett University System Center, which offers undergraduate and graduate courses from Georgia State University and the University of Georgia. Industrial and corporate parks sprouted up across Gwinnett County like a new cash crop. Dacula was increasingly a magnet for both economic and residential growth.

In addition, these employment options made possible by decentralization meant that the professional class was increasingly employed outside the traditional city. Golf course subdivisions signified the arrival of a new type of resident. These professionals were less likely to commute from their homes in the residential periphery to the central business district but often worked within the area's nearby office parks or edge cities clustered around Interstate 285, Atlanta's encircling freeway (see Clark and Kuijpers-Linde 1994). Also, other more modest subdivisions attracted young families—most of whom were dual income couples with children to be enrolled in Dacula's touted schools. These young families were also willing to drive longer distances to work, in order to afford their first home. To many of them, Dacula represented affordability, a sense of safety and community, and access to metropolitan Atlanta resources.

Until the 1970s, "the history worth telling" for most Dacula residents was about a relatively stable community with stalwart families—both African American and white—whose contributions to the local ethos were built on years of staying put. Since the mid-1980s, many newcomers, especially the young, have found little in the local history that ties them to this particular place. Students, such as Clay Lord, a sixteen year-old attending Dacula High School, plan to attend college and, like his parents, relocate wherever the jobs are. He commented, "I'm definitely not a slacker type. I want to have a house and family and stuff. I just don't know if I'll stay around here. Maybe I'll go to Raleigh or someplace else. I don't care one way or the other if I end up in Dacula." For Clay, whose family relocated to the area two years ago after living in Cobb County, Georgia; Tucson, Arizona; and Washington, D.C., Dacula is both a hometown and an exurb.

Demographic Changes

The demographic changes in Dacula represent the changes that are occurring in the region and the differences that are still evident between this exurbanized small town and Gwinnett County at large. While the city population of Dacula increased only 28.8 percent between 1980 and 1990,[8] the population in the local zip code area has grown by 40.2 percent during the same time period.[9] Throughout Gwinnett County, towns whose boundaries have stayed constant have not seen a tremendous population explosion. In Gwinnett County and the metro Atlanta area—like many deconcentrated urban areas—unincorporated growth has been the model for development since World War II, with counties rather than city governments providing the bulk of the utilities, law enforcement, and other services. This deconcentrated settlement pattern has had distinct implications for distribution of governmental power in the region—a reality that would came back to "bite" local leaders in conflicts about community growth.[10]

Gwinnett's demographic profile prominently featured white, middle-class families with children. In 1990, 44 percent of households included children. More than 70 percent of the residents lived in married-couple families. Homeowners constituted 68.4 percent of the residents in Gwinnett County. Residents were also more than 90 percent white. Over time as the population in the county has increased, the percentage of black residents has decreased significantly. During the 1980s and early 1990s, Gwinnett County became less racially diverse than at any time since its founding in 1818.

The growth in Dacula environs has been fueled, in part, by the availability of affordable housing. Family after family spoke about their declining property holdings through the years. For example, while tapping

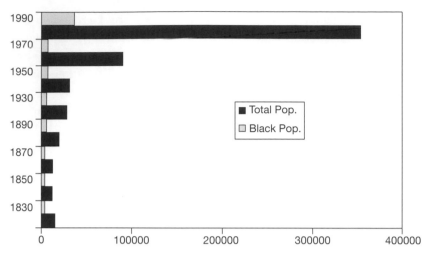

Figure 2.1 Census of Black Population in Gwinnett County, 1820–1990

her foot to the music at the annual bluegrass festival held at the Elisha Winn House, Elaine Foggs chronicled the altered patterns of property ownership in her family, as evidence of Dacula's exurbanization. The native Gwinnett County resident's grandfather had a big farm nearby with a cotton gin and sawmill on the premise. Her father had a smaller, fifty-acre farmstead subdivided from his father's land; now Foggs and her husband have only the few acres around their house just off a major highway in the area. Though local residents can now afford to own less land, more people can have their golden acre—or for many, quarter acre.

According to 1990 Census figures, the average home value of $96,950 in the Dacula region (census tract 506.01 and 506.02) was well below the values for Gwinnett County ($111,594) and the Atlanta metro area ($120,472). Yet these numbers represent a 132.85 percent increase in home value from 1980 to 1990 in the Dacula environs, an 89.59 percent change in Gwinnett County; and a 113.33 percent increase in the metro area (U.S. Bureau of the Census, 1990; Census of Population and Housing: Georgia). Surprisingly, though, as relatively inexpensive single-family homes have proliferated, another form of affordable housing has decreased dramatically: mobile homes. Mobile homes had been the first home of choice for an earlier generation of

Table 2.1
Population Growth in Northeast Gwinnett County, Georgia,
1980–1990[11]

	1980	1990
Number of persons	7,975	14,458
Number of Households	2,507	4,732
Average Household Size	3.18	3.0
Housing Units	2,603	4,919
Single Family	85.4%	91.4%
Multi-family	1.5	0.3
Mobile homes	13.1	7.5

rural residents who were land-rich but cash-poor. In the South, mobile homes also often carried cultural connotations of hardscrabble lifestyles; not something with which the newcomers to Dacula wanted to be associated.

Nonetheless, Dacula continued as a poor relation in the county with 4.9 percent of residents below the poverty level compared to 4.0 for both Gwinnett County and the metro Atlanta area in 1990. Dacula residents also lagged behind in income with the average family pulling in only $49,974 compared with $54,508 for Gwinnett residents as a whole and $53,016 for the metro area (U.S. Bureau of the Census, 1990). On the plus side, Dacula's crime rate was just over half the rate of Gwinnett County as a whole.[12] In choosing Dacula, many residents were thinking safety first, for themselves and their children.

Educationally, Dacula residents were also behind other Gwinnett inhabitants and other metro residents. In 1990, fewer than 12 percent of residents in the Dacula area had college degrees, whereas 30 percent of Gwinnett and metro Atlanta residents had completed degrees. Nineteen percent of Dacula residents worked in managerial or professional jobs, compared to 31 percent for Gwinnett County and metro Atlanta residents. Dacula had more households with children; more elderly residents and fewer persons born outside of Georgia.[13] Nonetheless, according to Georgia Department of Education figures, Dacula school children performed at or slightly above the level of their Gwinnett County fellows and other metro Atlanta youngsters.[14] Most Dacula residents—oldtimers and newcomers—wore this public recognition of their youngsters' scholastic achievement like a badge of honor. For instance, during an interview, Anita Beaman, a newcomer whose son and daughter were in the second and third grade respectively, recited Iowa Basics average scores for Dacula Elementary to me as though they were batting averages.

Richard "Dicky" Busby typified many qualities of Dacula residents. He belonged to the Dacula Masons; he fished when he had time, which was not as often since his daughter had moved back home with her thirteen year-old son. Dicky did not regularly listen to the radio, but kept on a country station for "background noise" when he was working in the garage.[15] Dicky was not unlike many of his neighbors in his preferences. Market research also showed that people similar to those who reside in Dacula were less likely to have a valid passport, own a personal computer, employ a maid, or have a premium credit card than were individuals who fit the profile of Gwinnett citizens at large.[16] Individuals similar to Dacula residents were about as likely as Gwinnett residents and other U.S. residents to play golf, drink domestic beer, and own a domestic car.[17]

In comparison with the population of Gwinnett County as a whole, the residents of Dacula and environs were more characteristically "country," less cosmopolitan, and less prosperous. Residents realized that their community had more in common with their rural neighboring counties, but they also saw the change as it came crawling down Highway 316—like a Chevy truck hemmed in by traffic.[18]

Infrastructure Changes

Transformation of the built environment of Gwinnett swept across the county beginning in the southwestern edge nearest Atlanta and rapidly proceeded toward Dacula. The evolution of Highway 316 from an unpaved town road to a county road in the 1960s and 1970s, to the University Parkway of the 1990s reflected the rapid infrastructural growth, driven by the area's economic prosperity and spread by Gwinnett's characteristic boosterism.[19] Dubbed the Golden Wishbone, the space between Highway 316 and Interstate 85 enfolds most of Gwinnett county's so-called vacant land and has been viewed as a prime location for incoming industry and residential development.

In hopes of promoting and controlling coming development, busi-

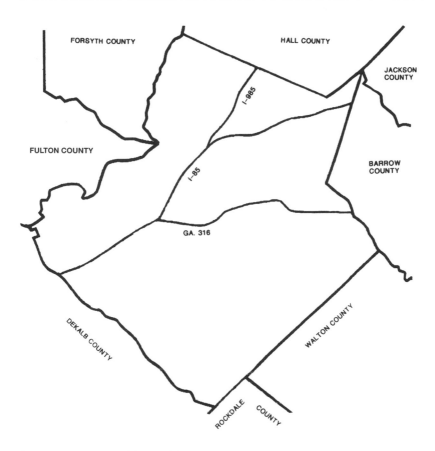

Figure 2.2 Map of Golden Wishbone

nesses and landowners in the Golden Wishbone and beyond cooperated in 1992 to found a nonprofit corporation, 316 Alliance. The group's
aim was to make sure that the forty-five-mile road from Atlanta to Athens blossomed on the eastern end in the same way that it had on the
western end near Lawrenceville. Marketing the Wishbone corridor as
an ideal location for high-tech industries, the Alliance sought to alter
the area's reputation for traditional low-wage, labor-intensive manufacturing jobs by attracting higher-paid, "human capital" jobs that rely on
the ideas and prestige of the University of Georgia and the Gwinnett
Technical Institute. The Alliance president suggested that the area
needed another development that would complement the Gwinnett

Progress Center—a light industrial, office, and new housing development stretching from the outskirts of Lawrenceville to Dacula along
Highway 316, and offering prime real estate at top dollar rates. Others
saw the necessity of a shopping mall to attract consumers and businesses
to the area. Thus came the developers' dream—the Mall of Georgia.
When finished in 2000, this new mall will be a five-hundred-acre development with an eighty-acre nature park and 8,600 parking spaces.
The developer has insisted that they have taken a page from Disney
and will seek to have the mall look as much like an ideal community
as possible. The news of a "new mall for the new millennium" was
greeted by local Dacula residents as an apocalypse. "Everything's going
to be different now. I suppose we can hold on for a little while, but pretty
soon, we'll just be Dekalb County [a more urbanized county near At-
lanta]," said Nowell Altoona, a long-time Dacula resident who moved
from an Atlanta inner suburban area in the 1970s.

The new mall will also be new competition for the Gwinnett Place
Mall, which when it was built in 1984, was a harbinger of change for
Dacula. Built off Interstate 85 on the site of a horse pasture and mobile home park, Gwinnett Place has been the county's number one income generating locale for more than ten years. Visited more than
twenty million times per year, Gwinnett Place had the highest traffic
count of any mall in the state in 1996. Billing itself as "downtown
Gwinnett," the area surrounding Gwinnett Place is a bustling magnet
for office buildings. The county's business and roadway infrastructure
funnels people into the vicinity of the mall. In a series in the *Gwinnett
Report*, entitled "Gwinnett Place: A Decade of Impact," the president
of the Gwinnett Chamber of Commerce during the mall's construction
is quoted, "Certainly from a retail aspect, it is the engine that drives
the county. Everything that came along behind it, including the hotels, were [sic] directly attributable to the mall. The bottom line is: there
was no such thing as a retail center [in Gwinnett] prior to the mall."

The Gwinnett Place Mall Corners is now a full-fledged edge city.[20]
The immense speed and scale of the localized development made it a
mecca for jobs, shopping, and entertainment. Growth corridors, such
as the Golden Wishbone, radiated from the area. By 1995 the Gwinnett
Place Mall Corners even had the chaotic, raw feel of a new urban area
as pedestrians mixed with traffic accompanied by the staccato of bleat-

ing horns. But the Mall Corners does not function like the downtown areas of the county's former small towns—where "all life's necessities could be gotten within a block" as Lula DeVries commented about Dacula's downtown during the 1960s, when she and her husband ran the grocery. For many of the nearby residents, Gwinnett Place Mall Corners is just one of several edge cities that determine their routines of belonging (Fishman 1990).[21] Now people wonder if the Mall of Georgia will displace Gwinnett Place as "downtown Gwinnett" and further deconcentrate these routines of belonging. The questioning is not benign in Dacula, where they have become accustomed to the residential development that sprang up in radiating circles around the Gwinnett Place Mall and they wonder what is ahead as residential development is planned for the new mall.

As development has rippled out to Dacula from Gwinnett Place Mall Corners, residents have failed to build schools fast enough to keep up. School officials contended in 1997 that since 1990, they have felt the impact of 3,500 students, or the equivalent of three schools, just due to approval of higher-density residential zoning. Gwinnett's high birth rate has also outpaced the county's estimates.

More buildings are regularly going up. High, middle, and elementary schools have all undergone renovation and expansion within the last five years. Dacula's elementary school exceeded capacity within a year of being built. Elaine Foggs measures change in terms of portable classrooms outside the school where she became a teacher more than two decades ago. She noted that these days "they build schools and within a year or two of moving in, we are having classes in trailers again." In the 1994–1995 school year, educators needed fifteen mobile units at the Dacula Elementary School to accommodate the more than three hundred students beyond the building's capacity. In 1996, a new elementary school was built nearby to handle the dramatically increasing population of youngsters. In 1994, Dacula Middle School added new buildings and remodeled its gyms, just in time to begin absorbing the population bulge that three years prior began moving through the elementary school.

Adding classroom space is not the only change in Dacula's educational system. For many Dacula residents, keeping what they see as traditional values means supporting the local school system where the

Dacula Falcons regularly walk away with awards in football and basketball. In 1993, the Dacula High School athletics director noted that the demand for soccer and volleyball had increased in the past years, "We've had a lot of phone calls from people moving into the area." But before the director would approve the addition of new sports programs, he wanted to make certain that the staples of football, basketball, and baseball would not be hurt by defections to new pastimes. "We've been playing football and basketball here for a long time. The community really gets behind us. I don't know maybe we'll have more people come out for soccer and volleyball in a few years, but for now it's football."

Even mundane activities such as taking out the trash have been changed as people have moved in. Landfills cannot be built fast enough to keep up with demand, and county government is woefully behind in adding routes for pickup. In the mid-1990s, the number of new homes in the area strained the county's police and fire, road maintenance, and sanitation and water systems. Calls to county offices were often met with a recording indicating the likely wait for a personal response—sometimes also a message indicating that "due to increased demand" some offices were taking no additional requests for services. In 1993 and 1994, housing starts outpaced building inspections. The county's director of development said, "Some developers are pretty irate because [the delay in inspections] costs them money, and the quality of the inspections may be suffering."

With the development has come increased fear of crime and increased demand for more police protection. Although residents' attitudes about the extent of the "crime problem" vary considerably, many oldtimers name increase in crime as one of the main problems of the growth. Many newcomers who perceive the county to be relatively crime-free have often developed a second-nature repertoire of crime-prevention strategies. Said one recently settled Dacula citizen who carried a handgun in the glove compartment of his Ranchero, "Think safe, be safe." Another long-time Dacula resident commented that she no longer drives alone at night in the county. "You can't be too careful," she noted. Like many, she is calling for a local Dacula police department to expand patrols. However, contrary to the perceptions of many, the actual number of criminal incidents in the Dacula area has been dropping in the past years as the area's population has increased. "Residents of the suburbs sprouting in the northeast corner of Gwinnett County can wake up knowing they have a 99.9 percent chance of not becoming a crime victim. Those communities and fifty-three others in northeast and west Cobb, southeast Clayton and southeast Gwinnett are home to 23 percent of metro Atlanta residents but only 2 percent of the violent crime and 6 percent of all crime."[22] Dacula—like most exurbs nationwide—is comparatively safe.

Although Dacula city officials are optimistic about the opportunity for growth in the area, they also feel Damocles' sword over their heads in the form of state legislation designed to require municipalities to provide five services from a list of ten. In 1996, Dacula offered only three, including zoning, water, and sewage (garbage disposal). If the town cannot ante up it may be disbanded and its services and assets taken over by the county. Former Dacula mayor James Worth was dismayed about Gwinnett County's failure to assist the city in providing residents with additional services.[23] "Even though the county can't keep up with its obligations, they won't give us the funds [from taxes and levies] to let us expand our services. We can't annex these subdivisions, because the county's against it. Yet they're not meeting their obligations."

Dacula City Council has attempted to bolster its town's status by engaging in a beautification project in downtown. New sidewalks, brick ledges, wooden planters, and trees and a gazebo were added. The effort was spearheaded by Steve Brady, a Dacula newcomer and part-time city employee, who was elected mayor in 1993. "I was going to surrounding counties and noticed that theirs looked so good, and ours looked so bad." Brady hoped that the beautification project would encourage Dacula residents to take pride in their town and, maybe, to start an annual festival. His vision paid off in 1994 with the town's First Annual Memorial Day parade. Lewis Norman, a Cubmaster in Dacula and member of Hinton Memorial UMC, organized a parade with a mix of the old and new Dacula, including the mounted Confederates, marching Boy and Girl Scouts, two high school bands, antique wagons and cars, and a phalanx of emergency vehicles. Said Lewis Norman, "I am not doing this as part of Scouts, but on my own. I am from Lawrenceville, but we have a committee of people [to organize the parade] in Dacula."

In addition to the beautified downtown and the town festival, Dacula has seen a steady increase in the number of professional and retail services offered in town. Ace Hardware came in 1986; the Dairy Queen in 1990; an antique shop in 1993; a Waffle House, Publix Distribution, and a legal office in 1994; more sit-down restaurants and fast gas joints in 1995; in 1996 a prototype supermarket for a nationwide chain; and more and more service organizations. "We're turning the corner," said David Suches, who established his legal practice in downtown Dacula in 1994. But just as with the town parades and festivals, the new is mixed liberally with the old. The Tanner Ford Hardware Company, an old-time general store, continues to keep its doors open. A pot-bellied stove heats the brick store as the town's oldtimers sit around shooting the breeze and talking about the fates of the local football team.

City leaders and residents expect the growth to continue. When Highway 316 was extended to Dacula in 1981, long-time residents held their breath expecting the hordes to arrive. But the growth through the 1980s was gradual compared to the rapid expansion of the 1990s. In 1990 "concerned citizens of Dacula," an *ad hoc* group of oldtimers and first-wave newcomers to the area, organized to oppose another large-scale housing development near Dacula. They distributed a flyer throughout the community alerting residents. It read: "Developer's Dream . . . Dacula's Nightmare! Did you know that developers are proposing to build a new city in your backyard, and they intend to use your tax dollars to do it? Backed by foreign investors, these developers are asking for high-density rezoning of 1,158 acres in the area surrounding the Elisha Winn House on Dacula Road. This development will include 2000 homes, cluster homes, offices, a 22–acre shopping center and a golf course irrigated by waste water. Bottom Line—More Taxes, More People, More Traffic, More Crime, More Pollution—Less of what we live here for!" The coalition succeeded in slowing development but not in stopping it. Developers received initial zoning approval in 1991, but delays caused by local lawsuits and the countywide economic recession resulted in the project's postponement until 1994 when county commissioners approved a scaled-down Dacula Project that includes 911 houses and a golf course. Three golf court tunnels now pass below Dacula Road. Said Alfred DeVries, "Good thing they're putting them underground 'cause nobody taught this old farmer who has the right-of-way—a tractor or a golf cart." Dacula Project developers are work-ing on Phase II of the project—a 227,000–square foot shopping center.

As the edge city of Gwinnett Place Mall Corners sprouted up, Dacula began to feel the rippling effects of infrastructural expansion. When Highway 316 made Dacula accessible to residents commuting to Mall Corners and other edge cities, inevitable residential growth soon followed. Now Dacula is likely to be sandwiched by another possible edge city, which will surround the Mall of Georgia. As part of urban deconcentration, privately owned mall complexes develop into edge cit-ies—making the urban landscape resemble pepperonis on a pizza. Al-though these edge cities often displace small towns like Dacula in terms of economic development, they nonetheless require small towns to ex-pand public services to residential developments—when counties can-not meet the challenge. Though its beautified downtown now hosts community festivals and parades, Dacula's business district is no longer a local economic force; but its neighborhoods are booming with new residents. These residents want cultural rather than economic services in their backyards.

Cultural Changes

The demographic and infrastructural changes in the area have changed the cultural life of Dacula. Increasingly one is likely to find a fusion of cultural styles and offerings, such as the Chinese restaurant and coun-try buffet serving lunch and dinner daily. After a busy morning of in-terviewing, I stopped in for a lunch of meatloaf and vegetable stir-fry. Eating nearby was a group of workers from Publix Distribution, several oldtimers from the garage next door, and the Asian proprietors. Other fusion offerings include Frank's Hometown Jamboree, which in 1993 began hosting karaoke on Saturday nights. On Saturday and Sunday afternoons, one will find long-time residents engaged in a lively game of Tennessee Nine in a court nestled behind a home on Drowning Creek Road outside of Dacula. Randolph Boyce comments about the weekly game, "It's just something we do. It's as old as Methuselah. It was a big thing during the Depression. People didn't have money to play golf, so they would come down to play marbles." But the game as old as

Methuselah is now being taught to a new generation of exurban young-sters from a nearby subdivision.

"Conservatism" fuses the disparate members of the community. Yet the term and its attendant actions vary considerably. For some local residents, conservative means resisting the changes of encroaching exurbanization; for others, conservative denotes an activist political stance; for nearly all, however, conservative means that they want government to keep its hands out of their wallet. Conservative values, safety, and a friendly way of life were the most common answers to my question about the cultural norms that residents appreciate in Dacula. Residents pride themselves on maintaining an outlook that frowns on rowdy and deviant behavior and subtly rewards Sunday-school manners and decent living. Some oldtimers believe that the area's newcomers are reinforcing those traditional values and adding a new one, inclusiveness. Harold Dill, who has lived in the county since the early 1940s, commented: "There's one big difference, when I first moved to the farm in 1948—I wanted to raise my children on a farm. And you couldn't be a part of the community unless you was born here. But that's changed. People are coming in, and people accept people better, and I like that."

The cultural changes underway in the county have spawned a robust exchange of exurban and country hick jokes, depending on one's length of residence in the county. From my years of interviewing it appears that everyone with whom I came in contact knew someone who kept goats, pigs, or chickens in the middle of a subdivision. On the other hand, long-time residents took no limit of pride in pillorying the unfamiliar lifestyles of newcomers. Norman Baggs, former editor of the *Gwinnett Post-Tribune*, often served as an unofficial intermediary between the two cultures. A lengthy quote from his 26 February 1994 column recounts his Letterman-style top-ten list about what newcomers and oldtimers alike need to know about subdivision life in Gwinnett County:

10. A great American once said, "United we stand! Divided we fall! Subdivided we can get 32 houses on that flood plain."
9. There is a book in the county library entitled "Two Million Dumb Things to Call a Residential Neighborhood." It is always checked out.
8. In cookie-cutter subdivisions where all the houses look alike, upon

accidentally entering your neighbor's house instead of your own it is considered gauche to kiss his spouse and ask what's for dinner.

7. Cul-de-sac is an Indian word for "couldn't get another house in there even if we do extend the road."

6. Not every successful person in the county is a land developer. Some of them loan money to land developers, and the rest do their legal work.

5. It is considered inappropriate to use a leaf blower to move your neighbor's grass seed into your yard. If, however, a natural wind does the same thing, it is OK to spread some hay to keep it where you want it.

4. "Phase II completed" means your kid's school will get three brand new house trailers next year.

3. Having a subdivision named after a body of water is no guarantee there's anything more scenic than a wastewater treatment plant within 15 miles.

2. The Atlanta Games in '96 will feature cul-de-sac basketball as an Olympic competition.

1. It really does make sense to plow down all those big trees and then plant little ones. The fifth family to own your home will appreciate the shade.

This good-natured joshing often does highlight the cultural fissures and connections that residents of Dacula and environs confront in daily life.

Despite some resistance to expanding school sports offerings, recreational programs provide a common cultural focus for oldtimers and newcomers. On Saturday morning at the ball field where I sometimes conducted interviews, I was reminded that for some softball is not a pastime, but a religion. During the sign-up weekend, parents camp out for upwards of twelve hours to insure their child's spot on a local team. The vigils are regularly covered by local television news and print journalists as evidence of exurban overkill. But the parents with whom I spoke said that they were doing it only partly for their kids. Getting their sons and daughters on the ball team whose practices are closest to their homes or offices means saving themselves from hours of chauffeuring their children to and from Little League. Plus the all-night tailgate party has become a parental rite of passage for some in the area. Dacula's long-time residents also find much to appreciate in evenings spent in lawn chairs watching neighbors or grandchildren pick off balls.

One evening as I joined First Baptist-Dacula for their weekly men's soft-ball game, I witnessed what appeared to me as a new type of "dinner on the grounds" as friends and family brought their picnic blankets, Tupperware containers of gooey bars, and coolers of soda for an evening of socializing. In these instances, the routines of belonging of oldtimers and those of newcomers seemed to jibe.

But for some of Dacula's long-time residents, the last two decades have felt overwhelming. As Sarah Coser, an elderly woman whose mobile home outside of Dacula was in the prospective path of a long-fought-over outer highway, said: "It started out good and slow, but now we're cooked and not a damn thing we can do about it." From the way Sarah saw it, dislocation was inevitable. Others, however, such as Miss Irene Abbott, the matriarch of Hinton Memorial UMC, thought change could be guided. She was among those who worked to slow the Dacula subdivision project by creating the leaflets and distributing them within the community. She called on her long-standing networks of belonging to shape the cultural and infrastructural changes in directions that she saw as being the common good. For oldtimers, Dacula is a particular place—its organizations shape their lives and they often prefer to live within its parameters.

For a generation of early newcomers, the changes have seemed particularly pernicious. Nowell Altoona regularly stopped me at church to share another "bit of devastation" happening within the locality. Lester Tweed, who had begun an organic herb farm near Dacula, also experienced the changes in the area as spoliation not only of the environment but also of a culture. This first wave of newcomers often found themselves at loose ends. Oldtimers did not consider them "one of us," but neither did they fit what they perceived as the values and patterns of the newest wave of Dacula residents. They seem to fit Cowdrey's (1983) portrait of how persons in places like Dacula respond to change: "For men and women who are middle-aged in the 1980s, as for their great-grandparents in the 1880s, there will always be the feeling that they are separated from their youth by more than years. The changes in the metaphorical landscape of culture have been mirrored in the physical landscape, whose forms, more than ever before, are shaped by super-abounding human power. Cotton fields have changed to pastures or to woods; marshes to soybean fields or rolling Gulf; wild land to neon strips. A generation after World War II, healthier, more prosperous and more numerous southerners confront common American dilemmas without altogether shifting the burden of a peculiar past" (169). For the first wave of newcomers, Dacula often represented a type of locality that is under siege as exurbanization alters the culture that they elected to adopt.[24] Their place in Dacula's culture was disappearing.

The newcomers who arrived since the mid-1980s experienced a dilemma as well. They came for the sense of history and tradition that they perceived along Dacula's main road. They came because they wanted a home of their own. They came because the schools were generally safe and high quality. They tried to do their part to make Dacula the place they thought it was—beautifying its downtown and sponsoring its parades. Yet with exurbanization came social and cultural tensions as small-town values, traditions, and practices, so coveted by exurban newcomers, were transformed by their arrival. The routines of belonging that these newcomers adopted were different from those that characterized the oldtimers. The networks of support and influence upon which they relied differed as well. For all of Dacula's residents, though, the challenges of life on the edge were ever present.

While Dacula, Georgia, is not a microcosm of the United States, the Sunbelt, the South, or even Gwinnett County, the concerns and experiences of Dacula residents resemble those of residents in many small towns whose patterns of life have been altered by the sociospatial changes of residential and industrial urban deconcentration over the past three decades (cf. Heenan 1991). Though caused by similar economic factors across the nation and globe, these infrastructural, demographic, and cultural changes are as idiosyncratic as the metropolitan regions in which they occur.[25] But they are all the transformations of particular places with local customs, historical narratives, and institutions that are reordered, renegotiated, and sometimes rejected in the process of change (cf. P. Abbott 1987; Oldenberg 1989).

Chapter 3

A Place to Be Religious

Organizing Ecological Change

O<small>N</small> S<small>UNDAY</small> <small>MORNINGS</small> when I pulled out of my driveway, I flicked on the local gospel station to keep me company on my forty-five-minute commute to church. The sounds of the Winans or the Smallwood Singers accompanied me as I made my way to a congregation in Dacula. By the end of my research, I knew how the people of Dacula "did church" and how to prepare myself accordingly. If I was going to Dacula Church of God, I knew to wear hosiery no matter how hot the day, and the Bible I pulled from my shelf was the King James Version. Sundays at Trinity Christian Fellowship meant more casual dress—even my Birkenstocks were entirely in keeping with congregational norms—and the Bible tucked under my arm was the New International Version. At First Baptist–Dacula, I needed to be prepared for an impromptu prayer in case I was called on to lift up the congregation's needs that week— my occasional note taking during the service seemed to the minister a sign that I was paying particularly careful attention. At First Baptist– Dacula even the prayers were in King James's English.

Jubilee Worship Center was a free-wheeling, multicultural, multiracial, spirit-filled adventure, which often took all of Sunday morning as well as most of the afternoon. While everyone carried a Bible, usually in a leather or vinyl Bible cozy, there wasn't one official version either in the pulpit or in the pew. Comfortable shoes were a must at Jubilee because one spent most of the service on one's feet. If my destination was Hinton Memorial UMC, I dressed in a suit and arrived early enough to spend time on the steps visiting. Generally, I was among the few that followed along in the Revised Standard Version pew Bibles. I knew though that I would be out by noon. If the minister went long, Vernon England was likely to mention it as he filed through the pastor's greeting line—not a happy prospect for any minister. I left home early if I was going to Hebron Baptist, not for visiting on the front-steps as at Hinton, but for finding a parking place and a seat in the sanctuary. Hebron's parking lots were managed by men using two-way radios and uniformed Gwinnett County police. By the time I reached the sanctuary of the megachurch, I was delighted to hear the mellow music of the worship band and the instructions to pray and meditate before the service begins. The tacit knowledge of the practices and ways of different congregations in the Dacula area assisted me as I discovered the parameters of the religious ecology of this particular place and the ways the congregations related to one another.

While in chapter 2, I focused on the infrastructural, demographic, and cultural changes happening in the environment, in this chapter I examine the congregations in this local religious ecology and explore the development of their internal identities. The changes in this religious organizational environment are attributable to both the local effects of urban restructuring, as Dacula exurbanized, and the consequences of religious restructuring, including the declining significance of denominationalism, the proliferation of new religious organizational forms, *de facto* congregationalism, and increased religious voluntarism. My premise was that in order to understand the effects of this contextual and institutional change, I could not look solely at individual religious organizations, I also needed to attend to the population of religious organizations, to connections among organizations, to status ordering, and to the informal ways locals related to these religious groups. During my time in these congregations, I also saw different patterns in congregations' efforts to adapt to alterations within the religious organizational ecology.[1]

Dacula's Religious Ecology

Until the early 1980s, Dacula's religious ecology had been a very stable one. Of the twenty-four religious organizations that I identified in 1995, eleven could trace their dates of founding back to the years before the town's establishment, for example, Hinton Memorial UMC (founded 1837), Hebron Baptist Church (founded 1842), Hog Mountain Baptist Church (founded in 1854), Appalachee Baptist Church (founded in 1863), and Mt. Zion UMC (founded in 1870). Four congregations were begun in the early decades of the twentieth century, including Pleasant Grove Baptist (founded in 1903), Felding Chapel Baptist Church (founded in early 1930s), First Baptist Church–Dacula (founded in 1931), and Church of Christ at Auburn Road (founded in 1940). Only one congregation—Dacula Church of God (founded in 1972)—was established in the 1960s and 1970s.

But the 1980s and 1990s have been decades of significant volatility within the religious ecology. Most notably, the number of new church foundings had risen dramatically—paralleling and perhaps exceeding the pace of the town's early years.[2] Eight congregations were established in the span of thirteen years within the Dacula environs. For instance, New Hope Baptist Church was founded in 1982; New Covenant Baptist began in 1984; Christian Central Fellowship in 1986; Jubilee Worship Center in 1987; both Trinity Christian Fellowship and New Life Fellowship Center in 1990; Perimeter Ministries in 1994; and the number kept climbing. Toward the end of my formal research, the number and variety of congregations, religious organizations, and special purpose groups seemed to change from month to month.

As Dacula became an exurb, the relatively established equilibrium in the religious ecology was unsettled as emergent groups targeted the area for church planting efforts; religious leaders mobilized to form new entrepreneurial units; established denominations selected congregations for redevelopment; and nascent groups emerged in response to national or local religious concerns.[3] Almost as if locals had placed a sign on Highway 316 designating the area "Church Growth Parkway," the ecology was transformed into a religious entrepreneurial locale. The contextual changes wrought by urban restructuring made Dacula ripe for local religious restructuring.

In part, this restructuring meant that those congregations on Highway 28 paralleling the railroad tracks or on Dacula Road were no longer the only ones to be considered within the religious ecology. The ecological unit had broadened to include more organizations—even as subdivisions on the outskirts of Dacula altered people's views of what constituted their town's territory, despite the fact that the city limits remained stable. Thus in addition to the changes within Dacula's immediate environment, other changes were happening that resulted in the partial incorporation of Dacula into the religious organizational life of Gwinnett County generally.[4] A short description of the changes in Gwinnett's religious environment is warranted.

In 1929, the county's church membership by denomination revealed that 65.8 percent of the surveyed church members were Baptist and 31.0 percent were Methodist (Flanigan 1943:287).[5] A perusal of the Worship Directory in the *Gwinnett Post Tribune* gives a picture of the current diversity in recent years. Denominations included Christian and Missionary Alliance, Anglican, Assembly of God, Church of Christ, Christian Science, Episcopal, Nazarene, Presbyterian, numerous independent full gospel fellowships, Southern and independent Baptist, United Methodist, and African Methodist Episcopal. In addition to the range of Protestant denominations, Gwinnett's religious organizations, include an Orthodox house church, several Roman Catholic parishes, two Jewish synagogues, a Hindu temple, various women's spirituality groups, a nascent Wiccan coven, a local branch of the Christian Coalition, and two Unitarian Universalist congregations—among others. A growing number of ethnic churches have also begun in Gwinnett County in the past decade. Several Spanish-speaking congregations meet in Methodist, Episcopal, or Baptist churches. A Romanian Pentecostal congregation also meets in a rented facility. Nonetheless, Baptists and Methodists continue to dominate in this northeast Georgia county. In 1992, 35.7 percent of religious adherents within the county were affiliated with the Southern Baptist Convention, and 17.6 percent of the county's total adherents were United Methodist (Bradley, et al. 1992:101).[6]

Gwinnett County, as a whole, is experiencing a burst of growth in religious organizational formation and expansion. In 1997, a market survey of religious organizations in the county identified the total number of groups as 475, with annual revenue of $99.6 million. According to this same poll, an increase of 43.8 percent in the number of religious organizations is expected by 2002.[7] Congregations—both new and old— are attempting to be not only spiritual centers for their congregants but also focal points for social and family life, and communal endeavors.[8] Many Gwinnett congregations—like countless nationwide—now routinely provide activities such as sports, counseling, and travel, for instance, mission trips. A few even offer live theater and movies in addition to worship and religious services. Gwinnett's rapid economic and residential growth has become the foundation for the development of new and expanded religious organizations.

These varied religious offerings have made it increasingly attractive for people residing in Dacula to look further afield for communities of faith, support, and service, in which they feel welcomed and aided. For example, Roman Catholics in the Dacula area generally worshiped at St. Lawrence in Lawrenceville or St. Benedict in Duluth. Both churches are located more than ten to fifteen miles from Dacula. Nonetheless, while a few Dacula area residents may travel a considerable distance for worship, the vast majority of those who seek religious fellowship do so among the organizations encompassed by the Dacula religious ecology.

Though the religious ecology in Dacula has expanded and diversified—exhibiting a diversity of denominational affiliation (and nonaffiliation), worship style, and theology—there have remained two overwhelming commonalities among them, theological conservativism and racial segregation. Changes in the area's population have opened the door for considerable innovative religious activity, but oldtimers and newcomers alike continue to support religious and cultural ideas and beliefs that are basically conservative. Though the meaning of conservative had almost as many nuances as congregants with whom I spoke, the basic notion, as applied to religion, included the idea that religious groups are responsible for establishing and upholding the norms of two-parent, intact families, "working hard for a living," and "walking on paths of personal righteousness." As Donnie Libert, pastor of the Jubilee Worship Center, said, "I believe that Christian fellowship is a great strength for individuals as well as families." Andy Sylvan, pastor of Ebenezer Baptist Church, which was founded in 1848 and where "most members are related to each other in more than one way," noted that congregants, "want to come together to know that they're the family of God and get a good Word to begin their week." For Ebenezer, conservativism meant traditional ways of doing things and familiar "old time" religion.

The other commonality in Dacula's religious ecology is also part of its conservatism: racial segregation. Segregation is certainly not unique to Dacula's religious ecology, yet it was clearly evident here. Of the congregations in the ecology, two were exclusively African American and one, Jubilee Worship Center, was multiracial, including Asians, Hispanics, and African Americans. Mt. Zion United Methodist Church, located within a half mile of Hinton Memorial UMC, a white congregation, was the oldest African American congregation in the ecology. Mt. Zion and Hinton conducted annual communal services, but otherwise had little interchange. Mt. Zion was also located near Hebron Baptist, but did not see Hebron as a draw for Mt. Zion's current or potential members. In 1994, Reverend Margaret Heych, the church's first woman pastor, commented that "really the only other congregation that Mt. Zion works much with is Appalachee Baptist Church"—another African American congregation nearby. Randall noted that the Mt. Zion was experiencing a moderate growth in attendance because "many oldtimers have been able to help their children start out by giving them land." She also mentioned that some long-time Mt. Zion members had become quite wealthy selling their homesteads to developers. Attracting extended families back to Dacula has meant that the area's middle-class African-American population has been growing slowly, but steadily. Appalachee Baptist Church has also been a beneficiary of this slow return migration of African Americans. However, Pastor Stephen Pearsall argued that the traditionalism of the congregation was preventing the church from attracting many newcomers. "This is a traditional church that wants to stay that way." Thus, Mt. Zion and Appalachee Baptist churches experienced moderate growth. However, neither congregation had a weekly attendance of more than seventy-five individuals during the time of my field research.

Jubilee Worship Center was, however, growing rapidly, drawing some of the African-American newcomers to the area. The worship style of Jubilee contained more popular Christian music than did the services of either Mt. Zion or Appalachee Baptist—a quality that Pastor Donnie Libert credited for drawing youth and young families. Libert, who is white, consciously drew African Americans into the worship and leadership team of the church, seeking to make the congregation welcoming. "For some folks going back to church where all your family is, actually isn't all that great. Here we want them to take leadership positions, whereas they sometimes have to fight for a place of ministry [elsewhere]." Jubilee Worship Center was experiencing dramatic growth, with a Sunday morning attendance of nearly three hundred in 1995, and consciously accentuated its multiracial quality in promoting itself.

That the religious ecology of Dacula is partitioned by race, to a large degree, is a result of the history of race relations in the environment, the circumstances of congregational foundings, and the histories of denominational practice—to name only some relevant factors. This partitioning has, thus, created different definitions of the religious ecology for the area's African-American congregations. Competition, mutualism, and status rivalry are, nonetheless, elements within this segmented religious ecology. Yet this partitioned religious ecology has remained relatively stable, in part, because the population influx to Dacula's environs is overwhelmingly Caucasian. What remains unpredictable, however, is the extent to which Jubilee Worship Center will attract an increasing proportion of incoming African Americans and the potential of other now primarily white congregations to promote internal racial diversity.

In the following pages, I identify six religious organizations whose relations to one another and to the changes in the community highlight some of the diversity within this ecology. As I discussed in chapter 1, within a frame of reference that highlights environments as having religious organizational ecologies, competition and rivalry is often seen; however, that is not the only possible response to change in the organizational environment. In this chapter, I examine six organizations: two types of generalist organizations (Hebron Baptist and First Baptist–Dacula), two types of specialist organizations (Hinton Memorial UMC and Trinity Fellowship), and two types of organizational demise or dormancy (Felding Chapel Baptist and Perimeter Ministries).

The account of Dacula's religious ecology is made more complicated and, I think more theoretically interesting, because one congregation is a megachurch. Thus, even among those organizations that developed specialist rather than generalist orientations, the impact of an organizational giant in their midst created tension.[9] Thus sometimes rivalry rather than direct competition was expressed by congregations who felt their status deflated, even if few of their members were actually lost.

Hebron Baptist Church: Making a Megachurch

Hebron Baptist Church is composed of several mobile classrooms, a small brick chapel that formerly served as the sanctuary, a Quonset-like gymnasium, a multi-storied Christian Living building, and a modern brick auditorium that seats approximately 1,300. Hebron is predominantly white. Across the street is a crowded old cemetery, the entrance of which occasionally doubles as overflow parking space. This architectural pastiche of old and new reflects the congregation's history and practice. In fifteen years, this country Baptist congregation transformed itself into a trendy, exurban megachurch.[10]

Founded in 1842, Hebron Baptist is a historic congregation that has successfully adapted to a dramatically altered environment. Fifteen years ago, it was among the smallest of the dozen or so small Baptist churches in and around Dacula. In 1995, drawing congregants from seven surrounding metropolitan counties, Hebron was a congregation of nearly 3,400 regular worshipers, surpassing the total number of residents within Dacula city limits. The congregation's story is a classic tale of church growth on a metropolitan frontier. In the 1980s, when Gwinnett was the fastest growing county in the United States, Hebron kept pace with the steady population inflow, becoming the primary beneficiary of exurban growth in the area. Its optimal location on the periphery of Dacula near the community's newly constructed elementary school and abutting several high-density subdivisions gave it high visibility among exurban newcomers. Likewise, denominational support (in the form of financial subsidies from the national and state Southern Baptist Conventions and the expertise of the denomination's church growth specialists) allowed this small congregation to take full advantage of the demographic transformations occurring around them.

The church's pastor, Bryant Quinn, whose nearly twenty-year tenure provided a high degree of leadership stability and consistent outward vision, was very deliberate in addressing the needs of newcomers by implementing programs designed to meet their familial concerns and by updating the congregation's worship services. In 1977, when the south Georgia native came to the church as a twenty-four-year-old Mercer University graduate, he began going out on rounds with the Dacula Fire Department. As he sat with families who experienced tremendous personal tragedy, he realized that many had no one locally to support them during difficult times. Cognizant of the history of residential mobility and concomitant absence of local support systems among many newcomers, Quinn led the Hebron congregation in aggressive evangelism in the area's burgeoning subdivisions. The church's slightly more than one hundred congregants began canvasing each neighborhood once or twice a month inviting families to attend special programs at the church. The evangelistic blitz spawned a new verb in the area, as locals inquired if new subdivisions had been "hebroned" lately.

Although some area newcomers responded negatively to the persistent outreach, many were swayed by age-graded evangelism, as youth visited other youth, singles other singles, and young families other young families. Dick Lee, who began attending Hebron in 1994, reported his visit from the congregation's members upon moving into a subdivision nearly ten miles from the church: "One thing that happened immediately, just immediately was a visitation. They were just so good about it. Tuesday night they came. We had about ten or eleven people in our age groups in this [living] room. I was out shooting baskets in the backyard, and my son and twin daughter came and said, 'Dad, there are some people here to see you.' And they were from Hebron. Then the doorbell rang and another group came in. And then the doorbell rang a little while later and another group came in. They didn't know that the other groups were going to be here. Just a lot of laughing and things. You could tell that they just really worked at this." Being a police officer, Lee was immediately invited to attend the public safety support group, in which he soon became quite active helping to make arrangements for several high-profile Gwinnett County police funerals held at Hebron in 1994 and 1995.

For religious organizations in this exurban area of commuting and multiple schedules, getting in and staying in touch with people is vital to organizational survival and vitality. Hebron's leadership adopted the resources of up-to-date technology. Desktop publishing and computer labels were real God-sends. Hebron used these relatively low-tech and inexpensive means to produce a newsletter to stay in contact with a range of individuals who were not regular attenders but who consider the congregation their home church.[11] In 1996, the regular weekly newsletter, "The Vision," was distributed to three times the number of regular worshippers (totaling approximately seven thousand recipients) who came to the church each week.[12] One individual who received the newsletter but attended services at the church only occasionally, commented, "I love the newsletter because it always has a good word, I can read it when I have time, and it keeps me in touch with MY church." Many Hebron congregants spoke of the encouragement they received from Quinn's short spiritual commentaries in the newsletters. These messages included encouragement to find a place of service in the congregation, a testimony of spiritual support received, or a celebration of the church's impact on the community. The church newsletter became an important way for Hebron to keep marginal members tied to the church and to encourage committed and peripheral participants alike. It was a communication tool that allowed this generalist organization to reach more people than would regularly participate in services located at the church's facility.

On-line communication was the next means the congregation adopted for this purpose. In 1995, Quinn commissioned a web site and arranged for congregational chat-rooms and listservs for various support groups. Quinn noted that he did not want to get "hung up" in the medium for the message, but that he wanted to use whatever people are using to get the congregation's theological vision out to area residents. This megachurch pastor did not, however, see the newsletter or computer-driven communication as a total substitute for physically gathering for worship and mutual support.

Hebron works hard to induce marginal members to become more active with a range of specifically targeted religious offerings. The church's success in attracting and retaining white, lower-middle- to middle-class exurban families with children (whose numbers make up the bulk of the congregation) in addition to a significant number of area oldtimers, has been due, in part, to its innovative and extensive programming and celebrative and spiritually challenging worship experiences. Balancing conservative Baptist theology with a therapeutic personalism,[13] Hebron has sought to address the stresses of living on the edge (cf. Bellah et al. 1985).[14] Particularly successful in incorporating new members have been occupation and special needs support groups. Initiated by a police department chaplain and associate pastor at Hebron, the support group for public safety personnel and their families has provided peer and professional counseling, seminars in stress management, and topical discussions about their work and family experience. The support group also reaches out to other public safety families, especially those who have experienced loss.

The church provides many services for people in the throes of personal crisis. Grief Relief, a group designed to assist individuals who have lost a loved one, whose business has failed, who are in poor health, or who have lost an identity, encourages "unhurried healing to help bring life back into focus after the blur of pain, confusion, and bewilderment caused by loss." Another group, Creating Awareness, spearheads the congregation's efforts to address the needs of people, especially children, with disabilities. The group developed special Sunday school programs for children and adults with disabilities and succeeded in having headphones installed and initiating signing for the hearing impaired during services. Other support groups have included Divorce Recovery, Christian Alcohol Recovery, Christian Al-Anon, and Adult Children of Confusion—a group for children of non-Christians. The church also has operated the AlphaCare Therapy Services, an on-premise professional counseling group which provided free or low cost "Christ-centered" individual, marital, and family therapy. In addition to ongoing support and service groups, Hebron regularly offers one-night LifeSkill Seminars designed to develop practical skills and theological perspectives in such areas as parenting, finances, dating, and sexuality. For example, a seminar in 1994 was entitled "Building a Marriage Partnership for Life—Managing Expectations" and was described as follows: "Couples often approach marriage with an ideal that turns into an ordeal so that they want a new deal! What they expect from each other and from marriage has only produced frustration and conflict that keeps tearing down each other and the relationship. This seminar will approach this problem by helping couples identify realistic expectations for the relationship and each other. It will then assist couples to set positive goals for their marriage that they can begin to pursue together. The emphasis will be on communicating and working together to make relationships a new deal for both spouses."

Offering counseling services under the auspices of the church, Hebron reinforces its theological stance of developing a personal relationship with God with the notion that this same God is concerned about their other personal relations. It also provides a setting for discussing Hebron's view of gender as it relates to love and marriage.[15]

With individual staff members for handling singles, senior adults, high school students, middle school students, and preschool children, the church is able to offer a sophisticated array of age-specific programs including choirs, Sunday school classes, and support groups. In 1995, Hebron supported a youth program with a membership of approximately five hundred. Led by a minister who had been a football hero and valedictorian in Dacula's only high school, the youth program offered Christian films, special guests—such as football players and NASCAR drivers—fellowship and discussion groups, summer and winter retreats, Discipleship Now weekends, and numerous impromptu and planned parties. Young people from Hebron also started prayer groups at several local schools, among them the Second Chance prayer group at nearby Duluth High School. The annual Vacation Bible School, supported by an extensive bus ministry, drew more than five hundred children in 1995 and 1996. Daily visits from Captain Hook and Arte the Aquaman, drawings for boys and girls bicycles and other prizes, Bible stories and songs, and a Hippo-party-mus were highlights of the 1994 Vacation Bible School. The Young at Heart, for elders fifty years and beyond, offered separate weekly Bible studies and fellowship gatherings for men and women, as well as coed meetings.

The congregation's single largest event, the Starlight Crusade, which typically falls the week before Memorial Day and runs Sunday through Friday nights at the Dacula Football Stadium, features age-graded special emphasis dinners. For the 1994 gathering, the college/ career and singles groups had a cookout; public safety officials from northeast Georgia had a banquet-style dinner; middle and high school students had a pizza party; and hamburgers were served to children from fifth grade and below. The revival under the stars often draws more than six thousand people to enjoy the 180–voice Hebron choir and nationally known contemporary Christian musicians, such as NewSong and Michael English, who perform each evening. Quinn had attended the Billy Graham School of Evangelism where services in an open-air setting were encouraged. He remarked in a 22 May 1993 article in the *Atlanta Journal and Constitution* (Gwinnett Extra), "Starlight is an opportunity for people to come and hear really great Christian music and positive preaching in a neutral environment. We rent the stadium. Second, it's a lot of fun. Our people want folks to be able to come and be totally relaxed without any requests for money." The cost for the Star-light Crusade (over $45,000 in 1994) was paid by the congregation, which takes up a special "love offering for the community" during Eas-ter. The congregation's annual budget ($1.9 million in 1993, $2.3 mil-lion in 1994, and $4.5 million in 1996) has permitted a great deal of programming innovation. The church is not, however, spendthrift, since Quinn refuses to go into debt for any projects, including on buildings—which explains the institution's architectural pastiche.

Despite good planning and execution, the congregation's innova-tive programming sometimes fails. In April 1993, Hebron began a Sat-urday evening worship service and Bible study designed in particular to serve public safety employees for whom a Saturday service was con-sidered more convenient. Quinn promoted the Saturday services as one more way that Hebron could accommodate the lifestyles of its busy exurban members. "In doing this, we are showing that Hebron is will-ing to break with tradition," said Quinn, in an article published in the *Gwinnett Post-Tribune*, 7 April 1993. "Like I have said: We have to un-derstand that the message of Christ is the same, but the methods of delivering that message are not sacred." Despite more than 350 pledge cards from people saying they would be attending the Saturday services, the participation was well below that total. By mid-summer 1993, Hebron stopped holding Saturday services.

The failure of the Saturday evening service scheme may have been due, in part, to many congregants' preference for services with a big group. An integral element of this congregation's identity is the wor-ship atmosphere made possible by its large size. One Hebron member commented, "I don't mind the crowd, except sometimes the parking. In fact, I like the way things sound and the feeling of support I have among that many Christians." At the 8:30, 9:45, and 11:00 Sunday morning services, the auditorium, decorated with simple brass chande-liers, powder-blue carpet, and department-store drapes, is generally crowded with predominately white, middle-class young families, middle-aged couples, and teenagers. (A children's worship is held elsewhere on the grounds.) Most Sunday services at the church begin with at least one and sometimes as many as four baptisms, performed by one of the church's eight pastors dressed in a black clerical robe. Accompanied by the fifteen member orchestra and seventy-five person, robeless choir quietly singing a contemporary chorus, such as "Let's Just Praise the Lord," the new convert is immersed as the pastor recites a traditional baptismal formula. The baptized believer rises from the water to the vigorous applause and loud "amening" of the 1,300 congregants. Such a welcome to the company of Baptists is both unnerving and energizing.

Afterward, the pastor of music ministries quickly rises from his blue-padded platform chair to lead the congregation in several fast-paced contemporary Christian choruses, which are printed in the bulletin. Often between the first and second chorus, the minister instructs congregants to "turn to your neighbor and tell them how good they look—even if they don't." Most congregants quickly shake hands and return to singing, ignoring the proposed conversation starter. But when Quinn approaches the microphone to encourage members to greet newcomers, congregants then make the rounds. Leonard Boswell, a new member and a former Episcopalian, commented about his experience as a visitor, "When they introduced the visitors, everybody shook our hand—they'd come from other pews. It was a real friendly place. But the thing that was really good was the preaching. And the singing, too. It is conservative fire and brimstone, but with everything all together it isn't scary. It is just the truth."

Leaning nonchalantly against the oak cross-shaped pulpit, Quinn generally begins his sermon with jocular Christian small-talk with the congregation. After a downpour during Youth Night at the 1994 Starlight Crusade, Quinn commented that it had rained on Youth Night for three years. He teased that if it rains again next year, "we'll look for sin in the youth ministry camp." Often as he makes self-deprecating jokes, Quinn calls on individuals in the congregation by name to "back me up now." But when Quinn instructs congregants to "turn with me in your Bibles to . . . ," the mood turns serious. With the rustle of turning pages sounding like rain inside the sanctuary, Quinn offers a pastoral prayer for all those who will hear this message—"Father, just let it convict them of their need for You." Congregants followed along as Quinn read passages, usually from the New International Version, but other versions, including the New American Standard and New King James Versions were sometimes cited as having better wording.

Downplaying the congregation's denominational affiliation, despite his former role as president of the Georgia Baptist Convention, Quinn's sermons often reinforced Hebron's unique character both in the Southern Baptist Convention and in the northeast Georgia region generally.[16] Mentioning the number of baptisms in the church during the past month, Quinn commented one Sunday that there were more people saved at Hebron in a month than many SBC churches can claim in a decade.[17] Local churches, which are generally not called by name, also come in for unflattering comparison. Quinn sermonizes, "We can't afford to wait until [the area's newcomers] come and beat down our doors, we've been called by God to go out and get them. We're a church that's willing to take risks to do that." No one is outside his call for inclusion in this generalist religious organization.

Quinn's messages do not, however, simply reinforce the congregation's sense of mission and communality, they also frequently press congregants to be more conscientious employees and merciful employers, to win souls to Christ, to be more devoted parents, to grow in the faith, and to be more playful spouses. Quinn's sermons were similar in content to his former biweekly Spiritual Life columns in the *Gwinnett Post Tribune*, whose titles included "Only with God's help can we learn to love for a lifetime," "No matter what your status, God can use your talents," and "My encounter with personal pain taught me we don't suffer alone." Yet his sermons also go beyond these more public messages to detail for congregants the dire present-day and other-worldly consequences of failing to heed his and the Bible's call to "right living." Quinn intended this conservative fire and brimstone theme, as Boswell termed it, to press through the superficiality of contemporary life, and convince Hebron congregants that Christian commitment really matters, now and hereafter. The sense of gravity that his tone and topic often conveyed was welcomed by many congregants. Charlene Lemond, a teenager involved in the high school ministry and a member of a Soul Winning Accountability Team, an age-graded evangelism training and support group, commented, "He's not just another person telling you, 'Stop and listen to me.' What he's saying really matters."

Quinn concludes each service with an all-eyes-closed-all-heads-bowed altar call. Sometimes as many as twenty people file forward to pray with pastors arrayed across the front of the auditorium. After a brief time of prayer, Quinn announces the names of those who responded and their reasons for doing so. Applauding, the congregants rise to their feet, and a receiving line assembles at the front of the sanctuary, as converts, new members, and the troubled are hugged and greeted.

Hebron, like most megachurches, provides high-intensity experiences of communality with relatively weak systems for insuring individual religious accountability—the assurance of right without the punishment of wrong.[18] It offers personal affirmation and anonymity. As such it is well suited to attract a wide range of members. Its individualized and small group programming provide emotional and spiritual support, while the large services evidence an intensity made possible in a throng of like-minded believers. Quinn, like many religious leaders, uses small groups as a speedy means to incorporate and establish systems of personal support among an increasingly diversified and mobile population (Wuthnow 1994b). Yet the dramatic growth of megachurches in the past decade also illustrates an additional phenomenon. Increasingly many congregants are not only comfortable in large organizations, but they seek them out for their full-service support substructure and for the drama, some say theater, of the large group experience (Schaller 1992:62).

Hebron was uniquely well suited as a generalist organization seeking to service a range of individuals with a wide array of personal and spiritual needs. It utilized familiar tools, such as computer technology and weekly newsletters, to extend its reach and to hold on to marginal members. Finally, Hebron maximized religious choices under the congregation's "big tent." The congregation's adaptation of these structures, practices, and options was supplemented with a profoundly effervescent, mass experience in Sunday morning gatherings and with intimate encounters of care in support groups. There is no mistaking it; Hebron members came to have church.

Hinton Memorial UMC: Specializing in History

Until the 1960s, Hinton Memorial UMC and Hebron Baptist each held services only every other Sunday, and congregants regularly worshipped together. Alfred and Lula DeVries, former Dacula shopkeepers and retired farmers, vividly recalled holding joint meetings with Hebron.

Alfred's father led singing at the combined services. Yet the recent histories of the congregations have diverged dramatically. While Hebron became a generalist congregation, Hinton Memorial UMC increasingly identified itself as a specialist congregation appealing to first wave newcomers and those who have relocated to the area in the past decade and who want to maintain a strong sense of the area's earlier history and ethos. This stance of cultural specialism evolved after a schism (discussed at length in chapter 4) made it clear that Hinton Memorial had a particular identity that congregants wanted to preserve at nearly any cost.

Founded in 1837, Hinton Memorial, long known as Dacula's establishment church, evolved from a single-family dominion during the 1960s to a steadily growing congregation in the late 1980s.[19] But in 1990, the congregation experienced a schism when Reverend Gerald Gerhard, their pastor of six years, and more than half of the members left the Methodist church to found an independent charismatic congregation, Trinity Christian Fellowship. Prior to the split, the congregation had tripled in size in five years, growing from a weekly attendance of forty to one hundred twenty.

Several long-time Hinton members contended that an attempt to compete with Hebron's generalist approach contributed to the schism. Nowell Altoona, head of the Trustees Committee during the schism, reported, "[Gerhard] was seeing that Hebron Baptist Church up the road from us, which is growing by leaps and bounds, and talking with some of the people there. I know he was having regular dialogue with Bryant Quinn and several others. He got depressed that things weren't going like that down here. He was not accomplishing what he thought he needed to do as fast as he wanted to do it. He felt as though the music needed to be different. Then things really started changing drastically."

Wounded by the schism, some Hinton Memorial congregants believed that they had been raided by Hebron. Lula DeVries expressed bewilderment that her children left Hinton, their family's church. "My daughter is a member there [at Hebron]. And our young son, he left our church and goes to Hebron Baptist. I guess they like it. There's a lot of activity there. Of course, when you have maybe two thousand members or something like that, or more, there's a lot of activity going on, and that's what young people like. Of course, with our limited membership, you can't have a whole lot of activity. You know the teenage kids; they like to be where all the other teens are. My daughter doesn't have children. But I mean, I think that's one of the reasons why Hebron has grown so fast. They have a lot of programs and all the teenagers want to go there."

Alfred DeVries, on the other hand, responded to Hebron's phenomenal growth and Hinton's loss of young families with a somewhat stunned admiration. "We have probably the stiffest competition in the world just up the road there—Hebron. Boy, they have tremendous services. And I mean they have a tremendous preacher. It is hard to compete with that fellow. And they've got a good program. We don't really have a good program for the children. We're trying to get one, but it's hard. I think we're doing real well with the senior citizens. We've got them participating and doing well. I think we need to try and appeal to the retirees moving into the area."

For many long-time members the primary aggravation was not the few members that Hebron attracted away from the membership rolls of Hinton. Rather, they begrudged their loss of status in Dacula's religious ecology. Long-time Hinton Memorial members felt their standing in the community and among other churches slip as Hebron grew in size, gradually becoming the area's congregation of note. Some Dacula oldtimers and Hinton members perceived that their community and congregation were subject to a self-described twin take-over—high-powered megadevelopers established real estate subdivisions as rival towns and an upstart megachurch shifted the status alignment in their local community.

From 1990 to 1993 as Hebron added more than one thousand congregants, Hinton Memorial stayed in a "holding pattern" under the pastoral leadership of Reverend Luther Dawson, a retirement-aged, traditional Methodist minister. The congregation, hampered by the financial strain of a heavily mortgaged parsonage and sapped of programmatic incentive, allowed youth and children's programs to die slowly. Though some efforts were made to attract the area's retirees, this population represented only a handful compared to the rapid inflow of young suburban families. The congregation relied mostly on new members from families who actively sought religious fellowship, who retained denominational loyalty (an increasingly uncommon circumstance among unchurched exurbanites), or who were contacted personally and informally by long-time Hinton members.[20]

In early 1993, however, as Hinton Memorial sought new pastoral leadership, the congregation was urged by their district superintendent to become a "redevelopment congregation." This program of the North Georgia Conference of the UMC was designed to enable congregations in the midst of changing communities to gain the financial resources, programming, and training in order to engage in active outreach. Denominational officials and consultants exerted considerable pressure on the congregation to participate. One official noted that if Hinton did not want to grow "there will soon be another United Methodist congregation on your doorstep." Although the Hinton members decided to join the redevelopment program, some members perceived it as the only option available to them if they did not want the denomination further to undermine their status in the community.

Hinton congregants, newcomers and oldtimers alike, did not relish the prospect of denominationally induced growth. They were determined to maintain their status as a small-town congregation with a strong sense of tradition that could be inculcated in a new group of folks, if only they were given some time. Newcomers, too, asserted that they joined Hinton exactly because they did not want to get lost in a large church. Many of the exurban newcomers who attended Hinton came after rejecting Hebron. Linda and Bill Lyle decided to attend Hinton, despite the superior programming that Hebron could offer their daughter with learning disabilities and their preteen son. Linda commented: "When Bill came here, he was like "Why don't we try the Baptist church?" because it's the biggest. He's worried about a youth program. Hinton doesn't really have one. It's growing though. But I've heard some really, really strange stuff about that Baptist church. It's too big. And they're not very nice. The Cub Scouts wanted to use one of their facilities, and they told them they couldn't do it because none of them were members. I mean, that's too big for your britches. Dacula isn't that big that they can't help. I mean if they're not going to help these kids, who are they going to help?" Being a community-focused congregation, with time and space to offer local civic groups was one of Hinton's reasons for being.

Despite inducement (or what some at Hinton perceived as coercion) to growth by denominational officials, Hinton Memorial has grown slowly. They have not attempted to match the programming and styles of Hebron Baptist, but they have increased programs that capitalize on what they perceived as their unique character. Bob Tracy, a coach at Dacula High School, believed that United Methodist denominational officials were naive if they thought that Hinton could compete with Hebron to become a mainline megachurch. He stated, "We can't fight that. So really the only people that we're gonna get are the ones who want to come to a small church where we are friendly." Billy Sue Hammond, a long-time resident and local real estate agent, maintained that Hinton, with its thirty to forty regular worshipers, should give up any notion of trying to "out Hebron Hebron" and instead invest its energies in finding something that is impossible for a megachurch to do.

As part of this strategy, Hinton members have been active in preserving the unique history of Dacula and in promoting a local boosterism. Congregants contrast their local focus with Hebron's appeal to the Atlanta metro area. Hinton trustees have sold plates and Christmas ornaments with etchings of the area's historic buildings; a Hinton member, an Ohio native and exurban newcomer, spearheaded the town's first Dacula Days and Memorial Day parade; and several Hinton members, including Linda Lyle, planned storytelling events at the church, in which congregational oldtimers tell mostly newcomers' youngsters what the area was like before it became an exurb of Atlanta. The congregation also revived, in 1994, the Methodist tradition of attendance at an annual camp meeting. In recent years, oldtimers and newcomers alike have fanned themselves under the open wood-framed shelter for a local camp meeting.

The congregation's newsletter, "All around Town," has provided a forum for the dissemination of the Hinton's specialist historical identity. Hinton employed its newsletter to inform the area residents of its commitment to "traditional" small-town values. The newsletter has for more than a decade been sent to everyone in the Dacula zip code area and has become the equivalent of a community crier and historical journal. The monthly newsletter publishes biographies of deceased local dignitaries and Civil War heroes, histories of abandoned local settlements, a "Roots" column sometimes detailing, for instance, the fictitious

reminiscences of two young boys named Bogan and Grunt, family recipes, and old photos of Dacula High School sports teams. This newsletter has reinforced and publicized the congregation's self-identity as a
traditional, small-town church, despite the rapid change in Dacula.
Hinton's "All around Town" has provided a means for getting out its
particular story and culture. Not coincidentally, getting this message out
has drawn local newcomers who are looking for exactly this type of
atmosphere.

Since 1993, under the leadership of an energetic young pastor, a
slightly growing number of committed, white, middle-class young
couples with children and the preponderance of elderly oldtimers at
Hinton have reckoned with the changes in their religious organizational
environment. But instead of aggressively pursuing growth as denominational officials had hoped, the congregation, hampered by continued
financial instability, has been slowly developing programs that exploit
their historical identity and that do not have to compete directly with
Hebron for participants. By developing a specialist historical identity
among the religious organizations in the area, Hinton has assured its
short-term survival and bides time for devising additional strategies and
resources for responding to its changing environment.

Trinity Christian Fellowship: Specializing in Diffusion

As evidenced by the bulletin board notice in 1995 that announced
"Souls saved in 1994—134; Goal—500," Trinity Christian Fellowship,
established in 1990 after the schism at Hinton Memorial UMC, has
been vigorously pursuing growth. By attracting the area's incoming white
middle-class exurbanites, the congregation has experienced rapid expansion, swelling from approximately fifty adherents following the split
to more than three hundred in 1997. TCF (as the congregation is known
to insiders) is an independent, interdenominational church affiliated
and in mission with Trinity Fellowship of Churches, a consortium of
charismatic congregations located mostly in the Southeast. After nearly
three years of itinerancy, often holding meetings in the Dacula High
School auditorium, the congregation built, and occupied in late 1993,
a new brick and sheet metal facility, located in a rapidly exurbanizing
area approximately six miles west of Dacula. Similar to Hebron Baptist

Church which defines its mission as "reaching northeast Georgia for Christ," Trinity Christian Fellowship identifies its area of influence as the "northeast metro [Atlanta] community." Despite this wide net, the congregation has continued to draw its membership primarily from Dacula and Lawrenceville.

With Gerald Gerhard continuing as pastor, Trinity Christian Fellowship has developed programming apace or slightly ahead of the demand created by the church's newcomers. In 1996 the congregation supported twelve age-graded Sunday school classes, fourteen small care groups, Fisherman's Ministry (a weekly evangelistic visitation ministry), fellowship suppers each Wednesday night, and age-graded mid-week family night programs, including Kid's Praise for children aged five through fifth grade, R.I.O.T. Youth Ministry, and L.I.F.E adult life-skills classes.[21] Although the congregation has not adopted the specialized therapy, special needs, or occupational support groups of Hebron, a therapeutic and self-help ethos was evident in the daily workings of Trinity Christian Fellowship. For example, fitness and diet guru Susan Powter's book *Stop the Insanity!* (1993) was read by the women's Sunday school adult class in 1995. The congregation's welcome letter, tied with a burgundy bow to match the auditorium's color scheme and distributed to all church visitors, excerpts the writings of an unnamed young African pastor. It begins: "I'm part of the fellowship of the unashamed. I have Holy Spirit Power. The die has been cast. I have stepped over the line. The decision has been made. I'm a disciple of His. I won't look back, let up, slow down, back away, or be still. My past is redeemed, my present makes sense, my future is secure. I'm finished and done with low living, sight walking, small planning, smooth knees, colorless dreams, tamed visions, mundane talking, cheap living, and dwarfed goals."

Although Trinity Christian Fellowship has explicit goals for annual growth, it seeks to diminish the negative connotations of expansion in its mission statement. The fellowship's brochure states its mission, "The vision God has given us is bold, exciting and full of opportunity. It is not our desire to be a 'Megachurch' with thousands of members. It is our desire to be a family oriented, nurturing, loving body of believers who understand the true goal of being Christian. . . . The goal of Trinity Christian Fellowship was to minister the love of Jesus to today's families."

Megachurch status, though it was unsavory to a few members, was perceived as a viable option for the congregation. Not only did Gerhard
have close association with Quinn, especially in the mid-1980s when
Hebron Baptist was just attaining mega-status, but Trinity Christian Fellowship had affiliated with Trinity Fellowship of Churches, a consortium of fast-growing charismatic congregations.[22] Thus Trinity's stated
intention of foregoing megachurch designs was not because either the
congregation or its pastor believed that such a goal was unattainable,
even in an religious ecology already dominated by a megachurch. Rather
Gerhard and Trinity members aimed to "mother" numerous other local
congregations.[23] In essence, the congregation expanded its sphere of
influence by decentralization, instead of centralization and consolida-
tion.[24] This specialized organizational strategy has allowed the congregation to understand itself as part of an array of complementary
organizations across the metropolitan area. It has also developed the
ritual of "sending out," as a significant part of many services. For example, a young couple from the congregation was commissioned in 1995
to pastor Promiseland Bible Church in Woodstock, Georgia—an exurb northwest of Atlanta. Sponsored by Trinity Christian Fellowship
and Trinity Fellowship of Churches, another congregant established an
affiliated Bible study and worship group at Georgia Tech where he was
a student. Members of TCF committed to making weekly treks to downtown Atlanta to assist with guitar playing and evangelism.

In addition to this "mothering" organizational strategy, Trinity's pastor has made shrewd use of existing organizations to get his message
out. In metro Atlanta, as in many urban regions, talk radio has been a
growth industry. It reaches people who are in their cars or at their desks
as a captive audience. Gerhard has been a regular guest on several Atlanta area Christian talk radio shows, one of which takes calls from
people on the way home from work. Gerhard regularly announced his
radio schedule, listing it in the Sunday bulletin, and encouraged congregants to keep the radio tuned to it in their cars and at work. Gerhard
also frequently indicated in his sermons and during his time on the radio that he had been listening to other talk show hosts, such as Rush
Limbaugh. By mentioning his status as a "ditto-head" (a title used by
followers of Rush Limbaugh to identify themselves as such), the pastor
of this conservative independent church tapped the fellow-feeling of

congregants and listeners and piggy-backed on Rush's legitimacy with his audience. For Trinity, talk radio provided a free forum for getting out their message and drawing interested parties to their meetings; and it helped this independent congregation establish links to an expansive cultural and religious movement with a ready-made audience.

The commonality between the mothering model of evangelism and political and cultural conservativism was the emphasis on family.[25] Not only did he see the congregation's mission as protecting and edifying the nuclear, "traditional" family, Gerhard used the mothering organizational approach both to reinforce the congregation's self-identity as a family serving other families and to establish strong patterns of evangelistic outreach, followed by vigorous discipleship programs. He stated often, "We can't give them birth and then expect them to grow up on their own." His sermons on missions were peppered with vivid physical metaphors and analogies comparing spawning nascent congregations to human parenting. Congregants were expected to do the spiritual equivalent of "wiping babies' butts," "burping out the gas," and "holding them through the night when they can't sleep."[26] But Gerhard abided no coddling of spiritual newborns. In a 1995 series of sermons entitled "Victorious Christian Living," he cited two reasons for Christians failing to mature and five keys to spiritual maturity. His reasons included that mature Christians permit spiritual infants to stay immature. He preached sternly, "God is clear. Here's the thing. You have to seek God and walk in right relationship with Him. If you're not doing that, GROW UP!" After a short pause for emphasis, he added, "I mean that in a loving way."

The congregation's altar call most clearly exhibited this "tough love" parental concern. One Sunday, he proclaimed "we're all family here and besides Jesus says confess your sins one to another and you will be forgiven." Gerhard often rejected the all-eyes-closed-all-heads-bowed traditional call, opting instead for the all-eyes-open-all-heads-up variety. As individuals filed toward the front of the congregation, and most did every service, congregants reached out to caress or hug their neighbors. Gerhard waited at the steps of the platform to embrace each person as he or she arrived. On their way to the front of the auditorium, individuals often grabbed facial tissues from the white baskets positioned under the first seat of every other row of chairs. They were needed as Trinity members wept together and confessed aloud their faults and pains. The altar service typically lasted no longer than ten minutes and was usually followed by several upbeat contemporary praise choruses, such as "I Just Came to Praise the Lord" and "My God Is an Awesome God," projected on the front wall. During this time congregants roamed the sanctuary patting, and hugging one another.

Trinity Christian Fellowship's ritual practice, such as impromptu offerings for needy congregations—including the (organizationally unaffiliated) Church of Christ on Auburn Road in 1996 when it burnt to the ground under suspicious circumstances—and commissioning ceremonies, conformed to its self-identity as a family whose mission it is to mother other congregations in its environs. Although the church perceived mega-status as an option, it had chosen a specialized organizational strategy of promoting a decentralized network of satellite congregations and groups. This arrangement had organizational benefits for a congregation with limited financial support from national or regional governing bodies, as Hebron had during the critical early years of growth. By capitalizing on its most ready resource—energetic young believers—the congregation sent people out to establish outposts in other areas, rather than bringing more and more people together in a single facility. This approach had the added benefit of diffusing leadership tensions within the congregation, as emergent religious entrepreneurs were given their own locales in which to ply their religious wares.

Organizationally, Trinity emphasized its small size as an advantage over Hebron. This congregation was a "family" in which knowing one another intimately was prized. They valued the family atmosphere, in part, because it allowed members to experience the fullness of the Spirit, including crying, laughing, and speaking in tongues, in a safe setting. Contrasting their small congregation with Hebron, Trinity members explained to me that they were not surrounded by strangers who would look askance at unconventional utterances and gestures. An independent operator within the religio-cultural milieu of conservative charismatic/Pentecostalism, Trinity had the advantages of establishing links to "baby" congregations elsewhere, and yet maintaining the autonomy and privacy of an intimate religious family. Within its organizational field, Trinity Christian Fellowship had embraced a specialist strategy for taking advantage of changes in its focal population while not engaging in head-to-head competition with an already established megachurch. Gerhard and TCF devised an organizational approach that was "schism" by design. The success of this tactic was related in no small degree to Gerhard's ability to mobilize people for spiritual parenting.

First Baptist Church–Dacula: Generally Holding On

First Baptist Church–Dacula was the congregation most hamstrung by Hebron's phenomenal growth in the prior decade. Even without Hebron nearby, First Baptist would have had stiff competition within its ecology from New Hope, New Life, New Covenant, Union Grove, Pleasant Grove, Hog Mountain, Alcovy, and Ebenezer Baptist churches, all located within a relatively thinly populated fifteen-mile radius. Although a saturation point for Baptist churches in the rural and semirural South has not yet been found, such a concentration of separate congregations bespeaks the area's checkered history of church splits and raids. Including Hebron, the congregations represent an even split between independent and Southern Baptist affiliation. Attendance numbers range from approximately fifteen people at Alcovy to Hebron's near 3,400 regular attenders. The majority of the congregations, however, have between one hundred and 150 Sunday worshipers.

Such is the case with First Baptist–Dacula, the only church of any affiliation located in what passes for Dacula's downtown. One of the independent Baptist congregations, the church is loosely affiliated with the General Association of Regular Baptists. Reverend Ivan Palmer, the church's pastor for the past decade, identified it as more theologically conservative than the Southern Baptist Convention. Palmer characterized the congregation as fundamentalist—"although we're not fighting fundies. It's just not my style." First Baptist does, however, have a long history of strident conservatism, breaking with the Southern Baptist Convention in the 1970s in protest over the denomination's leftward drift (see Ammerman 1990:44–71).

Much more than Hinton Memorial, First Baptist Church, founded during the Depression, was the true artifact of the area's recent rural past. Adjacent to Dacula's general store and ancient gas station, the brick facility was built in the mid-1950s by local farmers and factory workers. On my first visit in 1994, the small foyer entrance to the church sported a display case with David C. Cook publications and several dog-eared copies of "Closer Walk," a Christian sports newsletter. Most Sundays the wall above the display contained a carefully arranged collage of photos. In summer 1994, there was one of the church's family retreat at Amicalola Falls in the north Georgia mountains. The church's spare sanctuary could seat approximately 225, although at most services no more than fifty people were in attendance. At the front of the room were milky stained glass windows with a crown and a dove. The white pulpit was located immediately below the window. As the minister stood at the pulpit the crown and dove appeared to hover over his head. Overhead was a sign reading "'Til the Whole World Knows" which was left up all year, in 1995, after the annual mission conference.

Most Sundays, worshipers pulled up for services in their pick-up trucks and late model GM cars, as the church bells pealed. One Sunday in early 1995, when I climbed the stairs to the church instead of the tinny melodies played on an old upright piano that I had come to expect, I was greeted by the sounds of a modern synthesizer, electric guitar, and drums belting out the tune of a peppy contemporary Christian chorus. The church's part-time music minister, Palmer's son-in-law, was a recent music major graduate of Southeastern Bible College in Birmingham, Alabama. The contemporary music represented one innovation that First Baptist adopted in its efforts to draw Dacula's exurban newcomers. Some congregants enjoyed beginning each service with the praise choruses and worship songs, such as "I'm so Glad I'm a Part of the Family of God" and "In My Life Lord, Be Glorified," sung from the *Word* chorus books. However, Phyllis Kennington, a fifty-two-year-old long-time member, confessed that it "jangled" her nerves. She much preferred singing such standards as "'Tis so Sweet to Trust in Jesus," "There Is Power in the Blood," "What a Lovely Name," and "Victory in Jesus" from the hymnbook. She and other traditionalists in the congregation were accommodated with a hymn sing "set," as the music minister referred to the musical medleys of pietistic hymns. Even during the 11:00 Sunday service, congregants frequently called out the page numbers of hymns they favored. This juxtaposition of musical styles epitomized this heterogeneous body and its ambivalent responses to changes in its focal population and organizational ecology. First Baptist–Dacula attempted to maintain a generalist organizational strategy while the changes in the community made this bridging of cultures and styles increasingly organizationally complex. Thus First Baptist–Dacula seemed to mix and match stylistic and cultural responses in an effort to appeal to everyone, and in the process often slowly drove away nearly everyone.

Despite his efforts to update the congregation's practices, programs, and style, Palmer seemed more at home with a traditional storytelling format. He was wont to ramble and veer off during services to relate long and circuitous narratives. For example, one Sunday morning, Palmer recounted in detail his meeting with a member's brother-in-law who had recently lost his leg in an industrial accident, including a mention of the red velvet cake he was served. During the same service, he called on a woman in her mid-thirties to tell about her trip to Bolivia to see her missionary parents. Worried that he was putting her on the spot with his impromptu invitation, he told her "don't panic, it's just family here." With no evidence of panic, the woman followed Palmer's example and spoke for approximately ten minutes. Palmer also invited considerable spontaneous lay participation during the service, often asking a congregant to come to the pulpit to lead a song, offer prayers, or testify. Services here often ran nearly two hours.

Scripture passages were generally read from the King James Version. Sermons often highlighted the Bible's lessons for helping persons handle their anxieties and fear. Palmer preached a series of sermons in 1993 on how to establish a calm heart in a strife-torn world. He spoke about living in a nasty, fearsome world where no one and nothing could be counted on all the time. He used long, detailed examples of being out of work, health problems, business reversals, and betrayal. One Sunday morning after about fifteen minutes of enumerating the dangers of the modern world, he said, "But we don't have to focus on that." Instead he urged a concentration on the peace of heaven, although "the promise of heaven will not always ease the problems of today." Palmer's itemization of the hazards of this world was countered by his detailed description of the beauties of heaven. He spoke about the mansions in heaven, which, he said, most people erroneously think are like the homes on Harbins Road, an upper-middle-class neighborhood of newcomers near Dacula. Directing the congregants to turn to Revelation in their Bibles, Palmer assured them that "We understand that heaven will be more fabulous than anything we can imagine." In heaven, he reported, "There is plenty of room in the family for the young and the old," unlike the homes on Harbins. He also said that there would be no "pecking order" in heaven, as there is on earth.

In addition to speaking of the otherworldly comfort provided in the Bible, Palmer regularly highlighted the direction for everyday life contained in the word of God. He admonished congregants one Sunday evening that "All we need for life and godliness is found in the Bible" and that the Bible had "practical, down-to-earth truth with handles." He often spoke about people whom the world would "throw away," but that God never throws anyone away so neither can we. That commitment was acted out as services closed with an altar call, often with strains of "Just as I Am" swelling in the background. Congregants were assured that though changes in their community were often frightening and that they may feel like the throw-aways of the community's coming culture, there was always room for them, "just as they are" at the altars of First Baptist.

However, First Baptist's generalized organizational strategy has failed to take account of Dacula's realigned religious organizational field. Like the blue-collar workers who filled its pews, this church had been largely side-stepped by the area's growth and transformation. The congregation's attempts to modernize satisfied neither the newcomers who wanted both energetic worship experiences and additional programs, nor the oldtimers who were disoriented by the changes. Although Palmer implemented several new programs and services in the congregation, including an AWANA youth group, seniors meetings, and a nursery, he had little help from congregants. Many of the programs were staffed by Palmer's family. His two daughters and their families, as well as a nephew and his mother, attended the church. Lois Palmer, his wife, single-handedly organized the annual week-long Vacation Bible School.[27] The finances of the congregation, though meager, were not disastrous, primarily due to the building having been paid off.

This lack of programming, resources, and personnel made it nearly impossible for First Baptist to retain young adults, teenagers, and their families. Palmer commented bitterly, "Hebron has sucked teenagers out of here like a vacuum cleaner." Particularly critical of what he deemed to be the megachurch's over-programming which separated children from their parents at church and which took them out of the home too often, he accused Hebron of collusion in modern society's efforts to tear apart the family. This attitude was shared by congregant Joan Swallow, a "stay-at-home" mother and wife of a missionary sponsored by a Lawrenceville-based independent Baptist mission agency, who stated confidently: "Of course, I've heard that they've had two kidnappings over there. They're so big, you see. They don't know who's in the nursery and who's not."

Hebron leaders though deny that their nursery was plagued by kidnappings. Swallow's comment, however, revealed the level of threat perceived by First Baptist's members. Their children were being kidnapped, in a manner of speaking—drawn away by Hebron's programming and mystique.

First Baptist generally held on, but they were not in a position to compete on the basis of providing all things to all people—the way that Hebron could. Without a specialized sense of the congregation's history and connection to the community, it was unable to attract exurbanites craving a sense of embedded systems of support. Without a viable organizational strategy for manageable growth or institutional resources from a denomination or similar organization, its attempts to update worship and to implement growth strategies were often ill conceived and underfunded. In fact, by beginning to make changes in the church's cultural style before the church was actually attracting newcomers, leaders expended the congregation's limited resources and short-lived tolerance for change. This was dire given the long-term transformation of the religious organizational ecology.

Felding Chapel Baptist Church and Perimeter Ministries: Congregational Demise

Other congregations have been unsuccessful in holding or establishing a place in the religious ecology of Dacula. Felding Chapel Baptist Church, an independent congregation that met only on Sundays for worship, had no programs, no budget, and no paid pastor, has gone "dormant"—as one local identified the church's current state. It is an apt metaphor for this congregation whose primary constituents had been an extended family of farmers, who split from a nearby congregation during the 1930s over "modernizing" theology.

Until its demise, the congregation consisted of about fifteen members; any ten of whom were likely to be present for Sunday morning worship. Worshipers usually sang their opening revival choruses a cappella, although occasionally one of the younger men brought a guitar. The services were no nonsense and fast moving. After three or four choruses, the preacher for the day would rise to tell the congregation what bills they had received in the week's mail. This sum was the amount expected to come in during the offering. Prayer requests were expressed in verbal shorthand, since everyone present seemed to know the situation—except me. "Keep praying for Evelyn, you know, about the leg" was a request I heard one Sunday. After a time of prayer that was done in unison with hands raised to the Lord, the preacher launched into his sermon. Often delivered by Rodney Nason, a regular preacher, the sermon began with a variation on "The Lord just laid this on my heart last night, and I want to share . . . ." Family members settled back for a sermon usually lasting about thirty minutes. Unlike most other Baptist churches in the Dacula ecology, Felding Chapel members did not carry Bibles and follow along with the preacher. As the words tumbled from the pulpit, their familiarity seemed to be taken for granted, with "amens" offered for various verses read from the King James Version. At the conclusion of the sermon, the oak offering plate was passed around from pew to pew by congregants. (There were no ushers.) The service concluded, just after the noon hour, with the invitation to come up and "kneel for a time of prayer." Nearly everyone went to the front of the church, except the one or two teenage males in the congregation. After several minutes of praying at the front, members met at the coffeepot perched on a slatted wooden chair near the door. This time of informal sharing was as intimate as were the prayer requests. I wrote in my field journal after a Sunday at Felding Chapel, "I feel like I'm standing around outside of a hospital door, and everyone is speaking very softly. I didn't stay long. I knew I made them very uncomfortable." It was clearly a family moment.

The Felding family had built the church on their donated land. The cement block facility was tidy and spare. Electricity had been added only during the past ten years, and still the facility had a simple bare bulb in the center of the meeting room and one outlet for a coffeepot at the rear. Behind the church were approximately twenty grave markers—

many of them bearing the Felding name. Also to the back of the meeting hall were outhouses, still the only restroom facilities available.

Rodney Nason told me the year before the church closed, "We're just fundamental Bible people. We always preach the gospel and let them decide what's right. I just guess that there were more [members] that thought that they wanted more modern preaching and religion." Nason worked full-time as a mechanic for the Bartow County school system and was saddened to see the congregation dwindle. He had received his call to preach when he was fifteen years old and always tried to be faithful. He never worried much about his lack of formal biblical training because he was assured that God gave him the right words for the hour. When I contacted Nason again in 1996, as the church was closing, he felt confident that the closure was temporary. "God will help us rise up again." However, still in 1998, Felding Chapel sat empty most Sundays. Former members use the facility for family reunions, and Nason anticipated having the annual revival during the summer. One funeral had taken place at the chapel during the past year. According to Nason, most congregants had either begun going to the Lawrenceville Church of God, a megachurch in a nearby town, Hebron Baptist Church, or had simply stopped going to church. Rodney continued to pursue his calling to preach by filling in as preacher in small Baptist churches in surrounding counties.

Felding Chapel succumbed to the liabilities inherent in its founding some sixty years earlier. As a family chapel, the church had been imprinted with a particular identity that resisted alteration even as the environment changed (cf. Becker 1998). For this congregation, the intimacy of family was more important than organizational survival. It is likely that this scenario accounts for many other plots of graves now tended by strangers. Not unlike the abandoned homesteads that dot the northern Plains, these cemeteries and dormant churches remind the observer of a landscape whose population has changed. The private, kin-centered specialist churches have been largely transformed by the immense transfer of population that has happened in Gwinnett County. Few families have enough extended kin within driving distance to make family chapels a viable worshiping community. Some similar congregations have adapted to the changes in their environment by opening their doors more widely; others have closed their doors more securely. Felding

Chapel Baptist Church now is unbolted only occasionally and then for a variety of family homecomings or homegoings.

Perimeter Ministries was also eventually unsuccessful in establishing a place in Dacula's religious ecology, but for quite different reasons. Founded by a former football player who became a Pentecostal evangelist, the congregation initially located in the Gwinnett Progress Center. From Highway 316, the only evidence of the congregation was an illuminated, portable sign at the entrance to the park, reading "Perimeter Ministries—Meet God Every Time" and with the service schedule below. The sign was the subject of considerable tension with some of the businesses in adjacent office space.

Dan Johnstone, the pastor and founder of Perimeter Ministries, was associated with the Evangelical Free Church in the Midwest before coming to the Atlanta metro area for a short stint playing for the Atlanta Falcons football team. Johnstone had received his biblical training through a year-long series of seminars. When he rented the first building for Perimeter Ministries, the congregation consisted of twelve people, including two families with children (in addition to his own wife and two children) and several single young adults. The congregation had been meeting in the Johnstone home, but he believed that they needed the publicity that they could get with a building.

Perimeter Ministries followed a common pattern of worship among evangelical congregations. During Sunday morning Bible Study, Anne, Johnstone's wife, played the electric piano while the pastor and one other worship leader directed the congregation in choruses. When I visited in 1995, the blue molded chairs were situated in concentric half circles in front of the pulpit. The main door opened immediately into the worship space so that anyone who entered immediately became the focus of attention from the front. Johnstone greeted each person who arrived, either by name or with a general greeting, as the singing continued. The pattern created impromptu choruses as names were added to the song's lyrics in order to personalize the message. On another visit in fall 1995, singing lasted for approximately forty minutes, followed by a testimony time. The ten participants were each expected to speak up about what God had done for them during the past week. The testimonies could be either a comment consisting only of several sentences, or a detailed account of a dilemma resolved. For example, that Sunday, a brunette spoke—who looked to be in her early twenties, attending with her six-year-old son, who had learning disabilities. She related how she come to peace about home-schooling her child after months of struggling to find the right teacher for him in the public schools. After each person testified, Johnstone would approach the individual, lay his hands on both shoulders, and say, "We thank you, Lord!"

The small-group feeling of the gathering was facilitated by Johnstone's practice of sitting during his sermon, rising only to write on the blackboard when he turned to another passage of scripture. The sermon was interactive. Individuals commented if he was moving too quickly from one verse to another in the topical sermon. Questions seemed appropriate at anytime. After approximately forty-five minutes of Bible study, the service concluded with prayer for understanding and a direct appeal for each participant to give his or her life completely to Christ. As Johnstone issued the challenge, he called out names asking God to help these people break chains of darkness and bondage. The intimacy of the service was slowly dispelled as individuals wiped their tears, hugged, and turned to greet the only stranger in the room—me. The close surroundings of a living room was palpable even though the congregation met in an office park. This small group knew one another and had clearly shared much together.

Though I didn't visit the congregation again during my time in the field. I noticed that about six months after my initial visits, the electric sign was gone from the front of the office park. I contacted Perimeter Ministries to learn their fate. Pastor Johnstone explained that they had moved out of the Dacula area because more of their members resided in Duluth, another exurb north of Atlanta. Dan was sanguine about moving, "we'll probably be back with another church planted there in ten years."

This failure within the Dacula ecology highlighted both the significant vulnerability of congregations starting out without institutional support, such as comes from denominations, and the dilemma of organizational density. During the 1980s and 1990s many more congregations were founded in the Dacula area; many of these congregations survived because they were early innovators, culturally specific, or organizationally savvy. However, some congregations simply were unable to establish themselves in an increasingly crowded religious ecology.

Perimeter Ministries developed a generalist approach serving a broad geographical region. However, since other congregations, including Hebron Baptist and Trinity Christian Fellowship, were already located within the environment, relocating from a crowded ecology to a relatively open ecology allowed the congregation to survive while retreating (at least temporarily) from Dacula's environment.

Organizing Ecological Change

By 1995, Dacula's twenty-four religious organizations had been dramatically restructured along three lines: the status order among the religious organizations, the variety of religious organizational form, and the ways of defining cultural niches.

Status ranking or the order of power and prestige among religious organizations in Dacula had undergone a destructuring and was in the process of restructuring on the basis of alternate norms. As discussed earlier, this destructuring was attributable to the local processes of urban deconcentration and the fundamental religious alterations that occurred across the United States as well as in particular places. The hegemony of mainstream denominations was disrupted by new religious routines of belonging—voluntarism, the diversification of religious organizational forms, and the increased plurality of religious cultures. These alterations in religious life meant that power and prestige arrangements among congregations at the local level were in flux.

Long-held beliefs about the socio-economic and educational levels of church members ceased to determine the assignment of status—beliefs which in Dacula had buttressed the high status of Hinton Memorial UMC. Reed (1986) writes: "In the South, as elsewhere, each denomination (and, within denominations, each congregation) ministers primarily to a particular social stratum. . . . Although Pentecostals and Episcopalians may have the same creed, neither desires to worship with the other" (62). The publicly perceived socio-economic and educational statuses among congregations had been altered with the arrival of newcomers, who were generally more financially and educationally privileged than most long-time Dacula natives. This earlier status structure was also often based on the oligarchies of prominent families who when they graced the pews of local churches, upped their own and the congregation's reputation. Many newcomers were simply unaware of the historical accretion that had made some families prominent in the community.

Indeed, the earlier status structure had begun to unravel even before waves of newcomers arrived, as most mainline denominational superstructures buttressing local congregational standing went into financial and numerical decline and as communal denominational identities were increasingly superseded by conservative or liberal orientations within denominations (see Wuthnow 1988). The voluntarism of newcomers further hastened the destructuring of local patterns of status among religious groups. These newcomers were more likely to choose congregations for reasons not entirely unrelated to socio-economic and educational status but also more based on other personal motives, defined by their feelings of a congregation's spiritual relevance, its practices of community-building, and ethos of its worship (Hammond 1992). Thus the destructuring of the congregational status order was an outcome of the localized changes caused by exurbanization and by broad patterns of religious restructuring, which also caused significant local alteration.

The result was not status leveling among religious organizations, but rather status confusion and sometimes rivalry. The norms for establishing the order of power and prestige were no longer taken for granted. My interviews among a range of religious leaders and congregants revealed that the two most frequently criticized churches were Hinton Memorial UMC and Hebron Baptist. In casual conversation, I sometimes heard people mention Hinton UMC as "thinking too highly" of itself. Herb Payne—a long-time Dacula resident whose family had worshiped at Hog Mountain Baptist—commented, "Probably I'd say that Hinton [Memorial UMC] is the church where you go if you've got money. They'll make you feel right at home." Bobbi Jo Leander said about her own church (Hinton Memorial UMC), "Well, we've really contributed a lot to this town—in terms of taking care of civic life—and made sure that local people were taken care of. I don't mean that we did that up-front, often we just helped behind the scenes—making sure that those who needed help got it." Hinton's civic prominence and financial largesse had within a previous status order made it both the congregation of note and the target of antipathy among those locals who thought that the church had "lorded it over" others—as one pastor in the area stated it.

The hostility expressed toward Hebron Baptist was often much more vituperative. Hebron had gotten "too big for [its] britches," according to Hinton Memorial newcomer, Linda Lyle. New Hope Baptist pastor, Dana Alsop, said, "Now, I'm not saying it's bad, but sometimes it seems that Hebron can act without considering anyone else in the community. For example, when they have their Starlight Crusades they don't seem to care that other churches are having revivals, too. Our people can't even get through the crowds to come." According to my interviews, Hebron's size and institutional connections were the most frequent reasons given for the expressions of antagonism toward it. Hebron congregants often tacitly defended their church from these barbs. "We've really done a lot for the community," said Anna Grove, who had attended Hebron for four years at the time of her interview in 1995. "We've got so many groups meeting here you can't keep track. And people that don't even attend play on the [softball] teams." Many people complained about the increased traffic surrounding Hebron's facility at the corner of Fence and Hebron Church Roads. Some resented the fact that Gwinnett County police regularly directed traffic flow out of the church's parking lots.

Within Dacula, the congregational status order was determined by multiple norms, but increasingly organizational size and dominance became the primary norm for determining status, and historic prominence and presence of locally distinguished families slowly waned as a norm. The rivalry over perceived organizational status is an important dynamic within local religious ecologies. As I discovered, it was certainly the topic of frequent fellowship hall and dinner table conversation. Status rivalry develops within religious ecologies when disruptions occur. Religious restructuring involves establishing an alternate set of norms for determining congregational status within the local ecology, even while the vestiges of older norms have yet to be fully displaced. Thus within many ecologies various status-determining norms coexist—making it much more difficult for locals to decide who are the winners and who are the losers. Rivalry, rather than competition for a common set of human or financial resources, is the basis for these status tensions. As Park and Burgess (1969) contend, competition is "strictly speaking interaction without formal contact" (506). Within the religious ecology of Dacula, congregations rubbed up against one another and often hackles were raised. Under Dacula's circumstances of rapid change, rivalry expressed by congregations was an essential part of adaptation. Rivalry, when asserted by less dominant groups, brings the high status organizations down to their level and also raises their own esteem, often producing greater capacity for future adaptation.

A second line of destructuring and restructuring in the local community had to do with alteration in religious organizational forms. In Dacula, I observed three innovations in organizational form: the development of a megachurch, the proliferation of groups without congregational or denominational affiliation, and the practice of congregational "mothering." While many historians would argue that the occupational hazard of sociologists is to name something as new because we are newly aware of its existence, it can be argued that some organizational forms are new at least within particular places. For example, while megachurches may look much like organizational patterns of tall-steeple downtown congregations and complex Catholic parishes of a previous era and even of the twentieth century, they are new to exurbia. Made feasible by urban deconcentration and interstate highways, these very large congregations now can establish an organizational supremacy that sends shock waves through an entire religious ecology.[28] In Dacula, other congregations were challenged to position themselves vis-à-vis this early congregational success. In fact, the dominance of the megachurch was based, in part, on an ecology of slow-responders. That is, Hebron Baptist could not have developed such significant early dominance were it not that other congregations were not attracting followers as the demographics of the area altered. Once the megachurch had developed as a generalist organizational type, other religious organizations were under greater ecological pressure to develop specializations.

Likewise, one would be hard pressed to argue that there are more independent groups and congregations in the Dacula area now than earlier in its history—given the locality's variety of small self-governing, kin-focused country churches and abandoned graveyards from congregations whose names have been lost to contemporary memory. Nonetheless, the forms and number of specialized groups has expanded with urban and religious restructuring. Some of these congregations were independent because of church splits. (Two others, in addition to Trinity Christian Fellowship, within this ecology fit this profile.) These newly independent congregations could transform their "seeming" failure into advantage by devising new patterns of translocal affiliation. Sometimes these loose, decentralized organizations continued their patterns of "schism"—now under friendly circumstances—in order to form new congregations. This became TCF's deliberate strategy for organizational diffusion, leadership development, and dissemination of their message (see also Miller 1997). However, some of these independent congregations, such as Perimeter Ministries, without the resources of denominations or other parenting bodies to assist them through the rocky early years, suffered an early demise. The liability of newness took its toll (Freeman, Carroll, and Hannon 1983). Thus TCF's "mothering" strategy continued a practice of caregiving and resource sharing which had enabled its own survival. This specialist organizational form was adapted to the risks of a volatile religious ecology.

Other organizational forms relatively new to the area were freestanding special purpose and support groups, including the Christian Business Women, Christian Entrepreneurs, Christian Weight Watchers, and the Christian Coalition.[29] The availability of desktop publishing, population specific address labels, and the relative ease of producing newsletters helped to bring together many religious groups that would ordinarily be too dispersed over the metropolitan landscape to form a coherent group. For example, in northeastern Gwinnett County, Hadassah, a Jewish educational, social, and charitable organization, began as a newsletter and evolved into a new chapter of this the largest women's Zionist organization in the United States. These organizations provided expanded choice for individuals within the local ecology.

Third and finally, local cultural norms were transformed in Dacula. Congregations had once relied on denominational identity to locate themselves and orient current and potential members. With denominational affiliation increasingly less salient for defining niches, some congregations have developed new cultural identifiers. It is in the local organizational ecology that congregations often develop these specialist cultural identities that distinguish them from one another as well as align them with a larger national or international religio-cultural milieu. For example, congregations identify themselves as "fighting fundies" or as the peace-loving sort, just as the pastor of First Baptist–Dacula identified divergent cultural approaches. However, sometimes these cultural identities are simply too inclusive. Those congregations that were continuing on without a specific focus population or specialized congregational culture often found themselves failing to attract new members and losing members who were resistant to changes that were attempted. In the Dacula environment, being a generally "peace-loving" fundamentalist congregation with a mixed bag of programmatic and cultural offerings presented little that was attractive for newcomers or oldtimers.

Some congregations, however, developed narrower cultural niches, such as "legacy cultures" that accentuated their ties to the locality in ways that made them repositories of local history, culture, and "tradition." Felding Chapel Baptist maintained such a narrow definition of acceptable tradition that they had no room for compromise with changing circumstances, thus this family-centered congregation became "dormant." Other congregations were successful in attracting a slow but steady inflow of exurbanites eager to identify with this particular place. Hinton Memorial UMC happened on this specialist culture in response to disruption in the ecology. The account of this congregation's ability to adapt to alterations in the religious ecology is the story of chapter 4.

As the number, composition, and activities of residents in the Dacula environs changed, local organizations experienced pressures and incentives to adapt in order to meet the new demands of the population. Organizations in this ecology dealt with these heterogeneous demands in multiple ways. Some organizations responded quickly with innovative measures to meet the challenges. These early innovators were often successful because of the failure of other organizations to respond quickly, and their success created new organizational pressures within the ecology. Residents within the locality were heterogeneous. Not all exurbanites or long-time Dacula homefolk wanted the same features in a religious organization. Dacula's diverse population posed complicated problems of organizational adaptation. Some organizations sought to replicate the successful approach of the early innovative congregations, while others developed alternate specialist organizational forms and identities, displaying diverse responses to ecological challenges. Other congregations were simply unable to find or hold their niche within this rapidly changing religious ecology.

Chapter 4

New Neighbors

Thou shalt love thy neighbour as thyself.
—Matthew 19:19, KJV

A Congregation in Transition

In the midst of Dacula's altered religious ecology, each congregation negotiated the dilemmas of welcoming or distancing itself from new neighbors. This chapter is an exploration of the internal dynamics associated with the coming of new neighbors within one congregation— Hinton Memorial UMC. The arrival of new neighbors altered familiar stories and rituals. Sometimes change resulted in wrenching controversy; at other times, though, the congregation's narratives and practices were modified almost unconsciously. The oldtimers' recipes for doing things were altered by the formulas of newcomers; and the stories that newcomers told picked up the themes offered by the oldtimers.

One story shows the transformation. For years, the exchange of surplus garden produce has been a common practice of neighboring in Dacula and a communal sacrament in many of the area's religious organizations. This practice can readily be interpreted in light of the area's agricultural past. The exchange continued even after farming ceased to be dominant in the area since long-time residents frequently "farmed their yards," as one oldtimer put it. These large homestead gardens yielded more produce than could be consumed by the shrinking families of oldtimers. So the exchange persisted.

During the summer of 1993—three years after the cataclysmic schism—the vegetables were again brought by many long-time members of Hinton Memorial UMC and displayed on a bench near the back door of the church. Vernon England shared from his bounty of yellow squash, Lula DeVries contributed cucumbers, and tomatoes appeared as if manna from heaven. After the Sunday morning worship service, several long-time members filed by filling their brown paper bags with the goodness. I was invited to do the same and departed that Sunday with the makings for a hearty vegetable stew.

The next Sunday during the announcement time, Reverend Luther Dawson, the congregation's retirement-aged minister, urged the congregation to make sure "you all pick up your veggies" because last week he had several rotten tomatoes on the bench by Wednesday. "I don't want to give anyone ammunition," he teased. Despite Dawson's admonition, tomatoes and zucchini were left on the bench to rot again that week. The ritual of the bringing of the bounty, which had been a communal event in the congregation for many years, soon stopped. It was replaced by the private exchange of goods as a few members brought individual brown bags to pass discreetly to one another rather than displaying the produce for all to appreciate and partake. This seemingly small change in this congregational practice highlighted the changes that were occurring inside and outside the church. The congregation was now attracting more area newcomers who did not have garden produce to share. Thus the ritual of exchange was meaningful for only some of the congregants. Without this shared understanding, the practice was altered to include only those for whom it still had significance.

For some Hinton congregants, the act of sharing their produce had deep religious meaning connecting them to their fellows across time. It was a significant part of the religious tradition of the place. Sarah Coser, an elderly women whose arthritic knees made attending services and tending to the garden outside her trailer home difficult, said of the produce exchange: "I guess it's just one way we tell folks 'hey.' Everybody that comes to church has to eat, don't they?" Religiously, the ritual confirmed her sense of participation in a community sharing in the bounty of God's harvest. For many newcomers, this ritual—though outside their range of personal experience and perceived by some to be a remnant of a distant past—represented a vision of a community with which they wanted to be associated. It was a symbol of the "simpler" life, for which many exurbanites had moved to the far reaches of the metropolitan region. However, despite their attraction to its charm, these newcomers did not have the practices and lifestyles that supported the vegetable exchange. One newcomer admitted to having purchased corn from her neighbor to bring to the exchange before it ended. Furthermore, they (unlike me) did not simply accept the bounty without reciprocating. Thus the practice was curtailed and privatized.

In Dacula, good neighboring is a time-honored tradition with extensive (if largely unspoken) protocols and reciprocal responsibilities. Their neighboring involves common stories, communal history, and symbols that represent and guide day-to-day patterns of interaction. Neighboring as a set of meanings "that fit a context of ideas and institutions" must be understood within its local environment.[1] In Dacula neighboring has been perceived as something quite different than what was done in Atlanta, for instance. It was interwoven with the particular history of the area and its local families. Finally, the stories people told about their neighboring were not only shaped by the past, they also fashioned the future, identifying potential neighbors and strangers and imagining dangers and possibilities. Dacula residents were at the mercy of the stories they told as much as those stories were at their mercy (cf. Bellah et al. 1985).

The existence of divergent interpretations of the religious ideas, practices, and mission of the congregation was evident throughout much of my time at Hinton Memorial UMC. The experience of church during this time of change varied for newcomers and oldtimers. It was within this intraorganizational context of negotiating the community's and the church's changes that the designations of "oldtimers" and "newcomers" became most significant. Though age was not the only determinant in designating oldtimers and newcomers, factionalism in the congregation was not unrelated to its largely bimodal age distribution. In 1993, the largest group of Hinton members were between thirty-one and forty.[2] The church had a relatively small number of middle aged (fifty-one to sixty years old) and a large number of senior citizens (sixty-one and over).

Generational differences were related to the ideas and routines of belonging for oldtimers and newcomers. For example, whereas newcomers tended to have social and religious networks that spanned the metropolitan region and were not coextensive with their residential neighbors (cf. Fischer 1982), oldtimers' social and religious networks

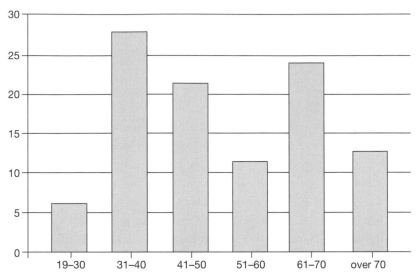

Figure 4.1 Age of Hinton Members, 1993

tended to be confined to residential neighbors. Secondly, oldtimers were more likely to emphasize ascriptive rather than chosen ties to religion. That is, they maintained a tradition of Methodism in their historical families, rather than seeking a congregation that most suited their current familial beliefs and lifestyles. Newcomers were more likely to be religious switchers and to expect personally relevant programming. Finally, oldtimers were deeply embedded in the fabric of the Dacula community and had strategies for responding to change that differed from those employed by newcomers. Forty-six percent of Hinton Memorial congregants had resided in the community for five years or less, likewise 46 percent had lived in the community for eleven or more years—many for more than twenty-five years.

Despite these differences, in many ways both newcomers and oldtimers wanted the same thing—to participate in a community that shaped edifying narratives. Nonetheless, the differences in their stories, the complex of ideas and institutions within which they made sense, and the visions of life these stories made possible often created fissures between oldtimers and newcomers that were revealed in the habits, comments, and practices of religious interaction.

Two caveats are worth emphasizing. My intention in using this distinction between oldtimers and newcomers is not to suggest that ev-

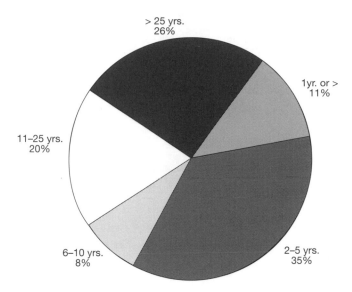

Figure 4.2 Hinton Members' Length of Community Residence, 1993

eryone in the congregation fell neatly into one or the other group. As I noted in chapter 2, the first wave of newcomers often distinguished themselves from those who arrived in the mid-1980s and 1990s, and, indeed, these initial newcomers did look somewhat distinct from the latter group. They tended to be more middle-aged and financially established than later newcomers. However, "oldtimers" saw both groups as "newcomers"—thus, I admit, that I am somewhat privileging the perspective of oldtimers in categorizing the first and second wave groups together. Nonetheless, many of the first wave of newcomers would agree that they were treated as newcomers. Finally, I do not propose that this dichotomy is the only relevant categorization of members. Rather the terms, "newcomers" and "oldtimers," were used by Hinton congregants and others in the community as relevant designations, highlighting differences in tenure in the community and in cultural character.

On Being a New Neighbor

For many newcomers, arrival at Hinton Memorial UMC was both familiar—sometimes harkening back to childhood religious participation—and alien, inviting and distancing. The record of my first visit at Hinton

Table 4.1
A Comparison of Oldtimers and Newcomers

	Oldtimers	*Newcomers*
Community Tenure	46 percent 11 or > yrs.	46 percent 5 or < yrs.
Length of Hinton Membership	34 percent 11 or > yrs.	52 percent 5 or < yrs.
Religious Switching	47 percent life-long Methodists	12 percent life-long Methodists
Network Patterns	locally interarticulated	geographically diffused

Memorial illustrates those competing experiences. Although I clearly was not a typical newcomer, I came to realize that my experience and perceptions as a newcomer were not uncommon for others. The passage below comes from my first fieldnotes and journal entries recorded after visiting Hinton Memorial in 1992 (cf. Wolf 1992).

> Hinton Memorial is on Dacula Road about one block off Georgia Highway 8. The church is set back from the road; it is a brick building with a steeple. The scene made me think of the Charlie Price song of a "little white church in the dell." The front doors open right into the main sanctuary. Anyone arriving late attracts immediate attention. Luckily I came early. Even so, everyone turned to look at me.
>
> I went to the vestibule of the church down a side aisle trying to look as though I was seeking a bathroom. The Sunday school classrooms and parlor are in the back of the church. They are small and stale-smelling. They reminded me of the church I attended as a child. Chewed up and broken crayolas were in a box on one of tables. There were no children in the rooms. I later learned that they let the kids go outside to play after about 30 minutes of Sunday school.
>
> The church is very neat and clean, but simple—almost stark. The bathroom, which I found adjacent to the kitchen, was newer than the building as a whole. [Since I was then using crutches,] I was glad to see that it had a handicap accessible toilet. A good thing about having an older congregation. There were few religious symbols displayed in the sanctuary. The only ones I could see were a wooden 2x4 cross behind the pulpit and

a baptismal font to the right of the pulpit. The sanctuary had padded pews and plush red carpet.

The pastor, Luther Dawson—a sixtyish man in a suit and tie—greeted me and asked me if I was from the area. People were quite friendly, smiling and nodding, but no one came up to talk with me. It was clear that they didn't have many visitors. I felt a little like I had made a find. There was a visitor's card, said an elderly man who was serving as usher, but they were not in the pews. Finally, after some searching he found one to give to me. I also received an orange carnation corsage since it was Mother's Day. I noted that I was not a mother and the usher said, "Well, you'll be one someday. Take the flower." So I did.

The 42 congregants were mostly aged, with three families with young children. More women were present than men. There were eight choir members in a loft made for 40 people. Six children went forward for the children's moment. The style of the service was a relaxed liturgical one with many congregants offering comments throughout, particularly during the announcements. At times the minister seemed barely in control of the service. The announcements were the single longest element of the service. The church is having a fund-raising chicken-que, bake sale, yard sale and car wash next weekend. So there was an impromptu meeting during the service about the remaining things to be decided. They talked a bit about the menu; several older women said that they did not like barbecued chicken and couldn't they just grill some without sauce. Another wanted to know what the side dishes would be. Others began passing around a sign-up sheet for helping with the tasks surrounding the day's events. They talked at length about the number of tickets that were left and how they could be sold and if the price was too high. One person suggested sending tickets to relatives in nearby towns and encouraging them to come and make a day of it. They also talked about "named cakes"—but I didn't know what that was. Anyway, I was getting hungry.

After some time the topic switched to the senior breakfast which was to be prepared this week by Billy Sue Hammond. Several people commented on what a good cook Billy Sue was. It really was a free-for-all discussion about the goings-on of the church during which the minister had little control over the flow. People regularly interrupted him. At one point, he was trying to get back to the order of the service, but someone wanted to make an announcement about the youth's part in the car wash and the need for everyone to come out with their dirty cars. A discussion of the corsages that were given to all women in the congregation followed. Looking around and appreciating the flowers went on for awhile. Reverend Dawson mentioned that now they were talking about Mother's Day as the Festival of the Christian Home. He bemoaned the change.

Finally, Reverend Dawson announced that it was time to pray. Prayers were offered for the trapped miners in Nova Scotia, the family of the police officer who was killed whose funeral was to be held at Hebron Baptist on Monday; and the LA racial riots were mentioned. "Seems like the whole world is going crazy," said Reverend Dawson.

The hymns were traditional, such as "Nearer, My God, to Thee," "In the Garden," and "O for a Thousand Tongues"; few congregants needed to follow the lyrics in the hymnal carefully. The pastor's daughter sang the offertory, "Faith of Our Mothers." The prayers were said with little affectation and in the vernacular. The sermon was about the loss of respect for motherhood and the concomitant lack of self-esteem among mothers. Scripture passage was about the good shepherd, and the connection to mothers as the shepherd of the family was made. The sermon was a loosely connected series of thoughts with little formal structure. Reverend Dawson mentioned several times that there were many lost children because mothers didn't care anymore. He also mentioned that mothers were heroes to their children. It sort of ambled along for a while and came to an end with an exhortation to respect our mothers and to make the home a safe place for all people.

After the benediction, I talked with Billy Sue Hammond about the changes at Hinton and Dacula. She said that the biggest change she had noted in the last decade was the movement of the church from the center of the community to the periphery. She said that her children lived in the area but they didn't attend church. She thought that most of the change was due to generational values—"our kids just don't think that church is as important as we grew up thinking." She thought that it was just going to get worse because of the growth that was going on in Gwinnett County.

In a conversation with Reverend Dawson, he said they had more housing developments and that they were becoming a "fringe of Atlanta." Slowly, too, people were trickling in to Hinton Memorial UMC. When asked what he did to attract new people, he said that he didn't do anything too aggressively. He worked to cultivate "people who seek us out." Right now, he was more interested in helping the congregation "rediscover our church." He mentioned several new families who had become involved in the church in the last two years. They were also relatively long-time residents of the area.

Miss Irene Abbott, who I was later to learn is the church matriarch and repository of its history, made a point of speaking to me after I had spoken to Nelson Hammond. Mr. Hammond, she said, was a real estate agent and appraiser and had been attending Hinton Memorial for only about ten years. She had heard him tell me that the thing that had changed the most was a few more housing developments. Ms. Abbott listening to my conversation with Mr. Hammond didn't think that I had received a clear picture of what was going on. She wanted me to know that they weren't passive in their resistance to change. They were friendly but they didn't want a lot of new people making their taxes go up and adding to the congestion and "compaction." She also noted that they sold the lots in 3/4 acre lots for these housing development where "you are sitting right on top of each other's heads." "The compaction is the thing that bothers Dacula people."

My experience that Sunday left me with pleasant but conflicting feelings and ideas. The congregants were friendly and warm, and yet closed and self-protective. I was welcomed and kept at arm's length. I learned that a man who had been in the community for ten years was still a "newcomer" and that "Dacula people" were opposed to newcomers as a whole though not necessarily individually. Nonetheless, there was a familiarity and folksiness to the service that evoked recollections of my childhood in a rural area. I was drawn to and baffled by their traditions.

Remembering the Past

Hinton Memorial provided one location for investigating the interactions between exurban newcomers and small-town oldtimers. In this congregation, the challenges of neighboring in the midst of a rapidly changing community were evident. The recent history of the church included a schism that divided it largely along the lines of oldtimers and newcomers. When I arrived at Hinton in 1992, congregants were trying to recover from the schism and still respond to the area's continuing influx of exurbanites. In addition, they had learned that the newcomers who sat next to them in the pew were not the only new neighbors with whom they had to deal. Changes in the denomination's organizational structure and the proliferation of religious groups in the area also created new challenges in neighboring. Congregants at Hinton wanted to respond to the alterations in their community. The question was not only how to institute new programs (although that also proved challenging for the financially strapped small congregation) but also how to make sense of the changes both in the community and in the congregation.

Within the Dacula community, Hinton Memorial UMC has been an enduring fixture. Its red brick building with frosted glass windows and copper steeple has been the site for three and four generations of baptisms, weddings, and funerals; and the annual barbecue held on the grounds is a community family reunion for oldtimers as children and grandchildren, former residents, and kin return to feast on smoked pork sandwiches and vinegary coleslaw—a menu that has remained unchanged for a decade (cf. Neville 1987).[3] Long-time Hinton members talk about their church as a faithful community that has persevered in the midst of many changes throughout its history. Oldtimers are especially proud that the church has met continually since its founding—a sign of its endurance. Its oral history is often retold in congregational meetings, in the "All around Town" newsletter, and in individual conversations as a sign of appreciation for the past efforts of their families and neighbors and as a tangible invocation to newcomers not to forget.

In 1837, twelve men and women met to organize a Methodist church in the Dacula area. A church was built and a cemetery established on land donated by Dr. Samuel Freeman. Freeman was the local physician and is believed to have had the first hospital in Gwinnett

County. The church's founder was a colorful, if somewhat miserly, fellow, and numerous legends surround Dr. Freeman including several about a buried treasure. According to one story, Freeman was often paid in small amounts of gold and silver, and the location of his stash became the subject of considerable speculation among area residents. After his death, the location of his hiding place was revealed when his property was purchased. A filling station was erected on the spot in the 1930s. It is believed that in the remodeling of the building, a set of instructions or perhaps a map was found. Owners found an empty iron pot in a rock pile in a nearby field. Rust and corrosion in the bottom of the pot convinced the finders that this was the treasure vessel. These stories of Freeman's wealth and sagacity for stashing it away provide an apt legacy for the founding of a church with the motto of "Earn all you can, save all you can." In 1857, Freeman deeded the church and the land in Dacula—a half block from his home—where it is now located. He stipulated, however, that the cemetery remain at the original site and that it continue to carry its original name. Thus the cemetery continues to be named Pleasant Hill Cemetery—though Hinton Memorial maintains it.[4]

During the early years of the congregation, the church was home to Dacula's tiny establishment of judges, schoolteachers, businessmen, and doctors. In 1910, the congregation became known as Dacula Methodist Church. In 1955, the church was renamed the Hinton Memorial United Methodist Church, in memory of Samuel L. and Alice Stanley Hinton who gave a sizable endowment to the congregation that would revert to the family if the name was changed. Until the summer of 1956, the church was part of a Methodist circuit. Reverend Jack Martins was the first minister to serve only this congregation. Martins was a favorite of the Hintons and had "holiness" leanings, according to some congregational oldtimers.[5] Harold Dill, a long-time member and Dacula shopkeeper, recalled Martins as their finest pastor. "He was super. He was super. Loved everybody. And he helped me with the Boy Scouts; he helped me with every kind of project. Then he had to sit me down and give me a sermon about me loving the preacher and not the god, worshiping the man. Because I worshiped him. I don't mean that I liked the guy, I mean that like I thought he was God on earth. I still do. I think every breath he takes is straight from God, he's just that kind of man." Billy Sue Hammond, however, contended that Martins' free-spending landed the congregation in financial straits and led to the Hintons' increased prominence because they were willing and able to assist the church financially. Martins served the church until 1960.

The 1960s and much of the 1970s was a time of "carryin' on," as one long-time member termed the feuding that characterized those years. From 1960 to 1977, the congregation had twelve pastors—none of whom stayed for more than two years.[6] Several long-time congregants referred to this period as the "Hinton time," meaning that during these years the namesake family, with whom they claim it was notoriously difficult to work, used their influence with the Methodist hierarchy to get unpopular, inept, or uncooperative pastors removed.

While it is impossible to say for sure whether congregants at Hinton fought more or less than the average church, the perception of persons inside and outside of the church was that the church and the Hintons, in particular, earned their reputation as quarrelsome. Feuding in the congregation and the rapid pastoral turnovers resulted in increasingly tense relations between the original Hintons and the North Georgia United Methodist Conference. According to the actions of conference officials during this time, the church's size and budget did not warrant the attention and special treatment, especially regarding the appointment of ministers, that the Hinton family thought was its due. The significance of their bad reputation was not lost on the Hinton congregation when in the late 1970s, the bishop and district superintendent forced the congregation to take one of the North Georgia Conference's first "lady preachers"—Reverend Janelle Shea. According to long-time members, Shea's tenure was distinguished by considerable tensions both about her as a female minister and about what some members held to be her confrontational style. She was strongly opposed by Miss Irene Abbott, the congregation's matriarch, although some women in the congregation, including Mrs. Lula DeVries, confessed to appreciating the woman's point of view coming from the pulpit. During Shea's pastorate, the namesake family, whose descendants still live adjacent to the church, stopped attending services at Hinton. One member said, "There was no way the Hintons were going to have a women in their pulpit."

Neighborly Restructuring: The First-Wave of Newcomers

After the Hintons' leave-taking, Shea spearheaded efforts to prepare the congregation for the changes that she was sure were coming to the area. She described Dacula and environs of the late 1970s in this way, "It was primarily still rural. There were beginning to be a few people coming out and buying relatively large—although under forty or fifty acres—pieces of land and building houses. People were beginning to move out. There were a few of those people, and they were bringing new flavor to the community. But for the most part it was still a fairly rural community." The few newcomers to the area to arrive during the first wave of in-migration were people who, Shea believed, would not be attracted to a congregation that was run "like a family business." These people were better educated, more financially secure, and more cosmopolitan than the typical member of Hinton Memorial. Shea worked to make the liturgy less "folksy" and more traditionally Methodist, by including a unison prayer of confession and expanding the congregation's repertoire of hymns.

For the most part, however, Hinton congregants seemed unconvinced that they were in for rapid change. The city's population rose a mere 4 percent from 1975 to 1980. That was not the skyrocketing growth that was beginning to characterize Gwinnett County; and without sewer connections, Dacula residents did not expect that the town would see large increases in population or jobs. Change, Hinton congregants supposed, might be coming, but it had a long way to go before it got to Dacula. Nonetheless, a few newcomers did begin to trickle in to the congregation. Shea described these individuals, emphasizing their dissimilarity from the typical Dacula resident: "The people that I'm thinking of who came to be a part of the congregation while I was there were, of course, not people who had grown up in that area. They had a different worldview. Many of them were people who had been professional people, had lived in an urban or suburban area, who were what I call the 'early retired.' Most of them had a certain amount of education—college graduate, some of them postgraduate work. And that was not the norm. True, there were persons in the Dacula area who were educated persons. I would not imply that there were none. But that was not the norm. And you know what happens when new people come into a community, and they're outsiders and don't know everyone. And they didn't grow up being kin to everyone. It's a different flavor."

For most congregants at Hinton though their similarities to these newcomers were also strong. The newcomers who began attending the church, such as Nelson Hammond, Alvin Wilford and his mother Anna, and Elaine and Nowell Altoona, had strong Methodist or mainline denominational backgrounds and a similar generational perspective, despite their generally higher education level. Strong cultural affinities helped to create solidarity. Under Shea's leadership, Billy Sue and Nelson Hammond and Alvin Wilford became important leaders in the congregation—bridging the views of oldtimers and first wave newcomers. Although Nelson, a life-long Episcopalian from Atlanta, was perceived by some to be a newcomer to the area, Billy Sue, a divorced mother of teenage children and local merchants, was native-born and a long-time member of Hinton. Alvin, an architect who began a small business in the area, began attending with his mother, Anna, and later his mother- and father-in-law. Alvin's evident commitment to extended family and his preference for small-town ways made it relatively easy for him to fit into the congregation. Billy Sue, Nelson, and Alvin provided the congregation with important financial and long-range planning skills that would later help them face the future in their changing community.

Shea was succeeded by Reverend Ron Bisby, who is described as a "big bear" of a minister. According to members, Bisby was not much of a preacher, but his warmth impressed congregants. He was renowned for making long, friendly visits to each of Hinton's congregants nearly once a month. He was also less intent than Shea on attracting the growing number of new residents in the Dacula area. However, during Bisby's tenure from 1980 to 1984, Georgia Highway 316 was completed to Dacula, and the in-migration began picking up speed. A 13 February 1980 article in the *Gwinnett Daily News* highlighted changes taking place in Dacula. "In an about-face from its former image as a wide place in the road (and the subject of dire warnings of speed traps), the city of Dacula will be undergoing a massive facelift in about six weeks." Although the town was preparing for change, Hinton Memorial carried on business as usual, gaining a few members and losing a few. Congregants claimed that Bisby's years as pastor were comfortable, but prepared them little for the changes that were just down the road.

Making More Methodisms: Charismatic Newcomers

In 1985, Reverend Gerald Gerhard came to the church's pastorate. During the mid-1980s, the congregation began to experience significant numerical growth as young exurban families moving into the area were attracted by the church's young energetic pastor. Gerhard was a talented preacher; and his involvement and programs, targeting newcomers—such as serving on the local school advisory committee and sponsoring an alternative Halloween party—quickly earned him the allegiance of young families moving into the area. Gerhard saw all around him the signs of the community's change and was determined to see the congregation increase its membership apace with the in-migration.

The changes in worship and mission initiated by Gerhard were dramatic. In a report in the Conference newspaper, *The Wesleyan Christian Advocate*, 11 November 1987, Gerhard reported the alterations that had occurred in the congregation after just two years: "Morning praise and worship service has doubled in attendance. Thirty new members have been received since the new vitality began and a third of these have been by professions of faith. . . . Budget has doubled in three years with $38,000 raised above the budget in two years for special projects. Sent a mission team to Mexico in 1986 and another to Brazil in 1987."

The "new vitality" that Gerhard touted was, despite its success in attracting newcomers, provoking many oldtimers at Hinton.[7] Increasingly, the families that began to attend the church were not traditional Methodists or even mainline Protestants. According to the report of one oldtimer, Gerhard began bringing lots of new people into the church from "all different kinds of churches—mostly more fundamentalist ones and even some people who just didn't go anywhere." Secondly, Gerhard began slowly to put these newcomers into important leadership positions in the church, including choir leader and Sunday school superintendent. Gerhard had also begun new programs, including spiritual life workshops and Mother's Morning Out, to attract area newcomers; and older programs, such as the United Methodist Men's Fellowship, were changed and revitalized. On the whole, these new programs were staffed by newcomers to the church and community and seemed, at best, superfluous to many oldtimers. Finally, Gerhard who had come to the church a "regular UMC pastor" had adopted charismatic theology and worship practices not long after his arrival. Despite Gerhard's contention that the church had a great past on which to build, many oldtimers believed that his advocacy of Holy Spirit baptism, the upheaval in patterns of leadership, and the influx of non-Methodists were changes that did not build on the past but rather repudiated it.

In the third year of his tenure, tensions that had simmered in the congregation reached a boiling point. The changes had come too many and too fast, said several oldtimers. Gerhard had advocated and enacted changes in the "traditional" Methodist worship style of the church.[8] He altered the church's long-standing liturgical practices to include numerous worship choruses projected on the cinder-block wall of the choir loft and substituted unstructured praise and prayer for the Apostles Creed and the Lord's Prayer. Referring to the new worship style, Nowell Altoona charged: "I got to the point to where I felt like we were doing Holy Aerobics. I used that term, and of course Gerry didn't like that too much. But it was more of a show. I really felt as though I was playing in a production. We were capitalizing on certain people's emotions, instead of what I considered true thinking and true understanding of the Word." Gerhard also replaced the choir, composed mostly of congregational oldtimers, who preferred traditional Methodist hymns, with a worship team of newcomers, including charismatic drummers and guitarists.[9] Elaine Altoona identified the views of many oldtimers: "A lot of the people who did not feel comfortable with that type of worship, chose not to attend for quite some time. Nowell and I felt that if people want to worship that way, that's fine. But it got to the point that those families that had been in the church for quite some time were sort of having it shoved down our throat that we were not worshiping correctly."

Tempers flared in nonworship congregational gatherings as well. One potluck ended early when newcomers began speaking in tongues during the prayer. Several oldtimers filled their plates and retired to the sanctuary to eat while the charismatics continued to pray. Disputes also erupted over religious symbols. Several charismatic young women objected to the statue of Mary in the church's rose garden and the ceramic likeness of Jesus in the parlor, arguing that they could easily be perceived as idols. Lula DeVries said, "They might just as well call us 'heathen' or 'idol-worshipers'." Members of the Trustees Committee steadfastly refused to remove the figures contending that there was "nothing in Methodism" that forbade the use of representational art and that they had been given to the church by godly (now deceased) members.

Part of the tension between the traditionalists and the charismatics, who some Hinton congregants called "fundamentalists," related to the use of a "technical" language for religious experience. When charismatics talked of being saved or "born again" and baptized in the Holy Spirit, traditionalists felt threatened and condemned as religious illiterates by the charismatics. In response, the traditionalists accentuated the actions that they had always seen as representing Christianity, in turn calling the charismatics hypocrites because their exclusionary language and practices did not demonstrate acceptance and love.

Fights also flared in the congregation about the payment of charismatic evangelists who regularly filled the pulpit. Gerhard recalled one Pastor and Parish Relations Committee meeting in which Miss Irene Abbott, Alfred DeVries, and Nowell Altoona accused him of not doing his job. "Here I am working day and night, sometimes neglecting my family—I'm sorry to say—and all they can do is sit and criticize me because I'm not in the pulpit every Sunday." Miss Abbott recalled that same meeting saying that Gerhard was paid to preach and that he should not have been "wasting the church's money" on "wild preachers."

Gerhard had established a rigid committee system and a leadership flowchart that broke with the practice of informal *ad hoc* leadership that had been the norm at Hinton. Oldtimers had vigorously objected to what they perceived as Gerhard's plan to consolidate his authority by filling leadership positions with his cronies. In the end, however, the committee structure enabled the traditional Methodists to continue to have a say in the operation of the church, through the Pastor and Parish Committee, during the last year and a half of Gerhard's pastorate. As Billy Sue Hammond said, "The only thing that saved us under [Gerhard] was the book—the [United Methodist] Book of Discipline that is." Bickering, name-calling, and insult-trading characterized many congregational meetings, as groups divided along battle lines of traditional oldtimers and charismatic newcomers.

In addition to the changes in the congregation's form of worship and organization, Gerhard began altering the congregation's place within the institutional complex of the United Methodist Church.[10] After Gerhard had experienced the baptism of the Holy Spirit, he had also become increasingly involved with Trinity Foundation, a charismatic evangelistic organization. He attended their seminars, reading books by the Foundation's leader, and conferring with fellow charismatic pastors about the strains at Hinton. Oldtimers also were conversing about the congregational tension; Hinton's administrative board invited the district superintendent to their homes for "eating" meetings to get advice (cf. Chaves 1993).

Despite the protestations of Gerhard and a growing number of baby boomer charismatic congregants that charismatic theology and practices were authorized by the "Guidelines" passed by the UMC General Conference, congregational oldtimers maintained that charismatics were not traditional Methodists and were simply not consistent with the congregation's past and small-town context. In their view, the inclusion of charismatic theological organizations and offerings within and on the margins of the denomination meant that the United Methodist Church began adopting a "new line" of denominationally sanctioned product— one that was often seen to be in significant opposition with their "old line."[11] Anna Johnson, a long-time Hinton congregant who described herself as "a blue-blood Methodist—with papers," stated: "Those of us that had been Methodist most of our lives, not that you have to have a pedigree to be a Methodist, but, like my parents and grandparents were all Methodists, and I have a brother who's a Methodist minister. And it was kind of like the Methodist church was not important to those people coming in, and it was important to those of us who had been there for a while. And we just felt like we wanted to stay a Methodist church." Vernon England also recalled: "It was not a Methodist church. We quit going. It was like a Holiness church—carrying on. Worship wasn't out of the Methodist thing at all. We didn't follow any of the Discipline. I don't miss that clapping hands and almost jumping over the pews and all that."

Especially for small, Southern UMC congregations, like Hinton Memorial, the inclusion of charismatics disrupted the Southern small-town religious status order where Methodists occupied the upper echelons of social respectability and Pentecostals (all varieties) clustered near the bottom (below Baptists, both SBC and independent). At Hinton Memorial UMC, oldtimers perceived that they were being forced to worship with those Pentecostals. Many oldtimers, like Vernon and Marie England, preferred to cease attendance rather than brook such indignity. As the oldtimers' dissatisfaction heightened and the number of disaffected members grew, they petitioned the bishop for aid in restoring "traditional" Methodism to their congregation.[12] The bishop intervened requiring the pastor to offer a traditional Methodist service, inclusive of a printed order of worship, recitation of the Lord's Prayer, and hymn singing. Gerhard did as he was told, but scheduled the gathering for 8:00 a.m. Sundays. The bishop also mandated severed ties with Trinity Foundation, although the evangelistic agency continued to be a part of the North Georgia UM Conference.

By then the road to schism had been paved not only by the recourse to divergent denominational and extra-denominational resources and structures, but also by the small and large insults of face-to-face conflict. The two service scheme lasted only four months, before the bishop again intervened, at the behest of the traditional Methodist congregants. The bishop decided it was time for Gerhard to move on. Gerhard perceived a punitive motive in his appointment to an even smaller, more remote congregation despite the increased membership and improved financial condition of Hinton Memorial under his leadership. In 1990, the newcomer charismatics left, taking with them much of the financial resources and programmatic enterprise that had fostered the congregation's growth.

Renovations: Recovering from Schism

In 1990, Reverend Luther and Anna Lee Dawson arrived at Hinton Memorial with the self-described mission of "piecing things back together." The approximately twenty-five members who had continued to attend through the last years of Gerhard's tenure felt as if they had weathered a devastating storm. The stories they told about the persecution they had endured by the hands of the schismatic charismatics were vivid, expressing their feelings of betrayal. Elaine Altoona shared this: "I was teaching the kindergarten, first and second grade Sunday school class. That last Sunday I said something about who was going to Gerald's church next week. And [a young girl] said 'Ms. Altoona, will you be there?' And I said, 'No, I think I'll stay here and go to this church.' And she just looked at me and said 'What? What do you mean?' and this was from a six-year-old. She said, 'But this church won't be here next Sunday.' I said, 'Well what do you mean?' She said, 'Well, Gerald's starting a new church, and this church won't even be here. This church will be gone.' So her parents had told her that our church wouldn't even be around."

Miss Irene Abbott held that a visit from Gerhard had precipitated the death of an elderly parishioner. After a meeting in 1990 during which the traditionalists had criticized Gerhard's innovations and noted that many oldtimers were no longer attending, Gerhard had, Miss Abbott said, demanded to know the names of those who were no longer coming to the church. She picked up the story. "And I said, 'Well, the Lechsaus don't come anymore. Why do you think not? They don't have a whole lot else to do.' So he goes to see those people the next day. He marches down to Mrs. Lechsau's house. Hadn't been there in months. Was not concerned about why they weren't coming. Two hours after he left, she suffered a massive heart attack. Went to Gwinnett Medical Center, and the only thing she said that night—you've got this all on tape—was 'I don't want him in the church at my funeral.' And she never came again." One Hinton congregant admitted to guilty pleasure reading a 22 June 1991 *Atlanta Journal and Constitution* article reporting that Trinity's plan to celebrate its one year anniversary by erecting a sign on their future home outside of Lawrenceville was thwarted by a restrictive covenant that barred clotheslines and signs. These and other accounts of Gerhard's actions and Trinity's fortunes forged a solidarity that motivated Hinton congregants' commitment to ensuring the church's survival.

After the schism, they felt that they had to turn their energies to taking stock and salvaging what they could. In 1993 Nowell Altoona described the postschism situation at Hinton: "It was pretty rough, and we're still not over it. There are still ways to be healed, I guess, even now. But money-wise we were hurt. Because when that group left, they closed all but two accounts at the church and they took the money with them. At that point when they left, we were having trouble getting enough money just to pay the pastor's salary. And that was a real struggle."

Hinton Memorial was in dire financial straits after the schism. The congregation had bills for new worship materials and David C. Cook Sunday school materials ordered by Gerhard and for renovations begun during the growth, and they needed more money to bring in a seasoned pastor to help with the aftermath of the schism. Nelson Hammond recalled, "We needed help financially because when [Gerhard] came our budget was something like $23,000, and the year that he left it was $85,000. And when they left, I mean, we just had to scratch the whole budget and we called on the Methodist organization and they helped us financially. I mean they actually sent money." "Not a great deal," interjected Billy Sue. "Well, not a great deal, but $1,000 was a lot of money when we were having trouble," said Nelson. Despite the stopgap help from the denomination, it was clear to Hinton congregants that they could not count on substantial financial assistance from the denomination. They would have to do this on their own, they believed.

Despite chronic financial shortfalls for more than four years, the congregation held on. After the schism, the church was unable to make its full apportionment payments to the denomination.[13] The matter of apportionment was a source of annoyance in the congregation. Congregants held that the denomination instead of supporting them "when we are down" continued to make unreasonable demands on them. In 1992, the annual operating budget was $45,000, approximately one-third of which was owed in apportionment to the UMC. The congregation appealed for individual giving for specific expenses. Some members paid the parsonage mortgage out of their own pockets; others purchased smaller items for the church advertised on the bulletin board near the fellowship hall. "The classified ads," as the display was titled, included bug spray, toilet paper, and other necessary supplies. On the whole though, the financial burden was not shared evenly among the members. Approximately one in five of the adult respondents to the 1993 survey gave between $100 and $599 annually, whereas nearly two in five gave $2,400 or more. On the average, congregants contributed 4 percent of their income to the church. Despite these differences in giving, congregants shared a common rhetorical commitment to sacrificing so that the church would survive.

Numerically, Hinton's attendance had been slashed to about twenty-five regular attenders, rising slowly to an average of fifty in 1993. The church roll (with as many as 190 until the church removed approximately 30 names at the annual charge conference in 1993) though was greatly inflated since many of the members who left with Gerhard did not transfer their membership.[14] During the months of battle that preceded the schism, many long-time members had ceased attending. Several oldtimers who had stopped attending said that the church was not the congregation they remembered and that, in fact, it was no longer Methodist. Their departure, however, created tensions with those members who remained and fought for control of the church. Liza Mayeux described their situation: "This is what the older people would do. They quit coming. And some of the newer people. I didn't have a whole lot to fight with me. You know, people don't want to get involved. And I thought, 'nobody's going to do this, and they're going to take over that church.' And they were very, very close. One more year and it would have all been over with. Because I didn't have *anybody* to fight with me." Despite feeling abandoned by some of their fellow "traditional" Methodists, Hinton congregants needed to draw their fellow traditionalists back to the church. Furthermore, the church's return to smallness made their appeal to these long-time members more enticing. The oldtimers who had left again felt that their contribution—financial and otherwise—was needed.

Reverend Dawson was chosen to appeal to the congregation's long-time members. He commented on his appointment to the church, "I was told by the District Superintendent from whence I came, and the one here, and then later in a conference with the Bishop, that they needed a traditional Methodist minister to get them on the beaten track. For good or ill, I was placed here for that reason." Dawson and his wife, a retired schoolteacher, traveled the area visiting each of the oldtimers—both those who had stopped attending during Gerhard's tenure and those who had stayed on, reassuring them that Hinton would again be a "traditional" Methodist church. Over a period of three years, these defectors slowly trickled back to the church.

Until more long-time members began returning, the remaining congregants hunkered down and did what they needed to do. Dawson assigned people to serve on committees, such as worship, nurture, and evangelism, without attention to willingness or preference. The jobs of the church had to be done, and many oldtimers saw serving without complaint as their Christian duty. During the difficult postschism years, the congregation survived on volunteer labor and loans of equipment. After the church typewriter broke, Eve Ansley, a local nurse and legal secretary, began typing the bulletin. Harold Dill did all the printing for the church in his quick print shop. Donald Pearson, a sixty-four-year-old General Motors worker, did all the yard work, using his own equipment. Jane and Merle DeLoach, a retired couple in their late sixties who lived near Athens, drove the thirty-five miles to the church twice a week—once for Sunday service and again on Saturday to clean the facility.

The view that it was congregants' duty to serve without regard to inclination or aptitude was not, however, universally shared.[15] Tensions arose when the few younger newcomers who had stayed at the church through the schism or who began attending soon after were quickly slotted into committees and jobs with the same disregard for choice. After two visits to the church in 1991, Lewis Norman, the Cubmaster who helped organize Dacula's First Annual Memorial Day Parade in 1994, was given the job of usher—a task for which he felt ill suited—and ceased attending for several months rather than do the ushering. Other visitors to the church were discouraged from attending when they were asked to take responsible positions in the congregation, such as Sunday school teacher or organist, after only one or two Sundays at the church. Many newcomers were simply not enamored by expectations of high commitment at Hinton during this postschism period. Thus the congregation had many visitors who quickly passed in and out of the church.

Hinton also responded to the schism by becoming very tied to the traditional "mainstream" Methodist resources. Whereas under Gerhard they did not use UMC Sunday school literature, under Dawson they began to use it exclusively. In fact, in 1993 the Seniors Sunday school class gave all families in the church a copy of their UMC adult Sunday school quarterly for personal study. Dawson actively promoted United Methodist Committee on Relief as the nation's "most efficient" charitable giving organization.

Congregants who had united around "traditional" worship styles of

Methodism, contrasted their worship rituals with the "chaotic" and "pumped up" practices in which the charismatics had engaged. Alvin Wilford described his feelings about the charismatic ritual practices: "They were starting to conduct healing services on the stage. We had one member, in particular, who had been a long-term member with phlebitis. They slapped their hands on and you know, 'Heal, heal!'— giving it the Oral Roberts–type treatment. Really, we had an Oral Roberts–type church. We never would say the Apostle's Creed; we'd never have a bulletin that had responsive readings. We never did anything that was traditional in the Methodist church." On Dawson's visits, he assured absentee members that the congregation would again recite the Lord's Prayer, return to the lectionary schedule, print an order of worship in the bulletin, sing hymns from the hymnal, and use Methodist literature in Sunday school.

Under Dawson, services quickly did return to a more traditional style, which was comfortable for the congregation's oldtimers. The congregation was no longer to be directed in worship by a team, rather Nowell Altoona began hymns from his place on the piano bench. Everyday needs were often expressed during the announcement time in the Sunday morning services—a practice that had been stifled under Gerhard. One Sunday Sarah Coser shared the misfortunes of a broken freezer during peak harvest time and petitioned congregants for a place to store her frozen goods until the repairs were made. The songs of Wesley again figured prominently in the printed order of service. The sanctuary filled with individual cadence and intonation as the congregation recited the Lord's Prayer. In contrast to the in-depth personal sharing that had often characterized prayer time under Gerhard, names were simply mentioned aloud, indicating a prayer need. Congregants who knew one another intimately knew the need, and others, traditionalists held, had no business knowing.

This practice, however, had the effect of confusing and sometimes alienating newcomers unfamiliar with these norms. One Sunday in 1993 controversy broke out when one of the church's newcomers mentioned in the service that Miss Abbott was to have surgery and inquired about the name of the hospital. Dawson told the congregation that Miss Abbott had specifically told him that she did not want her business mentioned in church. The embarrassed newcomer said that she felt rebuked for expressing her concern. This practice of not discussing needs in public became difficult for oldtimers and newcomers alike when the congregation discovered that Tony Slade had terminal cancer. Congregants watched without mentioning the obvious as he lost weight and weakened. Finally, about a month before his death, Slade requested prayer for strength during a Sunday service. Congregants prayed, and for some tears trailed down their cheeks, but no one moved to touch or lay hands on him, as would have been customary for the charismatics. Though I do not know whether or not Slade experienced the lack of touch and public recognition of his terminal condition as alienating, numerous church members expressed their concern that they were not sure that they had met his spiritual needs during the final months of his life. Perhaps for some in the congregation, the church's return to traditional practices meant that some felt more isolated in the midst of their personal trials.

The traditionalists at Hinton believed in conducting their Christian lives methodically, rather than following the "whims" of emotion and waiting for the Spirit to tell them everything that they should do. The oldtimers who remained after the schism expounded orderliness, propriety, and balance as chief among the spiritual virtues. Harold Dill stated his religious views: "I'm glad they got away from [Gerhard's] life-in-the-spirit, jump-up-and-down-and-holler thing. There wasn't nothing to it. . . . I think it's best put in the 111th Psalm, on the tenth verse. It says 'Fear of the Lord is the beginning of wisdom.' I've got to be afraid of what God will do, I've got to be afraid of what the police will do, I've got to be afraid of what my friends will do, and then maybe I'll gain enough wisdom not to do [the wrong]." Understanding one's responsibility to God, the authorities, and others provided all the motivation one needed to do the right thing. According to Hinton congregants surveyed in 1992 "living Christian values" was the Christian practice rated essential. When asked what were "Christian values," Hinton traditionalists often responded that they were summarized in "the Golden Rule."[16]

"Doing unto others" also meant being a "regular Joe" as one long-time Hinton congregant put it. Shirking one's responsibilities was seen as a sign of moral failure. Plain-spoken goodness and a populist appeal were signs of Christian commitment among these oldtimers. Alvin

Wilford tells a story contrasting his experience with members of a club that his wife, a high school French teacher and opera aficionado, had wanted them to join and his experience at the church. "It's not a very stilted church. People are genuine. What you see is what you get. And nobody puts on airs." He contrasted this with the gourmet club, in which there were three judges. "I consider myself to be fairly eloquent. I'm not a George Will or anything like that, but I get around, and I've got a pretty good command of the language. But some people, they speak in such stilted tones, that you can tell they're just trying to construct sentences and use verbiage to try and tell you 'hey, I'm better than you are because I can out-talk you.' That's how [one judge] would come about. Well, we hadn't seen him for ten years, we met him again about a year ago, after he had been appointed to the state bench; and he just one day left his wife a note saying 'I'm leaving, I've got a twenty-two-year-old girlfriend in town, the marriage is over, you can take care of the kids, I've spent all my life nose to the grindstone, shoulder the wheel, and now it's time to enjoy myself.' This is what happens with screwballs like that. That, to me, doesn't happen in our church because they're good folks." Religious commitment was a matter of living right, not talking right.

In contrast to the charismatics, the traditional Methodist remnant at Hinton engaged in very little unsolicited discussion of their views of God's will for their lives or God's actions in the world. Lula DeVries mentioned how uncomfortable traditionalists like herself had been with the charismatics, in part, because they were always invoking God. "They wanted to pray before deciding what color [of] carpet to put down," complained Lula. Another common story illustrating the perceived witlessness of some among the schismatic charismatics told of several young women who asked for divine direction for everything, including what they should eat for lunch. Most of the oldtimers spoke about making rational and commonsense decisions.

Congregants at Hinton wanted their church to support "traditional" values of neighborliness, frugality, and orderliness. Irene Abbott noted that it is the sense of "family" within the congregation that keeps her coming back. Nowell Altoona narrated his family's Methodist genealogy to explain his continued church participation. Thus the schism was particularly painful for Hinton congregants who had family members who left. Some traditionalists have made visits to these "dearly departed," as Alfred DeVries called them, to try to get them to return to the church. Miss Abbott described a visit that she and Alfred DeVries made to Caroline Barr, the daughter of long-time Hinton members. "We thought we would try and talk her into coming back to our church. After Mr. DeVries heard that she wasn't going to Gerhard's church anymore, he thought maybe we should invite her back to our church. So he asked me if I would care to come along. I always got along nice with Caroline, and I always respected her. She was a very hard working woman. She did a lot of work for the church. So anyhow, we tried to ask and invite her back. I said 'Well, you know, Caroline, I really think this is your church, because we miss you so much; and you are living close by; and we would really love to have you back.' But then she said well, she'll think about it, but most likely she'll stay [at Trinity]. The children like it there, and I guess there are more children." For the most part, such attempts to solicit former members to return failed.[17]

For many oldtimers, the schism altered their loyalty to the church. The nastiness that immediately preceded the split saw many confidences betrayed, according to Hinton members, and had made them more wary of newcomers. Oldtimers became particularly leery of newcomers who used unfamiliar, as Sarah Coser said, "high-falutin," religious language. A common complaint against the charismatics was that they were always talking about being saved, born again, or baptized in the Holy Spirit. Most traditionalists at Hinton did not have a carefully constructed story about a time of salvation or being born again. Rather they saw God as helping them do what they were already doing, only better. They believed that one ought to know what the Bible says and try to follow it, that it is good if you can be baptized as a baby, and that joining a Methodist church or attending church regularly helps, too. But none of those things were mandatory for being a good Christian. Being fair and treating people right are the criteria for living a good Christian life.

When Hinton traditionalists did speak of God, they often referred to him as a loving teacher who wants his disciples to become adults and take care of themselves. Since so many in the congregation were current or retired teachers and coaches, this model of God was particularly salient. The large number of teachers in the congregation supported an understanding of teaching as a vocation. Liza Mayeux, a former teacher and currently a stay-at-home mother, said that her careers were pretty much the same. "My job is still making sure children become decent adults," she said. Margie Golick, a teacher who works with at-risk students, also spoke about teaching as a civic and a religious responsibility. She commented about her experience: "I took a little girl home today, and I thought that when I was growing up I was poor. She had missed the bus, and they don't have a phone, so I dropped her off at what I guess was the landlord's house. I think they have electricity, but I'm not even sure of that. And they have chickens for their own eggs. I didn't even know people did that any more—we did that when I was growing up, but that's forty-seven years ago. . . . I think sometimes you get in there and get the chalk dust on your hands and you just can't get another job. You get chalk prints all over everything. But I guess it's because you feel like you're doing the right thing—for yourself, for them, and maybe even for God—who knows." Teaching for Golick was doing the right thing, perhaps even the Christian thing.

Though Hinton members also saw teaching today's youth as more difficult than in years past—drugs, disrespect, and divorce are named as problems that are leading to increased moral decay in the schools—they often noted that teaching was their way of serving the community and, to some extent, God. "You know, it's givin' something back. It's definitely not for the money," said Larry Golick, who was teaching high school science and math.

These traditional Methodists preferred that "politics" be kept out of the church. Although many agreed that religious values informed their voting, they did not like the pastor getting involved in telling them how to vote. They had disliked the anti-abortion messages that sometimes were included in Gerhard's sermons. They opposed abortion, but believed that one must respect "the law of the land." Some traditionalists also objected to Dawson's sermonic condemnations of the state lottery in Georgia. At one family night supper, Alfred DeVries said that he could not find in his Bible where playing the lottery was a sin like the preacher had been saying. He agreed that it may not be a good idea, but he thought that talking about it as a sin was going overboard.

The matter of mixing politics and religion, as Hinton traditionalists stated it, was really brought to a head in 1992 and again in 1994 when during Sunday morning services prior to the elections someone leafleted the cars in the church's parking lot with Christian Coalition voters' guides. Several congregants surmised that Hebron members had done these distributions, although they had no evidence that the megachurch was behind the actions. Miss Abbott, who was particularly distressed by the leafleting, said that she may agree with how they wanted her to vote, but that she was not going to do it just to spite them now. Linda Lyle, a congregation newcomer, expressed her dislike of politics, in general, and especially politics in church: "I hate listening to politics. I don't watch the news; I don't watch movies about certain things that happen. I don't want to know. I mean, I don't want to stick my head in the orchids—I know what's going on. Whenever I do watch the news I just get disgusted. So I'm not going to sit there and watch it. And I don't want to hear it at church. That's not what I go to church for."

Though many Hinton congregants were generally politically conservative—many indicated that they mostly voted Republican during elections—they objected to mixing politics and religion. As Donald Pearson said, "You just can't go and make God a Republican or a Democrat. You just got to be a little careful about that." The merging of politics and religion and talking about it from the pulpit was seen by Hinton congregants as a sign of "fundamentalism"—a label with which they did not want to be associated.

Participatory and populist principles were seen as important for the governance of the church as well. Although the church returned to "traditional" Methodism, it did not revert to the informal patterns of leadership that had predominated before Gerhard came to the church. Under Dawson, congregational leaders wanted to insure that "they let everyone have a say-so," but they also were committed to the established Methodist committee structure. During the postschism period, Hinton leaders argued that deviating from denominational guidelines had nearly resulted in the loss of their church once, and they were determined that it not become a threat again. So although rules were sometimes relaxed to insure participation and extensive discussion of issues, the United Methodist Book of Discipline was followed more closely than in pre-Gerhard regimes. Incorporating newcomers into the leadership structure of Hinton has been problematic. Early practices of overwhelming visitors with responsibility were followed by a reluctance to include newcomers fully in decisions about the direction of the congregation.

Making Tradition Anew: Creating a Legacy Identity

Several young families did stay at Hinton through the schism, although their loyalty was sometimes tested. Ann and Steve Nelson, a newcomer couple in their mid-thirties with three children, stayed at Hinton Memorial, despite their disappointment that many of their friends departed and that the services became less engaging. Ann shared about their experience: "When Gerry first left and Luther came, we kind of went 'eh.' It's not that we don't like Luther, but we thought, 'oh golly.' Gerry in his prime was a terrific preacher. He had us on the edge of our seats listening to every word. And Luther, bless his little heart. . . ." The couple argued for several months about departing, "Steve was like 'Ann, please!'" But Ann persuaded Steve to stay at least a year following the schism. "I thought if this church falls apart, it's going to kill Miss Abbott. It will kill her. That's one of the main reasons we stayed, was for the old folks. It's just like how Dacula's becoming so big. I feel bad for them. They were here before any of this other was here."

Ann and Steve stayed that year and continued to attend as several other young couples became involved in the church. The Nelsons also noted that the attention that their children received from the older members fostered their ongoing involvement. "It's like they have all these grandpas and grandmas," said Ann, whose parents are divorced and live out of state. However, some younger couples who remained at the church through the difficult postschism years, including Ann and Steve, could envision not attending Hinton if their children wanted to go to another church that offered more age-graded programming. For the time being though, these younger members decided to attend a small church where they knew everyone, rather than go to a larger church where they could choose from more programs. For these younger members loyalty to Hinton was neither as strong nor as primary as for most oldtimers.

One way newcomers who stayed through the schism or who began attending after 1990 fashioned a place for themselves in the congregation was by developing programming which was relevant for them and their children. From 1990 to 1993, little financial surplus existed for programming. Many programs that were begun under Gerhard were eliminated or curtailed in the early postschism years. Programs that began in 1992 and 1993 did so largely without the church's financial backing. In 1993, Bill and Linda Lyle began the congregation's United Methodist Kids (UMK), which met once a month for crafts, storytelling, and games. Linda Lyle anticipated that they would get around to talking about the Bible after they had met for a few months. Dawson, though supportive of the Lyle's efforts, emphasized traditional Sunday and Vacation Bible School programs, like the Bible give-away and the Sunday school pins, to encourage families with children to become involved at Hinton. Several younger mothers established formal and informal opportunities for developing more supportive relationships in the church. Other newcomers organized couples-oriented activities, such as "Destination Unknown" outings and Valentine's parties, during which the church provided nursery services.

Activities that became popular among newcomers in the congregation were what Darlene Shelton, an area newcomer and young leader in the congregation, called "twofers"—meaning they combined a recreational activity with a necessary daily event like dinner. For example, the family night suppers at the church became quite popular with newcomers. As they gained popularity, however, their character changed. Instead of continuing as traditional potlucks, the meals were catered. Shelton, who opened a nail studio in a nearby town, expressed her appreciation for the opportunity to feed her two early teenage daughters—who came to the church directly from softball practice—and to meet other people who lived in the area. Twofers were popular because most newcomers to Hinton said that they have enough things going on in their lives and did not need or want more church activities. One congregational misfire was the Sunday evening Bible studies. Begun by Dawson, these services found a following neither among newcomers, who did not relish another evening activity, nor among oldtimers, who did not want to get out at night, and they were soon discontinued.

During the early postschism years, Hinton Memorial congregants sought to turn necessity into virtue, as they emphasized the benefits of smallness. Oldtimers expressed their relief at having their regular pews and parking spaces back. The small congregation was also attractive to some area newcomers who could shape programs to meet their specific needs and were not pestered to fill every evening with church activities, as they perceived the demands of the purported family-friendly programming of Trinity and Hebron Baptist. Further, by emphasizing the congregation's adherence to traditional Methodism, Hinton leaders returned to a theme that resonated with oldtimers and some first-wave newcomers. After the charismatic hiatus, Hinton oldtimers were especially attuned to the meaning and rituals of traditional Methodism. The rhetoric and rituals of continuity also helped oldtimers to focus on those beliefs and experiences that remained the same, while at the same time they began tentative steps toward addressing again the transformation of their community. For newcomers, the rhetoric and ritual of traditional Methodism appealed to a way of life that they perceived as abstractly superior to their own.[18] Altered slightly to accommodate the preferences of newcomers, Hinton's rituals, such as family night suppers and the cadence of the Lord's prayer said in unison, had the form of tradition for newcomers (cf. Connerton 1989).

In addition to turning smallness into a virtue and reinforcing its continuity with Methodist tradition, Hinton responded to the challenges of the postschism years by emphasizing its historic and Southern character. For example, the adult Sunday school class discussed an article by Tex Sample urging the church to "switch Bach for country." Newcomers and oldtimers alike agreed with the theologian's statement, "in the world of working people, the themes of country sound and look like the world they know. They have to walk the line because they were never promised a rose garden." Dawson also sometimes played cassette recordings of selections from two area old-time and bluegrass bands, the Pea-picker Boys and the Skillet Lickers—who he called the Beatles of Hillbilly music—for special music during Sunday services. He filled bulletins and the backs of the monthly calendar with witticisms such as "Golf is the game that turned the cows out of the pasture and let the bull in" and "Some families can trace their ancestry back three hundred years but can't tell you where their children were last night."

For newcomers who decorated their homes with the mass-produced crafts of a rural past and spent Saturdays shopping for antiques, the congregation's history and country ways were attractive. Newcomers and oldtimers alike packed the church's jury-rigged van to travel to an "old-fashioned" camp meeting near Covington, Georgia, and later revived the tradition in their own hometown. When the air conditioning stopped working in July 1993, several congregants urged the printing of the hand fans as keepsakes. During Sunday worship services, Dawson implemented a testimony time that became a roll call of congregational forebears, after Miss Abbott was put in charge of getting people to stand up. Donald Pearson testified to his mother's "untiring strength," the "Christian faith that made her immovable," and her "fine meals." Others recalled the personal virtues of former members whose names adorned the memorial placards throughout the church. One particularly well-attended family night supper at the church concluded with several hours of old-timey riddles and demonstrations of Tennessee Nine marbles.

The congregation also transformed the *All around Town* into a combination community crier and historical journal. Billy Sue Hammond, who was interested in keeping the newsletter going since it provided valuable advertising space for her company, began soliciting historical vignettes and photos to include in the monthly newsletter. Publishing biographies of deceased local dignitaries and Civil War heroes and histories of abandoned local settlements became a record of the area's memories and heritage. *All around Town* also ran a series of old school photos and heirloom recipes for buttermilk fried chicken and homemade banana pudding as "true Southern ladies make."[19] "Roots," the front-page column in the newsletter written by Nelson Hammond, featured fictional accounts of the trip of two Dacula youngsters to Atlanta in 1904. The tone of the articles highlights the magnitude of the changes that had occurred in the area in less than a century. "Bogan and Grunt had left Dacula at 7:15 on a cool Saturday morning. The trip was a gift to both boys as a present from Bogan's papa honoring his son's fourteenth birthday. The forty-five minute buggy ride had taken eighteen minutes by train. Grunt was openly impressed. Bogan was just as impressed inwardly. . . . Bogan asked Grunt, 'Do you believe in movies?' 'What do you mean, do I believe in movies? I've heard of them but I don't know nothing about them.'" The article goes on to quote from a 1904 city of Atlanta ordinance prohibiting the operation of an automobile above the speed of eight miles an hour within the city limits. Also common in the newsletter were memorial columns about parents or relatives of oldtimers. One column begins, "Her name was Nina Lorie Cochran Triplett. I called her Mama. . . . She mothered all of us. She mothered her sisters and brothers. Her grandchildren and great-grand-children. She would have mothered the whole world had her arms been long enough." As the congregation's oldtimers and newcomers recol-lected, myth and history merged into one.

Since the newsletter was sent to all households in the Dacula zip-code area, it was received by many area newcomers—several of whom were actively involved in the Gwinnett County Historical Society. Ac-cording to the past president of the Society, members were extremely pleased to find a church interested in its history. "Too many of them would rather pave over their cemeteries for parking," she commented. Hinton, by becoming the purveyor of local history and lore, became the focus of much Historical Society interest. The Gwinnett Histori-cal Society, established in the early 1980s by the first wave of exurban newcomers, soon sought to offer genealogical-search classes and local history seminars at the church. The interest of Society members in their stories of the past also fostered notions in the congregation that their history was a resource for drawing new people to the congregation and for raising funds to support the church's budget.

In 1993, the Trustees Committee of the church began selling Christ-mas ornaments in the community with etchings of the area's historic buildings, including the church. The project raised a substantial supple-ment to their budget. Congregants also revamped their annual church barbecue—doing much more advertising in the community and as one oldtimer said "cuting" it up by having cloggers and bluegrass music. The cooks at the barbecue pit were asked to wear their blue-striped overalls "for effect." (Since this was their typical work attire, these oldtimers would probably have worn them anyway, requested or not.) The bar-becue also was a perennial money maker for the church.

Hinton's emphasis on traditionalism, their Southern "recipes" for doing things, and the solidarity borne of the schism resulted in the creation of a "legacy identity" which proved to be a successful special-ization strategy for attracting newcomers and oldtimers alike. As con-gregants organized and attended storytelling events, wrote and read about the travels of Bogan and Grunt, and created and sold "historic" ornaments, they fashioned a public memory that helped them understand their niche in this changing community. They affirmed themselves not only as traditional Methodists but also as arbiters of the cultural heritage of the area, preserving, conserving, and reworking Dacula's folklife. In telling and retelling its real and imagined history, the church highlighted its character as a community of memory (Bellah et al. 1985).[20] Ironically, by publicizing its history, the church also attracted more newcomers who opted for that narrative as well. The popular history recounted in the congregation created a Southern identity based on a sense of the area's own provincial traditions and also brought closer together oldtimers and newcomers, who sought in the area the ideal of rural past.

Congregants also used their history and their valorization of the extended family to encourage all to develop relationships with the newcomers who were attending the church in greater numbers by 1993. As the percentage of newcomers in the congregation increased, so did the number of individuals without nearby relatives. Hinton oldtimers who spoke often of all they had learned from grandparents, aunts, and uncles were urged to replicate those relations with the church's young families. Newcomers Ann Nelson and Liza Mayeux were invited to "adopt" the congregation's elders. Ann Nelson, who worked three nights a week as a nurse, began to have regular coffees with Sarah Coser; and Liza Mayeux, whose schedule as a stay-at-home mother was flexible, regularly dropped in on Anna Wilford after her son Alvin's death. Most newcomers to the congregation, however, did not have flexible daytime schedules that permitted such visits. Several of the young couples did regularly visit elderly congregants on the weekends, especially the DeVries who sponsored an annual hayride at their farm and allowed the church's children to treat their farm as a "petting zoo." Occasionally, older members at Hinton did assist with children's programs or assisted with after-school care. On the whole, however, these alliances were not long lasting.

More enduring was the common ideal of a community that supported family life. Long-time members worried about the dangers for young people that had been "introduced" into their community and reiterated their commitment to the family as their primary mission. Though most newcomers—both men and women—worked full-time in careers that demanded more than the traditional 9-to-5, they too stressed family as their most important priority and bemoaned the modern pressures that decreased their family time. Additionally, both newcomers and oldtimers spent much of their leisure time in family-related activities. Individuals with school-aged children were active in T-ball, Girls and Boys Scouts, and parents and teachers association. Elderly adults were also busy with family, including caring for their grandchildren or taking care of the house for children who worked full-time.

Serving one's family and one's nearby neighbors was again emphasized as the congregation's primary mission. Whereas under Gerhard, the congregation volunteered in downtown Atlanta at a homeless shelter; after the split, that ministry was stopped. Anna Lee Dawson promoted the congregation's involvement in the Meals On Wheels program. She thought congregants needed to focus on "helping their neighbors." Dawson reported regularly getting calls from all over Atlanta for benevolence help. So the trustees resolved to assist only people that were known to congregants. The church did on occasion take special offerings for groups outside their community, promoting giving to the United Methodist Children's Home and the United Methodist Committee on Relief. Yet even these were sometimes controversial as congregants contended that especially now they needed to keep their money "at home."

Hinton Memorial UMC under Dawson's leadership engaged in what some congregants termed a "holding pattern," but which was also a period of retrieval of and return to tradition in the service of innovation and change.[21] Following a period of contested identity at the church, the congregation focused on its history as a resource within a volatile local religious ecology. The resulting religious particularism emphasized the local, Southern character of the community and the church.[22] In so doing, they developed a specialist identity as a "legacy congregation" by drawing on the resources of the physical, historical, and cultural particularities of the place, and by adapting and recreating these structures, memories, and practices for new purposes and changed circumstances.

In part, this organizational process and this identity construction are similar to that engaged in by people whom Warner (1988) calls "elective parochials." At Hinton, though begun by long-time residents, cultural gentrification has been carried on by newcomers to the area who have made their own cultural syntheses, in part, by buttressing and adopting what they perceived to be traditional Southern values, traditions, and practices. They have done what James Clifford has noted: "Everywhere individuals and groups improvise local performances from (re)collected pasts, drawing on foreign media symbols and languages" (1988:14).

During this time, the congregation returned to the interests and practices of the mostly elderly congregants who had remained with the church after the schism. In contrast to the structured yet casual charismatic style of the past, congregants returned to a style of worship that maintained a dignified formality that church members felt exemplified the traditional religion to which they adhered. Instead of moving forward with plans to remodel the church schoolrooms, the congregation gave them a new coat of paint and expanded the rose garden. They sought to preserve their traditional space and place in the community.

Hinton's local identity tapped a network of alliances that had already formed around the evolving interests and coalitions of interests, especially related to preservationist issues.[23] Hinton's stance resulted in an affinity between members of the Gwinnett Historical Society, whose interests coincided with the congregation's resources, and Billy Sue Hammond, whose retail interests also corresponded with the congregation's concern to maintain a small-town feel in the church and community. But it was not until newcomers began responding to this congregational identity that members developed a self-conscious organizational identity as a "legacy congregation." From 1990 to 1994, Hinton Memorial attracted those few newcomers who joined, in part, because it had at first unconsciously, and then more deliberately, positioned itself within the local ecology as an "authentic traditional Southern church." This identity had been publicized through "traditional" programming, such as old-fashioned hymn-sings and family night suppers, congregational outings to local historic areas, dinners on the grounds, and storytelling events for the congregational youngsters. In addition, the congregation promoted its emphasis on what one new member called "traditional commonsense" religion, including worship that was "formal and solid" as Todd Penner, a newcomer to the area who joined the church in 1993, described it. By fashioning a specialist identity based on smallness, traditionalism, and local history, Hinton Memorial made a particular place for itself in the midst of its changing local religious ecology.

By appealing to migrant exurban families who wanted to support and build communities that preserved and reinvigorated regional, local culture, the congregation happened upon a strategy for growth that drew together oldtimers and newcomers. Hinton congregants nursed disdain for the "cookie-cutter" exurban "sprawl" of Trinity and Hebron. By defining themselves as doing something different from what these other congregations do, they could emphasize their lack of age-graded programming as a virtue of traditional family-oriented religion. In relation to the insular country churches, Hinton relied upon residual status distinctions that placed the Methodist Church at the top of the local status order when compared to "countrified churches" at the bottom. By continuing to emphasize its civic orientation and middle-class standing within a religious status order that was up for grabs, Hinton could buttress the middle-class status of newcomers who were often holding on tenuously to the middle-class expectations of home-owning, SUV-driving, upwardly-mobile exurbanites. Finally, unlike generalist congregations, like First Baptist–Dacula, which did not project the polished and self-conscious quaintness that was attractive to newcomers, Hinton knew its specialty and actively projected it into the community.

Though Hinton's specialist cultural orientation promoted organizational survival during a period of significant organizational vulnerability within a rapidly restructuring urban and religious ecology, it also had an ambiguous edge. The specialist identity adopted and encouraged by Hinton Memorial also subtly reinforced the existent racial segregation in the local institutional environment. In 1995 in the Dacula environs, a white resident was more likely to live on a plantation than were inhabitants 150 years ago. For example, the Auburn Oaks Plantation has been home to many of the Hinton's new members. Though the Southern and traditionalist congregational specialty provided a "fit" with the political, economic, and residential choices of many Hinton members, the Southern identity that was being upheld by Hinton was not the "New South" image of Civil Rights and the multiracial identity of a "city too busy to hate" (Ayers 1992; Bullard and Feagin 1991). Rather it was of an older South which combined, on equal footing, the images of Scarlett and Rhett, the hillbilly populism of the Skillet Lickers, and support for the Georgia Flag. [24] In an interview, one new Hinton member (an Iowa transplant) told of her husband's experience of presenting a watermelon-eating Mammy refrigerator magnet to his African-American secretary, which he had gotten during his vacation to Charleston, South Carolina. When his secretary expressed her displeasure with the gift, the woman's husband was confused and hurt. "But she likes watermelon," he had contended. In her telling, the Hinton member expressed frustration with the "touchiness" of African Americans in the South.

In its "legacy identity," Hinton Memorial actively adopted and adapted Southern regional values, practices, and history. The members have invented tradition. But in order to do so, they had to be taught the particularities of the place by the oldtimers.[25] By encouraging these responses among non-Southern exurbanites, the congregation has developed its special place within the community's religious organizational ecology. Hinton's response made sense within the local religious institutional environment. The identity was well suited to the cultural and social world of Atlanta's racially segregated exurban rim. The suburbs and exurbs, long reputed to be domains of modern conformism and homogeneity, are increasingly sites of particularistic innovation and religiously-based community building.[26] Contrary to the predictions of such social theorists as Wilkenson (1988) who suggest that the massive suburbanization may have led to a move on the part of most Americans away from extensive community, urban deconcentration and social mobility has been an incentive to engage in community building around particularistic group identities.[27] These particularistic identities offer the possibility of close personal relations and a degree of social embeddedness (cf. Warner 1993:1064). In particular, as this case supports, migrant exurban families are embedding themselves in local culture through supporting and building communities that preserve and modernize regional distinctives for both good and ill.

Facing the Future

Under Dawson, the congregation created a place for itself within its religious ecology and attracted a particular subpopulation of newcomers by returning, in part, to the tried and true "recipes" of behaving from the past. The congregation returned to familiar practices of neighboring, emphasized traditionalism, tried to follow the golden rule, and turned to the past to determine its future mission. When Reverend Luther Dawson announced his impending retirement in 1993, the congregation was forced to think again about its future as it made recommendations about the type of pastor it wanted next. Given their track record, congregants were far from confident that the denomination would send a minister to their liking. Nowell Altoona and Billy Sue and Nelson Hammond believed that the conference had given Hinton "bottom of the barrel" preachers for the last two decades. Despite their satisfaction with the general church's direction, some oldtimers and newcomers alike held that when they were sent Dawson the conference had given them leftovers. They believed that in order to get a pastor to their liking who would help the church get fully on its feet again, they would need to advocate strongly for themselves at the conference meetings. Others who had weathered the schism also felt at odds with the denominational hierarchy because they believed that they did not have the ear of the conference leaders. "Nobody's looking out for us," said Nelson Hammond.

This distrustful view of the denominational hierarchy was confirmed when in 1993 congregational leaders approached the church's new district superintendent about their future pastoral leadership. Reverend Jefferson Metz stated that Hinton Memorial was going to have to rethink its plan for the future, if it wanted a pastor to their liking. He stated in an interview with me: "what the church has as its goal and its dream is such a large fact in the kind of person that we need to look for as the pastor there, because if the church wants to just kind of sit on its hands and not do much, then that affects the kind of person that I'm going to look for. If the church is really wanting to be vital and reach out in ministry to all the people that are moving in and are going to be moving into that area, then we need to look for another kind of leadership. I think the community is just going to burst open around it in the next five years and if the church is not ready for it, it's going to get bypassed." This subtle threat was also perceived by the congregation and reinforced when the congregation was also informed that not only would they not receive the type of pastor they were requesting but also may not get one at all unless they paid up their apportionment to the conference. In November 1993 at the annual charge conference, Alfred DeVries, the church's treasurer during the bleakest postschism years, tried to make Metz understand the church's predicament: "If you will bear with us we will catch up. We are doing the best we can. We can do better and we will do better. We will be making payments on the apportionment and paying it up. I'm an old farmer, and I think that if you have a debt you pay it, but we've been in a drought. But we're coming out of it now."

To congregants, the options were either to continue with the mission they had fashioned for themselves, possibly without a full-time pastor, or to do as the denomination wanted them to do. The denomination was keen that Hinton Memorial begin to reach out enthusiastically to the general population of newcomers and to embrace the change that was occurring in the area, possibly preparing themselves to build and relocate to the outskirts of town within several years. To accomplish this vision, denominational officials promised financial assistance and aid with program development if the congregation committed itself to growth and outreach.

In 1993 after much debate, Hinton congregants affirmed their willingness to become a redevelopment congregation. This program of the North Georgia Conference of the UMC was designed to enable congregations in the midst of changing communities to gain financial resources, programming, and training in order to engage in active outreach. Congregations that join the program "covenanted" with denominational officials to accomplish certain programming goals, including doing research into the needs of community residents and implementing programs to address those needs.

The proposal to become a redevelopment congregation was controversial at Hinton, especially since it was understood that the congregation would have to pursue growth vigorously. Miss Abbott, though, contended that they could say whatever the denomination wanted to hear in order to get a pastor and then "just do what we've been doing." Hinton congregants valued their warm, family-like community and were concerned that the denomination wanted to force them to grow more than they would like and perhaps relocate to the outskirts of Dacula (cf. Becker 1998). Despite these persistent concerns, members approved participation in the Conference's redevelopment program, in part because the denomination would subsidize the salary of their next pastor. Without a pastor, they believed, they could not survive.

In 1993, Reverend Jeff Cox, a traditional Methodist pastor, came to Hinton Memorial from a small town not far from Athens.[28] More to the point for some congregants though, he was younger and had children—characteristics that Hinton congregants hoped would make him more proactive in meeting congregational needs, especially their perceived needs for better Sunday school and children's programming and for a youth group. In his inaugural sermon at the church, Cox spoke appreciatively of the congregation's history and its perseverance after the schism; and he said that now "we must look forward with hope rather than fear."

Cox wanted the congregation again to be more deliberate in reaching out to the area's newcomers. In September 1993, Cox wrote in his "All around Town" column, "From the Pastor's Desk," about "being new in the community." Singing the praises of the town's "unique downtown," its "teachers committed to the well-being and betterment of their students and community," "the loving caring fellowships," and "friendly neighbors," Cox spoke directly to newcomers who found little in Dacula worth mentioning. He encouraged them to find in the community a "sense of family" and a "depth of history." Also in inviting newcomers to worship at Hinton, he cited his own experience of difficulty when "little ones are born or someone gets sick, or something great happens and your mom and dad or brothers and sisters are one and a half hours away, or several states away, or even halfway around the world." He, like these mobile newcomers, needed the church to be family, history, and home. Cox, in speaking straight to their needs, explicitly sought to translate the offerings of Hinton Memorial into their language and concerns.

The internal incentives to attract more newcomers to Hinton were strong. After more than three years of chronic financial shortfall, Hinton layleaders such as Larry Golick and Nelson Hammond, joined Cox in publicly asserting that in order to escape their financial strictures the church had to grow. They held that the number of congregants needed to establish financial stability was one hundred to one hundred twenty-five. Most Hinton congregants, oldtimers and newcomers alike, affirmed that number was not too large as long as the approach was one of managed growth, meaning slow addition and full incorporation of newcomers. Several members, however, expressed strong feelings opposing membership drives, because of the aggressive recruitment strategies used by the charismatics and Hebron. Most Hinton oldtimers believed that people who should come to Hinton would come eventually, though newcomers were somewhat more skeptical of this theory. Newcomers, like Todd Penner, a marketing analyst and engineer for an oil company, believed that the congregation would need a strategy.

Cox, too, favored developing a plan for growth that would provide a new strategy for action. He enrolled the congregation as a charter participant in the Vision 2000 program, a United Methodist sponsored study designed to engage congregational leaders in Bible study, self study and planning for the future. The program began in 1994 and involved six months of study and weekly meetings. Cox also established three task forces that were charged with assessing the current programs of the congregation and needed improvements in worship, stewardship, and evangelism. These task forces sidestepped the standing committee structure of the congregation and enabled Cox to include many of the newer members and attendees in planning for the future without overwhelming them with premature leadership responsibilities, as had been the congregation's history. The task forces met twice a month for several months and then slowly disbanded around the time when the nominations committee made suggestions for filling committee openings.

With the arrival of Cox, the congregation developed an even more formal worship style. Few of the impromptu business meetings were permitted during the announcement time, as had been the hallmark of Dawson's tenure. Cox stopped several such discussions by suggesting that they would be more appropriate after the service. Nonetheless, the congregation continued to relish their fellowship time, and a power struggle emerged between several oldtimers, especially Alfred DeVries, and Cox about the length of the fellowship time. As Cox has attempted to prod people to take their seats after several minutes of meeting and greeting, Alfred twice said loudly, "Not yet, preacher." The service began with acolytes bringing in the flame and concluded with them processing out with it. This change was designed, said Cox, to make the children and youth a more integral part of the worship experience.

Cox also formalized the music program of the church. Nelson Hammond began serving as worship leader, and scripture reading by the laity was instituted. The choir was reorganized after disbanding in the third year of Dawson's tenure. A choir director was recruited by Cox from another United Methodist congregation in the area. In addition to regular rehearsals, the choir initiated fellowship activities that included oldtimers and newcomers. Since 1994, the choir has grown steadily and become an important group within the congregation. Cox changed worship, allowing for the involvement of both newcomers and oldtimers. The page numbers in the hymnal for the Lord's Prayer and the Apostle's Creed were printed in the bulletin; and confirmation and new member classes were begun. In contrast to Dawson's storytelling style, Cox orchestrated the children's moment and the sermon to highlight a common theme and targeted his remarks to the children more accurately to their comprehension level. Dawson, on the other hand, had often made the children's moment a religious version of Art Linkletter's "Kids Say the Darndest Things."

Cox commenced training programs for acolytes, ushers, and Sunday school teachers. After their training, the acolytes were commissioned before the congregation, ending the catch-as-catch-can nature of the acolyte position previously. The usher system has been less amenable to Cox's efforts for orderliness. Through 1996, ushers often were pull from the congregation on a last minute basis to fill in. Cox's plan for Sunday school training was also scrapped amidst the indignation of some long-time and professional teachers at his suggestion that they did not know how to instruct children and adults in religious matters.

Cox also added and augmented the church's children's programs as the number of children in attendance increased. These programs included an evening summer Bible school, United Methodist Youth Fellowship (UMYF), United Methodist Kids (UMK), United Methodist Tots (UMT), and monthly outings for teens, school-aged children and "tots." These gatherings attracted teens and children whose parents did not attend Hinton and resulted in the addition of several families to the congregation's membership rolls.

By late 1996, attendance averaged about one hundred fifty to two hundred in attendance for Sunday worship and seventy-five to eighty persons for Sunday school. The newcomers have been primarily young families of exurbanites. Despite evidence that many newcomers had wealth (there are now BMWs and Audis in the front parking lot), the financial situation of the congregation did not improve at the rate expected. In 1994, amidst considerable difference of opinion between oldtimers and newcomers, the congregation instituted a pledge system— "Pledge of Faithfulness campaign." In 1993 and 1994, the church was unable to meet its basic apportionment commitment that had been agreed upon by the congregation in the appointment process. Finances continued to be an Achilles' heel for the congregation.

Under Cox's leadership, the congregation's mission and identity again altered. Cox was keen to engage the congregation in a program of intentional reflection on its mission. The Vision 2000 project resulted in a new name, plans for new programming, initial plans for a building program, and the creation and adoption of a new mission statement. After much debate and with the realization that the name change would mean the loss of the Hintons' endowment, the church voted in 1994 to change its name to First United Methodist Church of Dacula. In many protracted church meetings, the meaning of the name change was discussed. Darlene Shelton favored the change of name to correspond to the Methodist congregations in other exurban communities. "Nobody knows what you are when you're a 'Hinton Memorial' but when you're First Church they know what to expect," she argued. Some congregants, like Shelton, maintained that being "First Church" named the church as the primary Methodist presence in the area. Cox also contended that the name change would give them the opportunity to represent themselves and increase their status in the community. Several oldtimers objected to the change, not because they were necessarily keen to keep the name of a family that had long since departed, but because it would cost the church financially. Finally, after several newcomers and one oldtimer agreed to replace the funds that would revert to the Hintons, the change was made. In December 1994 the church had a "grand opening" for First United Methodist Church of Dacula, announced in the "All around Town," *Gwinnett Post Tribune*, and flyers distributed in nearby subdivisions. In his column in the "All around Town," Cox told readers what they could expect.

> Our Ushers will greet, seat you, make sure you are comfortable,
>   and provide you with a service bulletin and hymnal.
> Our bulletin contains (printed for easy use) all the litanies,
>   Psalter, prayers, and creeds that are utilized in our services so
>   that all people may fully participate.

Also a result of the Vision 2000 project, the congregation began a preschool and Parent's Morning Out program. In the community study begun through the project, several newcomers canvased their neighbors and learned that affordable, nearby childcare was a need. Cox's wife, Annie was hired as preschool director, with aid from Redevelopment Program funds, and the old parsonage was remodeled to accommodate classes for two-, three-, and four-year olds. At this writing, First United Methodist of Dacula was in the process of planning a new construction at the edge of town. They expected to move to a new facility in 2000—at the latest. More change was on the way.

Conclusion

Hinton Memorial's adaptations to exurbanization and the concomitant changes in its community have been manifold. The first response in the mid-1980s was rapid growth by appealing to incoming exurbanites who were primarily attracted by the pastor's style and charismatic theology. This group differed in many ways from the long-time members of Hinton; and the rapid growth, incorporation of charismatic theology and worship style, and organizational tensions within the denomination resulted in congregational schism in 1990, when the charismatic pastor and half the congregation left the denomination to establish an independent charismatic congregation. From 1990 to 1993, Hinton Memorial stayed in a "holding pattern" under the leadership of Reverend Luther Dawson, a retirement-aged, traditional Methodist minister. The congregation was hampered by the financial strain of a heavily mortgaged parsonage and burdensome apportionment, and was sapped of programmatic incentive. However, by turning smallness, traditionalism, and localism into virtues, the congregation survived intact and created a strong "legacy identity" focusing on a myth of place and a longing for stability in the midst of change. This "legacy identity" continued to provide a focus while the congregation moved to recover financially and while it was forced by the denomination to become more proactive toward changes in the community. The congregation has put in order its internal structures and has again redefined itself and its mission in order to adapt to ongoing changes in its local organizational ecology.

The recent history of this congregation reveals to sociological re-searchers the importance of examining an individual congregation's re-sponse to change through considering (1) development of its religious identity at the local level, (2) changes in its organizational forms, and (3) shifts in its relation to members of its particular ecology. Especially in exurban locations, such as Dacula, which are in the midst of fast-paced change, organizational cultures change regularly in response to other religious organizations and new constituencies. Postschism, Hinton Memorial created for itself a specialty identity within Dacula's religious organizational ecology, which coincided with evolving coali-tions of interests within the rapidly changing community.

This story also underscores how the beliefs, rituals, and narratives of organizations are intimately related to their particular places. Ritu-als and practices of Hinton Memorial drew on recollections that had power for newcomers and oldtimers. The congregation drew lessons from its history to fashion its place in the community. As Dacula has con-tinued to expand, the financial, human, and cultural resources for iden-tity construction for religious organizations, such as First United Methodist of Dacula, continue to be altered.

Internal processes of accommodating change necessitate the cre-ation of new cultural patterns and the reinterpretation of older "tradi-tions" within new circumstances. While Hinton Memorial UMC was the setting for particular historical practices, it was not unique in the community. Such internal accounts could be given for each congrega-tion within the ecology.

Chapter 5   Making Faith

This is home. I don't care where—I might live in another subdivision or something, but this is home. My mother and father are buried about four miles from down here, and her mother and father are buried over here in Pleasant Hill. So we plan to be buried here also. So we won't be leaving.

Navigating within a Religious Ecology

—Vernon England

We moved out here [to Dacula] just because we found a piece of land—two and a half acres and we were going to build a house with a yard big enough for kids and safe. Todd was working in Lawrenceville then and it was real convenient for his job. But we didn't know a soul out here.

—Faith Penner

THE URBAN RESTRUCTURING underway in Dacula involves significant alterations in the ways in which home, work, church, and neighborhood are knit together. In this chapter the focus turns to how oldtimers and newcomers themselves have created routines of belonging within the organizations in their environment. From a description of the spatially situated practices of work, faith, recreation, and consumption of two families in Hinton Memorial UMC, one can gain an appreciation for the diverse resources and divergent norms that were at work within this congregation and community.[1]

Routines of Belonging

The household, productive, and consumer networks (Fishman 1990) of these families represent distinct patterns that are a result of living in a particular environment and creating practices of connectedness to the organizations of the environment.[2] Homes, stores, churches, and day-care centers are located in particular places. Family members who create their typical daily routines around these sites generally have reasons for doing so. That is to say, in most environments there are any number of homes, stores, churches, or day-care centers; individuals and families must order their days by relating to some and not to others. So how do people engage in these decision-making processes? They do so on the basis of logics and routines of belonging as situated within populations of organizations (Friedland and Alford 1991; Emirbayer and Goodman 1994). Thus we focus on particular organizational ecologies and on both deep-seated and emergent norms (or logics) regarding how people should live, consume, work, and live out their faith.

Analysis of these situated logics and routines of belonging provides composite pictures of the community relations and organizational ties of many newcomers and oldtimers in Dacula. Oldtimers and newcomers differed both in how they defined the relevant organizational ecologies and in the norms or logics they used to navigate them. To a great extent, the differences between organizational routines of oldtimers and newcomers related to how localized or dispersed they were in geographic space. For oldtimers, routines were more likely to have Dacula as the central locale for recreation, club meetings, church services, and shopping. For newcomers, routines generally were much more diffused in space—without an axis (cf. Perin 1977). Recreational activities, meetings, religious participation, and shopping were organized in relation to customized choice—not necessarily within a geographically localized place.

Oldtimers and newcomers at Hinton Memorial and Dacula diverged in the norms they implicitly and explicitly used to order their routines. On the one hand, many oldtimers emphasized community participation and cohesion, and, on the other, most newcomers accentuated customized choice and achievement.[3] Although many newcomers and oldtimers valued both sets of norms, their priority often differed. For oldtimers, the locality—Dacula—was generally perceived as a distinct social entity, a community standing apart from other communities nearby; and the church and the downtown area—such as it is—constituted a physical symbol of this distinct local ecology. Among these people, Dacula was regarded as a cohesive town whose organizations constituted the ecology. Norms of cohesion and commitment also provided criteria for assessing behavior and allocating social prestige.

Newcomers to Hinton Memorial UMC and Dacula, however, tended to emphasize the importance of choice and achievement. For many, Dacula represented a particular "type" of place where their visions of a simpler small-town life were realizable. They had chosen Dacula and Hinton Memorial UMC because of personal needs and familial considerations. They ordered their lives on the basis of their choices. The resources available to them were a function of their needs and time, rather than locality. Also for newcomers, the principle of choice and achievement provided the primary criteria for assessing conduct and determining their place in society. While local organizations were part of their ecology, they were placed within a much broader compass.

These dissimilar norms for ordering their days and their routines of belonging resulted in newcomers and oldtimers having divergent interpretations regarding how people should belong to organizations and how organizations should respond to them (Wellman and Leighton 1979). These dissimilar norms created both opportunities and dilemmas for organizational survival, adaptation, and specialization. Finally, these norms generated diverse resources and strategies for responding to changes in the local area, especially the conflicts that are addressed in chapter 6.

Choice and Religious Routines

The changes in the routines and norms of belonging that occurred at Hinton Memorial UMC and among Dacula's residents are not unique. Since the first large-scale wave of suburbanization in the post–World War II era, the homes of the middle-class have been located miles from their jobs; and those jobs have been increasingly in the more educationally demanding careers of service industries.[4] These changes affected neighboring as it became diffused.[5] People rely less and less on those living closest to them to fulfill needs of intimacy and sociability.

Religious organizations have followed their members to suburbs and edge cities (Hudnut-Buemler 1994). Early in the process of suburbanization, many religious leaders expected that these new settlement spaces would reinforce the religious traditions of suburbanites. A 22 March 1950 *Christian Century* article highlighted the views of many religious leaders: "The residents of Suburbia are, by and large, Protestant in tradition and by natural addiction. They want to have Protestant churches in their communities and will support them generously. They send their children to Protestant church schools, and more often than not maintain a church membership for themselves." However, fundamental in their move to suburbia (and beyond) was choice, which to a large extent undermined the expected compulsion of suburbanites to adhere to traditional patterns, including religious ones (Hudnut-Beumler 1994). Achievement rather than cohesion has been their principal concerns. Suburban relocation, in dislodging people from their hometowns or urban neighborhoods, also promoted more territorial mobility as people moved from city to city in pursuit of the good life. Families and individuals could make their own decisions about where to live, where to work, where to go to school, where to go shopping, and where (and if) to worship within the expanding matrix of particular places that made up the metropolitan region.

As choice became increasingly important to people's relationships with religious organizations, special purpose and support groups, independent congregations, and evangelistic organizations which offer pluralism within and across religious organizations flourished, crowding the local religious ecology with new associations and services (Wuthnow 1988; 1994b).[6] Contrary to Herberg's (1960) expectation, Americans did not readily conform to the religious "triple melting pot."[7] Although religious traditions are certainly still important in social location and self-identification, considerable diversity emerged within and across traditions and denominations, as people began to reconfigure religious organizations according to their choices (Wuthnow 1988; Hammond 1992). The religious independent sector increased; megachurches developed; and new quasi-denominations arose. These organizations emerged, in part, as the embodiment of customized religious choices. Like it or not, traditions, denominations, and local religious organizations became increasingly attuned to the suburban and exurban milieu in which choice was taken for granted and in which individual and familial needs and habits determined their selections.

Researchers have highlighted how these religious changes are related to education (Ammerman 1990), income (Wuthnow 1994b; Hoge, Johnson, and Luidens 1994), and generation (Hadaway and Roozen 1993; Roof 1993). Particular attention has been paid to generational consideration, that is, the impact of the baby boom cohort, relative to religious choice. Hadaway and Roozen (1993) write: "All of the evidence suggests that boomers' relationship to the church is fundamentally different from that of previous generations of Americans—that it is, to use the varied terminology of recent scholarly discussion, more 'voluntaristic,' consumer-oriented, and captive to the subjective, expressive dimensions of cultural individualism" (243). Marler and Roozen (1993) describe the generational change as one from tradition to consumer choice. Writing about baby boomers, Roof (1993) writes: "Increasingly within the Protestant, Catholic, and Jewish mainline, people identify themselves by adding on layers of experiential meaning to older, less relevant religious and denominational labels" (201). He summarizes the views of social scientists who have focused on generational changes: "Choice, so much a part of life for this [baby boom] generation, now expresses itself in dynamic and fluid religious styles" (5).

However, relatively little research has focused directly on issues of alterations in routines of belonging relative to the urban restructuring that occurred during this same time (D. Olson 1993; cf. Warner 1988; Ammerman 1987). The move to the suburbs and beyond was not simply a product of choice; it restructured choice. It fundamentally altered the ways in which home, work, church, and neighborhood are woven together. While I do not ignore the generational, educational, and income differences among oldtimers and newcomers, my focus is on the divergent ways in which newcomers and oldtimers embedded their routines of belonging within space and how this restructured their organizational choices. Oldtimers, whose routines are localized and are governed by norms of commitment and cohesion, are more likely to feel strong loyalty to a geographical locale or neighborhood church. They choose to maintain interarticulated, geographically local religious routines. Newcomers, whose routines are more likely to be diffused in space and organized by norms of choice and achievement, often relate to religious organizations by selecting convenient (though not always neighborhood) locations and religious services that meet their needs.

The routines of newcomers are often structured by the stresses of dual-income, exurban families with children. They express their desire for rituals that mark the changes within the family, including baptisms, weddings, and funerals. They also often articulate their needs for geographically accessible programming that assists them in balancing the pressures of the contemporary work world and their commitment to family. Additionally, these newcomers require support in the face of personal tragedy, loss, and pain, especially when mobility removes them from (or even prevents the development of) familial and kinship support networks. Although a phone call often helps, many of the newcomers with whom I spoke expressed their occasional need for a comforting shoulder—which was supplied by coreligionists.

An ecological framework emphasizes the importance of attending to how social organizations adapt, or fail to adapt, to changes within the local environment. By incorporating multiple levels of analysis within an ecological model, we see more adequately how familial choices both restructure and are restructured by populations of organizations. Families can and do create opportunities, as well as precarious situations, for organizations within the ecology by their routines of belonging. As was explored in chapter 3, religious bodies in Dacula responded to the arrival of newcomers within interdependent religious ecologies. Structuring their religious routines on the basis of these fluid and diverse personal and familial needs, newcomers often created more eclectic, multilayered routines of belonging which crossed traditional denominational and congregational boundaries (cf. Bellah et al. 1985, 1991; Hammond 1992; Roof 1993; and Carroll and Roof 1993). When oldtimers and newcomers, whose patterns of living out their faith differ, coexist within a single religious organization, the outcomes can be volatile, such as schism (as at Hinton Memorial) or organizational malaise (as characterized First Baptist–Dacula). On the other hand, congregations can develop strategies for interweaving these routines, either by providing a very "big tent" as did Hebron Baptist, or by devising bridging cultures, such as the legacy identity that Hinton Memorial later adopted.

In Dacula, oldtimers' and newcomers' divergent patterns for living out their faith was also altering relations among religious organizations locally and across the metropolitan region. The arrival of newcomers represented, and resulted in, new ways for churches to relate to one another. Newcomers simply did not live out their faith in the same way that oldtimers did. Newcomers at Hinton Memorial UMC were more apt than oldtimers to have routines of religious belonging that were multilayered and cross-denominational (Roof 1993:200–203).[8] For example, Anita Locking, a newcomer at Hinton Memorial, attended worship services at Hinton Memorial on Sunday mornings, went to Christian Weight Watchers at Hebron on Tuesday nights (where her husband was also a member of the softball leagues), took lessons in the spiritual discipline of yoga at the Pierce Institute (where she took birth training during her pregnancy) on Wednesdays after work, and enrolled her two children in a Church of God day care. Although her level of commitment to each of these religious institutions and its practices differs, Anita saw them all as important to her spiritual well-being. "There's no way to say that one is more important than the other; I guess I need them all, just in different ways." During my interviews with newcomers at Hinton, members of Hebron Baptist, and members of other congregations, I routinely found similarly multilayered and eclectic patterns of religious belonging. Through their patterns of interaction, families and individuals acted as conduits of information and practice between religious groups.

The stories of the Englands and Penners detail how newcomers and oldtimers relate religious organizations to one another and to the organization of their household, productive, and consumer routines. For example, Vernon England's leadership in the Dacula Masonic Lodge #433 and his role as treasurer for Hinton Memorial UMC related these local organizations when he announced the church's fund-raising barbecue at lodge meetings or when he invited a newcomer to the church to attend a lodge meeting. Faith Penner's choice to attend Grief Relief meetings at Hebron Baptist Church after the death of her mother and father and her decision to place her children in The Child's Place, a religious day-care center in Duluth near her gym, connected these organizations through her customized routines of belonging and through her use of ideas from these varied sources as a volunteer at Hinton.

Oldtimers at Hinton Memorial UMC, accustomed as they were to assuming commitment and cohesion as norms within the congregation—even after the schism—were increasingly related to fellow congregants who had developed a pastiche of religious organizational ties. These alterations, perhaps even more than did the schism, challenged the way in which oldtimers and newcomers alike lived out their faith locally. They were also challenging religious organizations to respond to such multilayered involvement among their members. Although competition and calls for fiscal and spiritual loyalty were responses evident at Hinton Memorial, another response was the development of affiliative relationships with other organizations, creating connections based not on denomination or broad cultural orientations but on local organizational cultures and services. Congregations in the midst of rapid change, seeking to accommodate both oldtimers and newcomers with their new routines of belonging, created new stories and cultures that situated the congregations within their altered religious ecology. Though for some oldtimers, in particular, these changes were bemoaned as a deemphasis on the norms of cohesion and commitment, they also entailed heightened attention to specific needs and the augmentation of congregational resources as the church sought to respond to the area's transformations. A close examination of the routines of the Englands and Penners provides a window into these changes within the Dacula community and the Hinton Memorial UMC congregation.

Vernon and Marie England

Vernon England, a short, balding man, leaned over the back of my pew to whisper in my ear, "How do you like them apples?" as he showed me that Sunday's copy of the church bulletin on the back of which was printed the week's selection of "chuckles"—a sampling from Reverend Luther Dawson's file of *Reader's Digest* funny stories and aphorisms. The one that Vernon highlighted with his thumb was "Jogging is a good way to meet new people—orthopedists, podiatrists, cardiologists, and ambulance drivers." The chuckle recalled a conversation that Vernon and I had earlier that morning about his doctor's orders to get more exercise. Vernon, a retired machinist, had said that he could not think of many more useless activities than running when you had no place to go. I suggested that he look up weeding in an exercise manual to see how much he would have to do to equal jogging.

Vernon was an avid gardener—one of the oldtimers who farmed

the cinnamon earth in their abundant backyards—but gardening, he feared, would only lead to more eating and did not really count as exercise. A few years ago when Marie retired from the Dacula school system where she had been a cafeteria worker and cook for thirty-five years, she ceded all the household cooking duties to Vernon. "I was tired of it; and he was bored," she reported. Vernon, a connoisseur of what he described as "good ole' Southern food," took up the task with gusto. During numerous visits to the England's home, I was nearly always treated to "cat-paw" biscuits or homemade cake. The problem was that Vernon's cooking was too rich for their decreased activity and advancing age. It was just one more thing that they were going to have to change, since Vernon did not relish the idea of donning jogging shorts and joining his new neighbors on their daily run down Dacula Road.

HOME

Vernon and Marie had lived in Dacula since childhood. Many of the old school photos published in the "All around Town" came from their family albums. The stories of their families were intimately connected with the history of this particular place. Vernon's father was a Baptist preacher in the area, and Marie's father owned an auto repair shop and later a jewelry store in town. Vernon and Marie had known one another all their lives and had been sweethearts since their late teens. "I got to carry her books for her. That was a mistake," Vernon said, laughing. Asked when they decided to marry, Marie admitted, "I can't remember just when he asked me to marry him." Marie nudged Vernon; "You did ask me, didn't you?" He replied, "Well, we're married aren't we? I must've." The couple married in a simple ceremony in Marie's parents' home when Vernon was nineteen years old and Marie eighteen years old. The photo of the event, which hung in a collage with nearly fifteen other family photos in the couple's living room, showed Vernon grinning mischievously and Marie stone-faced—an apt portrait of the couple.

In 1985 when Vernon retired from his job as a machinist, the couple moved into a home in one of Dacula's first subdivisions, a lemon-colored split-level just off Harbins Road, on the right side of the railroad tracks that divide Dacula. In spring when I first visited the England's home, the front yard was aglow with pink, red, and white azaleas. Later in mid-summer, day lilies flourished there. Inside the front entryway several plaques with Christian messages, such as "Bless this house" and "God is welcome here," set the tenor for expected interactions in the England's home. The furnishings in the house, which was built in the early 1980s, were an eclectic mix of furniture styles, Christian knickknacks, and country crafts. For example, a white family Bible with gold lettering was the centerpiece of the pine coffee table in the formal living room. The small room was packed with department store and antique furniture— four pink and blue wingback chairs, a velveteen sofa, and a cherry writing desk. Silk flowering plants were placed on most horizontal surfaces.

The home's focal point, however, was the family room and kitchen where Vernon and Marie generally entertained. The setting there was comfortable with the walls and glass-front cabinets filled with family mementos, all of which had a story behind them. If a visitor made time, Vernon or Marie would recount them. The china dog was from Marie's daughter-in-law, who knew of her mother-in-law's love for poodles; the lace curtains were crocheted by a school friend; and the photo of the bearded iris were from Vernon's garden in 1987—their best year. The television, two Lazyboys, and a plaid couch created a cozy family niche, out from underfoot but in full view of the kitchen.

For the first year of their marriage, Marie and Vernon lived in Vernon's maternal grandparents' small home about two miles east of Dacula. Then when Vernon was serving in the military during World War II, Marie lived with her parents on Dacula Road. Later after Vernon's father passed away and was buried in the Ebenezer Baptist cemetery near Dacula, Marie moved into the England family home in the heart of Dacula to care for Vernon's ailing mother until Vernon returned from overseas. 'Ama (for Grandma), as Vernon's mother was called, had severe back problems and was nearly bedridden after her husband's death. Vernon and Marie were primary caretakers of 'Ama England, until her death fifteen years after her husband, when she was buried next to him in Ebenezer's cemetery. After her death, Vernon and Marie and their growing family moved into Vernon's family home where they reared their three children and resided until 1985.

Vernon was keen to move to this residence after traffic began increasing in front of the old England home. Marie, however, was reluctant to relocate. Then their oldest son, Elliott, and his family pur-

chased a home in the same subdivision—just three doors up. So they
made the move. The old England home was divided into three apart-
ments and rented out. Marie and Vernon regularly baby-sat for the
grandchildren. They kept a toy box in the corner of their family room
and a swing set in the backyard "just to make sure they want to come,"
said Vernon. In 1992, Tom, their youngest son, moved with his family
to another subdivision near Hebron Baptist Church. Marie said there
was sometimes competition for their baby-sitting services. Ellen, the
couple's daughter, was the only family member who was "away." Her
family lived near Valdosta in south Georgia. But Marie and Vernon visited every two or three months.

With that exception, the couple's network of friends and family was
tightly bound to Dacula. Vernon commented in 1994, "We have some
friends that live here in town, and we have one or two in Lawrenceville.
And my brother lives down in Harbins. We have a dear friend up here
in town who's in real bad condition—in fact; he's in Atlanta at the VA
hospital. And Marie has waited on him for several years. People like
that—she talks with him every day, or he visits with me. We have quite
a few friends, and we share if we have worries or things like that." Most
of the couple's confidants were "Saturday night church friends," that
is, a group that had been going out every Saturday night for years. All
had to get back early enough to go to services on Sunday morning; most
attended Hinton Memorial UMC but several went to other churches
in the area.

The church friends from Hinton Memorial also got together once
a month on Tuesday morning (when they received the seniors' discount)
for the breakfast buffet at Shoney's in Lawrenceville. They generally
reserved a table in the restaurant's sunroom and made a relaxed morning of visiting and catching up. Once when I was invited to attend,
the group—including Miss Irene Abbott, Alfred and Lula DeVries,
Harold Dill, Jane and Merle DeLoach, and Luther and Anna Lee
Dawson—carried on a running joke about members' appetites. Alfred
credited his healthy appetite to his status as a farmer who had to keep
his strength up—though Lula reminded him that he was mostly retired.
But when Lula DeVries went back to the buffet, she commented that
the same goes for a farmer's wife. Finally, when Anna Lee made a third
trip, Alfred asked if she was planning to do any harvesting that day.

"Long time since I've seen a preacher's wife pitching hay." The teasing and collegiality of the group highlighted the members' shared local, generational, and cultural frame of reference.

Marie and Vernon maintained regular contact with more distant friends and family by telephone, which kept Vernon from having to get "out in the traffic" and kept Marie—according to Vernon—"busy yappin' on the line." Vernon was not always shy about getting on the interstates. Years of commuting to Atlanta and then Gainesville had given Vernon a steady hand on the wheel. Vernon and Marie made weekly visits to their friend in the Veterans Administration hospital in Atlanta and to Alvin Wilford who had been hospitalized in downtown Atlanta; and they made regular treks to Valdosta to see their daughter and grandchildren. It is just that Vernon, and to a lesser extent Marie, simply preferred to stay close to home, though the couple willingly ventured out to maintain familial and friendship connections and to care for loved ones.

NEIGHBORHOOD

Home and neighborhood blended easily for Vernon and Marie. Home, though centered in their split-level was intimately connected to Dacula's businesses, clubs, schools, and community activities. Their recreation revolved around local friends, family, and community events. The Englands had long been active contributors to Dacula's community life. For example, they regularly attended high school events, such as football games and carnivals, which were not restricted to the teachers and the students' parents. They went to elementary and middle school activities in which their grandchildren participated.

Since his return from the war, Vernon had been active in the local chapter of the Veterans of Foreign Wars (VFW), which often met at the Masonic Lodge in Dacula. He was regularly called upon to be in the color guard at fellow soldiers' funerals, and he donned his dress uniform annually to ride with other veterans on Hinton Memorial's float in Dacula's Memorial Day parade. Vernon was also a long-time member of the Masonic Lodge #433 into which he was initiated in the 1950s.[9]

Marie had long been active in several local clubs as well. Initially after her marriage, she participated in a sewing circle composed of young women who had grown up in the area and whose husbands were in the military. The group, called Ladies Aid, had continued to meet for coffee at least once a month ever since its inception. In the early 1950s, Marie helped found a local chapter of the Confederate Dames. The Dames, as Marie referred to the group which continued to meet in Dacula, was founded to help preserve the confederate graves in the area and to promote education about Southern culture. The Ladies Aid, Confederate Dames, the local VFW chapter, and the Masonic Lodge upheld the primary goal of promoting the interests of the community. Marie and Vernon's loyalty and participation in these voluntary associations were, in no small degree, related to this point of convergence.

Habit and commitment to local resources shaped the England's consumer routine as well. Their move to their cul-de-sac and their rental of the old England home was handled by Billy Sue Hammond Realty, which dealt almost exclusively with Dacula properties. Vernon shopped at Hill's Grocery at McMillan and Highway 28 in downtown Dacula, although he admitted that it did not provide the best selection of produce. (His vegetable garden and freezing though filled in most of the gaps.) The store, which advertised—"No Beer! No Wine! No Lottery!"—on its portable sign out front, was until 1995 the only grocery store on the Dacula side of Lawrenceville. The Englands purchased their meat from Wages Butchers near Dacula's Dairy Queen. Except for Saturday nights and Tuesday mornings when the couple went with church friends to restaurants in Lawrenceville or near the Gwinnett Place Mall Corners, Marie and Vernon dined out close to home occasionally at the Dairy Queen or the Waffle House at the intersection of Highways 316 and 28, or at home with a pizza delivered from Frank's, located in downtown Dacula.

They filled their prescriptions at Dacula Pharmacy, except for those medications that Vernon insisted were "so cheap it's a crime" through the AARP mail prescription service. They generally serviced their car at Earl's, where the gas is not cheap but the conversation was good. They rented videos at Stoplight Video adjacent to the town's one flashing stoplight. They purchased their home, life, and car insurance from Drue Steverson, the Allstate agent whose office was located on Winder Highway in Dacula. Marie had a standing Friday morning hair appointment at Kleen Kuts in the Dacula Square, adjacent to Hill's. (Vernon boasted that he just took the fingernail scissors to his thinning locks now and again to keep its stylish coif.) "We've even got our headstones picked out at Knight's," said Vernon, referring to Knight Monument, which had sold grave markers in Dacula for twenty years.

The one store that Vernon and Marie regularly frequented outside the Dacula area was the Wal-Mart in Lawrenceville where they purchased such things as birthday gifts for the grandchildren, toiletries, and automotive supplies. Marie would also have liked to visit the Gwinnett Place Mall more often than she did, which was once or twice a month. "I'd like to go to Gwinnett Mall, but he doesn't like to go. So sometimes I go with a friend. I enjoy that," she said.

Marie and Vernon's consumer routines were to a large extent reliant on the longstanding organizational ecology within their neighborhood—Dacula. They had long-term relationships with shop owners and merchants in their locale and were loyal to the community's commercial nucleus. "Some of these guys aren't going to make it, what with all the newcomers, but it sure seems a shame to see them go after all these years," said Marie. Vernon was especially determined to do his part in supporting local businesses, "I'm up to the general store most days, just to talk and what not. But I always buy a little something to keep them in business—like shoelaces or furnace filters."

In addition to expressing their solidarity through their pocketbook, the Englands were active in opposing changes in the community that they believed would adversely affect its merchants and residents. Vernon served on the Dacula City Council from 1977 to 1990. Though he considered himself temperamentally unsuited for public office. (He confessed, "I've got a temper when you cross me.") He was convinced that the town needed to take action to keep growth from occurring too rapidly. So he allowed his name to be "put in the hat" as Vernon described the local election. The Englands believed that Dacula needed someone to stand up for them. "The county was trying to get us to sign on to everything they sent our way so that they could dictate what we needed to do," complained Vernon. During the late 1970s and 1980s, Gwinnett County was rapidly increasing the number of water hookups and improving roads in the area surrounding Dacula. Vernon worried that the taxes would increase dramatically forcing his neighbors from their homes. Another city council member, who grew up on a farm outside of Dacula and had been forced to sell parcels of his family's homestead, echoed Vernon's concerns, "There's no way to pay the taxes with farmland. Land is too high to farm on."

Vernon was also opposed to the development of the Gwinnett Progress Center—the light industrial, office, and housing development that stretches from the outskirts of Lawrenceville to Dacula along Highway 316. He voted to oppose a centralized sewer system for Dacula and the surrounding area, hoping that the additional cost of laying sewer lines would discourage businesses from relocating to the area. The Center's developers saw such actions as "backward" and "shortsighted." One developer said of the Dacula City Council, "We try to have as little to do with them as possible. We prefer to deal with the County Commission. They understand our needs for timely action, and they are aware of the benefits that we can offer to a community like Gwinnett." Vernon remained suspicious that the concerns of particular places like Dacula were at worst ignored and at best misunderstood by the Commission. "They are thinking what's best for the whole county—the numbers—they aren't so concerned with what's going on in each little place."

During his tenure on the Dacula City Council, Vernon was not, however, unsympathetic to ventures that would bring new jobs. Though as a citizen he hoped Dacula would stay a small town rather than getting built up like Lawrenceville, Norcross, or Lilburn, as a city council member he considered it his "duty" to think about local jobs. He supported the development of several local distribution warehouses. These industries, argued Vernon, would employ local high school graduates. "I'm not saying that the Progress Center won't give jobs to people here, but most of them will come from away to work in these places." His calculation of jobs for local people versus competing businesses and more newcomers influenced his vote on each project. He was the first to admit that his reasoning was not an exact science, rather the local wisdom of a long-time resident. "I just did the best I could," he said. "And prayed a lot," added Marie. Vernon mentioned in an aside that the mayor, council members, and city workers were all Christians. "We appreciate that—helps keep out the graft." This contrasted with his estimation of the Gwinnett County Commission "that's wasting so much money it's criminal."

Vernon's calculations (and prayers) about his civic duties also led him to work to halt development on the Dacula project with Native American burial mounds located on the grounds. He believed that the developers' plans for a shopping center and a school in the subdivision would create "a town all its own." "That's the last thing we need now— another town right there on top of us," he warned. In this estimation, Vernon captured the feelings of many in the community. In 1993, Dacula Elementary School's principal, who had served the community for more than twenty years, said, "We need some relief, but the point is not to put a school wherever there is the most money, but to put it where it would do the most good. Another school two miles from us would not do the most good." Nonetheless, the new elementary school is within four miles of Dacula Elementary.

Vernon always took seriously the concerns of Dacula's educators in considering his civic and neighborly duties. He was particularly proud of the Dacula's school system. For years, when Marie worked in the Dacula school cafeterias, she knew the children by name and generally knew their parents and grandparents as well. Marie and Vernon had been active in the PTA in their time. They had attended ball games, sponsored science projects, and chaperoned school trips. A trophy from the state champion football team on which their oldest son played was among the keepsakes in the glass-front cabinet in the family room. Their children all graduated with honors and went on to attend college at University of Georgia or Georgia Southern College. Elliott was a sales agent for a developer; Tom managed a branch for a national bank, and Ellen managed the books for her husband's plumbing firm. The Englands were immensely proud of the educational attainment of their children and attributed their success in large part to the Dacula schools. They also hoped that their grandchildren would be the next generation in a long line of Englands to graduate from the Dacula schools and go on to Georgia colleges and universities.

But they worried, too. Marie feared that drugs and crime were becoming increasingly common in Dacula schools, "I know it is in high school, and I've heard that it was in middle school. I don't know about that, but I do know about high school. Even in small towns." She was concerned that her grandchildren would not have access to the same quality of education that was available to her children. Finances also figured in her worries about their future. "Colleges seems so much higher now. We could do it with both of us working and loans, but I don't know how the kids will be able to afford it."

Fear also affected the England's perception of their beloved neighborhood. "Used to here, we didn't think about locking the door. You didn't think about leaving your house open when you went to town. But you don't now. But back years ago that's the way it was around here. Everyone knew everyone, and I guess everybody knew everybody's business, but we were neighbors. Everyone knew if someone had trouble, we all had trouble. We worried about each other, or were happy with each other. But it has changed a lot. But I love it this way, too. I wish people could live the way we lived, if they would like it. It was a happy time back then. Children didn't have a lot to tempt them." Their neighborhood was, in their view, embattled, and Vernon and Marie focused their efforts in maintaining the organizations and resources they valued, preserving them for their grandchildren.

WORK

Vernon's commitment to bring jobs that employed local residents to the area was related to his own employment history. For most of his working life, he had lengthy commutes to work because the local opportunities were limited. Vernon joined up early at the onset of World War II. He recalled, "I thought it was the right thing, 'course I've thought that about any fighting we've been in." He was one of the first twenty-year-old Marines in Gwinnett County. "I was on the first busload to leave Lawrenceville in '42. I went to North Africa, Sicily, and Italy. I was sent to Manila when the war was over." Vernon spent three years serving in the military before he was wounded in battle.

During his absence, Marie began work in the cafeteria dishroom of Dacula's combined elementary, middle, and high school. Marie remembered those years of Vernon's absence as miserably lonely. Dacula was "picked clean" of young men, she said, leaving only the older men and women and young wives who "dogged" the mailman for news of their fighting men. Working provided not only the financial support she needed, but also a way to fill the time.

After the war, Vernon returned to Dacula for several years to work with his father-in-law initially in the garage and then in the jewelry store before beginning an apprenticeship in machine tooling. Vernon describes how he began in his craft, "Marie's father was a machinist, and he got me started in it. He had tools and so forth, and I found this place that would put up with me, so I did it." After completing the apprenticeship, Vernon took a job with a company in the Five Points area of Atlanta where he worked for fourteen years in the 1950s and early 1960s. Vernon's commute to downtown Atlanta was not uncommon among the men in Dacula during this time. He said, "At one time Doraville was about the only real company to pay the employees anything—General Motors. Everybody had to drive somewhere to work. It was even worse if you didn't have a trade or college." Vernon often gave rides to Hinton Memorial's young student pastors who attended Candler School of Theology.

In the mid-1960s Vernon took a job in Gainesville—thirty miles northwest of Dacula—where he practiced his trade until he retired. For many years, Vernon was an apprentice overseer for several young men from Dacula. He recalled, "I enjoyed it. I enjoyed my work every night, but I didn't enjoy it when I got older. Too much stress and tension. This new bunch comes in after I'd been there for twenty years and they changed the place all up. Everything was changed. But it wasn't just myself." The changes on the job were the result of the company's buyout by a multinational firm, which sought to increase production in the shop so as to match cheaper global competitors. Vernon took early retirement, and he found a part-time job. "I just wanted something to get me away from things. I started driving for a bus company for two or three years. I enjoyed it. I had never been out anywhere. I didn't know where nothing was. All I knew was work and back, work and back," he said. Finally in 1988, Vernon retired for good.

Marie had continued to work in the Dacula school cafeteria, after a hiatus of about ten years while her children were young. She worked in the cafeteria, she said, both because she wanted to put money away for college, but also because she liked the company. She especially liked working in the school system because her schedule corresponded to her children's. She also liked the feeling of being at the center of the community. She said, "I don't think I could have done like Vernon and gone someplace else to work. I needed to stay close to home." Like Vernon, Marie began to become frustrated with her work environment before her retirement. The Dacula schools were growing rapidly, and the cafeteria staff was expanding apace. New workers and additional oversight from the Gwinnett County school system disrupted the intimate crew of long-time workers. When Vernon decided to stop bus driving, Marie also retired. While they were both working, the Englands had an annual income of nearly $65,000. They were frugal and provided well for themselves in their retirement. "It's not like we're flush or anything, but we do OK."

For most of his working life, Vernon's employment took him far beyond Dacula, but never did he seriously consider moving his family to reside closer to his work. Work sites, he believed, would change, but the family needed a place to call home. Furthermore, Marie worked locally, both for financial and personal reasons. The couple's production routines, while they were more dispersed than the household and consumption routines, were still firmly rooted in Dacula.

CHURCH

Vernon and Marie's active involvement in Dacula Methodist Church (as Hinton Memorial UMC was then known) began in the early 1950s. Marie had attended congregational events while Vernon was in the military, and many of the women in the Ladies Aid were Methodist churchgoers. After Vernon's return, the young couple visited several churches before settling on Dacula Methodist—the only church in which they held membership. Vernon characterized their participation in congregational events before the birth of their children as sporadic. "We'd be there pretty often but—I don't know—it didn't seem all that important," he explained. Elliott's birth, however, marked the period of the family's scrupulous religious participation. "You start to thinking that you want your children to have good values and friends, so you start getting more involved," Marie explained.

Though Marie's religious background was Methodist, Vernon joked that he was still a closet Baptist (though he admitted that he had not been inside a Baptist church for ten years except for funerals). Nonetheless, the couple attended an adult membership class while the children underwent confirmation. Marie recalled that their children were particularly faithful in their attendance: "Back then we had six-month pins, one-year pins, five-year pins, and ten-year pins for perfect attendance. And if we went somewhere, we had to take them to church, so they had to pay for it. So they'd get their pins. I think Elliott got his ten-year pin." Ellen, the couple's daughter, was a pianist at the church when she was a teenager.

The Englands also became more involved in assisting with children's and youth programming. Vernon recalls: "We had ball teams and all when Elliott was young. Then later Elliott coached, and Tom would play. I guess Elliott was about fourteen. They played within the church league for a long time. And we had the Cub Scouts, which was pretty good. I don't think they had the Boy Scouts, but we had the Cub Scouts." Vernon remembered his role in the youth activity and his on-going contact with those youngsters. "But I'd take as many as I could pile in, sitting in the car, in the trunk, on the hood, and take them up to Lake Lanier and come back to get another load and another load to have a campout. Boy, we had great times. But the thing about it is some of them still call me, from all over the country. Wanting me to tell . . . two of the stories especially, that I used to tell, so they could record it for their children. I found an old book, in a falling-down log school over here in the woods. I was hunting. And it was completely . . . just rotted. But I opened it, and I could still read two stories in the center. And the book disintegrated. But I memorized those two stories, but I tell you what, they still want me to record it for their children. It was good."

Vernon was also active on various boards in the church, serving most consistently on the Trustees Committee but also assisting on the Pastor Parish Relations Committee and the Administrative Board, from time to time. Beginning in the mid-1950s, he was appointed to the Pleasant Hill Cemetery committee, composed of church and Dacula leaders, formed to oversee the upkeep of the grounds. He served on the cemetery committee for more than forty years. Marie was active in the United Methodist Women and could always be counted on to prepare food for funerals or to visit the sick, though she steadfastly refused to take more formal jobs, such as Sunday school teacher or committee member.

Until the schism and the community's change, Vernon and Marie believed that Hinton Memorial UMC was at the center of this locality, dominating civic affairs and playing a key role in social events in the community, including the annual barbecue, Thanksgiving services, and the Christmas program. Vernon recollected: "We'd have bonfires, and weenie roasts on special occasions, or before football games or something. There were lots of important things around here then, that's right. And you knew everyone around back then, all your neighbors. There was just always activity." Marie remembered Hinton's church bell that rang the noon hour daily and at eleven o'clock on Sundays as setting the watches of local residents.

According to the Englands, many circumstances conspired to undermine their church's prominence in the community. Vernon recalled being embarrassed to tell people that he was from Hinton during the last year of Gerhard's pastorate. "Everybody'd think that I was a runner and a roller," he said. The Englands ceased their attendance at Hinton Memorial during the most contentious final months prior to the schism. "It was not a Methodist church. I'm going back to three years ago, before Luther got here. It was not a Methodist church. We quit going. We went to [another Methodist church]. [Hinton] was like a Holiness church." Though the couple stopped participating in church services, they remained involved with their church friends and even then considered Hinton Memorial their church home. Unprepared to enter the bruising church battles that preceded the schism, the Englands hoped that if enough long-term members left then the Conference would be forced to act (cf. Baumgartner 1988).[10] In the end, they say, their strategy worked.

Vernon and Marie were back in their pew at Hinton the Sunday after Gerhard and the charismatics departed. Vernon took on the unpaid job of church and parsonage handyman, and Marie delivered for Meals On Wheels. They faithfully attended Sunday morning worship, family night suppers, the short-lived Sunday evening Bible study, United Methodist Women, and the new United Methodist Men. Vernon was chief cook for Hinton's annual fund-raising barbecue. Marie teased that she was the "chief bottle-washer." The couple maintained their involvement in and sizable donations to Hinton Memorial. Except for funerals, they did not attend any other religious services in Dacula or the metropolitan region.

They responded to the arrival of an increasing number of newcomers in the 1990s not only with appreciation for the vitality and finances they contributed, but also with some bewilderment at their lack of loyalty to the church. Marie commented, "It's hard. You'll see one couple for a few Sundays then you won't see them again until they come to join the church. I think that we've got to have some way to find out if they are serious." Vernon also found the habits of some newcomers puzzling: "Some of them you never see together. One will bring the kids one time and the other the next time. The other thing is that you don't know what some of them are, like with Gerhard. They are all the time changing their denomination." Though the Englands understood the busyness of a dual-income couple and the negotiations of an interdenominational marriage, they also expected that denominational and congregational loyalty should undergird a family's religious participation.

In their relations to home, family, neighborhood, work, and local organizations, Vernon and Marie developed routines of belonging that reinforced the norms of commitment and cohesion. They developed a highly interarticulated system of relationships and organizational ties that, with the exception of Vernon's work, centered in Dacula. Though they had numerous opportunities to relocate in pursuit of employment advancement, the couple opted to stay in Dacula, where they have buried their dead and reared their young. Their commitment to the community also structured their consumer patterns. In the face of increased consumer choice as Dacula became an exurb, the Englands were determined to support local small-town merchants whenever possible. Their religious participation at Hinton Memorial—except for the short hiatus during Gerhard's final months—was stable.

The loyalties and deeply embedded community ties of the Englands epitomized the routines of belonging among many Hinton Memorial and Dacula oldtimers. In the face of local changes, their habits reflected little significant alteration. Despite the gradual breakdown of Dacula's status as a distinct small town, they continued to structure their routines around it as figure 5.1 illustrates.

As the locality increasingly lost its distinctiveness as a small town, drawing nonlocal commercial enterprises, such as Wal-Mart and prototype supermarkets, the Englands attempted to maintain familiar routines of belonging. However, as Dacula's fate increasingly rested not

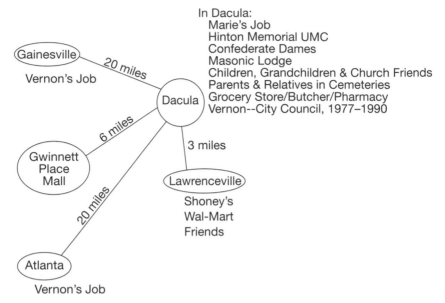

In Dacula:
Marie's Job
Hinton Memorial UMC
Confederate Dames
Masonic Lodge
Children, Grandchildren & Church Friends
Parents & Relatives in Cemeteries
Grocery Store/Butcher/Pharmacy
Vernon--City Council, 1977–1990

Gainesville
Vernon's Job

20 miles

Dacula

6 miles

Gwinnett
Place
Mall

3 miles

Lawrenceville
Shoney's
Wal-Mart
Friends

20 miles

Atlanta
Vernon's Job

Figure 5.1 Routines of Belonging for Vernon and Marie England

within the local community but in agencies, institutions, and processes outside the locality, the Englands had few connections to commercial, governmental, and denominational centers of power beyond their community.

Todd and Faith Penner

On a sultry summer morning in 1993, the Penners stood at the front of Hinton Memorial's sanctuary holding their two children to receive the baptismal charge. The air conditioning in the church was broken. All the doors and windows were open, and the sound of the train rumbling by made Reverend Dawson's words nearly incomprehensible. Dressed in a peach silk pantsuit, Faith Penner held their eight-month-old daughter, Alisa, who wore a flowing lace baptismal gown. Todd held the couple's four-year-old son, Andrew, who like his father was dressed in a suit and tie.

This Sunday father, son, and daughter were being baptized, and the couple was joining the church. Dawson held first Alisa and then Andrew as he dabbed water on their foreheads and offered prayers of thanksgiving for their young lives. When Todd's turn came, Dawson joked that he was not going to try to "hoist him up on my hip." Dawson prayed that Todd would follow the dictates of the Lord all his life, be successful in balancing the demands of work and family, and find peace in God in the midst of his stressful lifestyle. After the baptisms, the congregation stood to recite with the Penners the rite of membership from the Methodist hymnal. Dawson charged the congregation to care for and protect the faith of the Penners. The Penners vowed their support to the congregation with their time, talents, and finances. The ceremony concluded with the Penners standing before the communion table at the front of the church to receive the welcome of each Hinton member.

The Penners, who were in their mid-thirties, had lived in the Dacula area for four years when they joined Hinton Memorial UMC. They resided within three miles of Dacula. Todd and Faith met during college at University of Florida, Gainesville. They dated for three years before moving in together and relocating to the Gwinnett Mall Corners area. Todd, who had majored in engineering, had a difficult time finding a job that suited him. He returned to Lawrenceville, where his family had lived for six years during his junior high and high school years, to manage his father's rental property. Todd's father was also an engineer who had relocated the family frequently and lived just then in San Jose, California. His mother and father divorced in 1989, and his mother, a schoolteacher, resided in Columbia, South Carolina, where she was reared. Todd was the oldest of three children, but had little contact with his younger brothers who lived in Peachtree City, south of Atlanta, and Miami, Florida. "We call now and then, or Brad [the brother in Peachtree City] and I get together for a Braves game," Todd said. He noted that the family had never been very close.

Faith, on the other hand, was very close to her older sister, Tricia, who lived in Tacoma, Washington. They carried on lengthy phone conversations at least once a week and visited one another often. Tricia flew in to be with Faith for Andrew and Alisa's births. The sisters' relationship was intensified when their parents were killed in a plane crash while Faith was in college. Her father, a hobby pilot, and mother were flying to the Florida Keys for a weekend get-away when they crashed. Faith recounted the horror of not being able to find the plane for several days. "They were supposed to have an emergency signal on board, but something went wrong. All Tricia and I could think about was them being eaten by alligators or something. We just sat together in the house because [the aviation search team] told us they would call. Todd was there or I think I would have gone crazy." In the aftermath of the tragedy, Faith's uncle helped the young women liquidate their parent's accounting business, sell the family home in Gainesville, and set up trust funds.

Within a year Faith moved with Todd to an apartment near the Gwinnett Place Mall Corners. In 1988 they married at the Little Gardens Restaurant in Lawrenceville in a small family ceremony. Faith remembered the event as a bittersweet one during which she tried very intently to be happy, because she was sure that she was doing the right thing, but could not put her loss from her mind. Looking at the photos of the event, though, one can scarcely detect the emotional disturbance she reported. In the couple's wedding keepsake book, the pictures of Todd and her seemed the epitome of the happy couple. Faith, whose sable brown hair contrasted dramatically with her ivory brocade gown and toile blusher, smiled demurely; Todd in his black evening wear looked the confident young executive. The only photo that reveals Faith's distress is one in which Tricia and she are hugging, tears glistening on their cheeks—yet even here they could be mistaken for tears of joy.

NEIGHBORHOOD

Faith and Todd were intent on purchasing a home soon after their wedding, and Faith's trust fund provided a generous down payment. The Penners sought out locations in the Atlanta area with good schools and peaceful surroundings. The region around Dacula was then in Todd's words "nearly like North Georgia—wild and open." The couple purchased a large gray stucco and stone home on two and a half acres outside of Dacula. Initially, Faith was skeptical about moving so far into the country. She preferred the area around the Gwinnett Place Mall. But in Dacula, Todd argued, their money could buy more house. The couple's plans to begin a family made ample space especially important.

Equally crucial for the Penners was good access to interstate highways. Faith was then working in downtown Atlanta at a national banking firm. Although she had not completed her degree at the University of Florida, she had landed a good job in the bank's trust department. She did not mind commuting, but she did want a home near the interstate. "I worked downtown on Peachtree Street. I'd just take 316 to 85, and I was there in thirty-five to forty minutes. It wasn't bad because I didn't have to be in until 9:00 so I could leave here at 8:15. So it's real convenient as far as having a job downtown because we're so accessible to the interstate," said Faith. Todd was especially keen to find a home on a large lot, yet he wanted to be close enough to the city to make attendance at Hawks and Braves games and other cultural events relatively easy. "I know I'm generalizing, but I think that most people like to have a city there, where they can go to the games, the theater and things," said Todd.

He was, however, adamantly opposed to a home in one of the newly developed subdivisions in the Dacula area. He said of those residents, "I think that they're being fooled into thinking that they're going to get away from the traffic. And that's a joke, traffic's coming with them. I think a lot of people want the peace and quiet of country life. It's been very interesting to us that people want to be out in the country, but they want to all get together in a little subdivision. It sort of defeats the purpose, because if you notice, when people start building, then everybody joins around them and they get a subdivision. So they don't really want to be alone, but they think they do. So I think that's one thing that people have in mind, they want to get out, away from the hustle-bustle, hectic life of the city. They don't really know that they don't really want out. I think you can have a little more space, rather than a postage stamp lot."

Faith, on the other hand, had been reared in subdivisions in Dallas, Texas, and in Gainesville where "everybody knew everybody and everybody socialized with everybody." She initially perceived their Dacula location as too isolated and remote. As the surrounding area changed though, Faith realized how much she had appreciated the quiet and lack of congestion. She said, "There are a lot more subdivisions out here. There are a lot more houses now."

The Penners, however, did not typically associate with their Dacula neighbors. Faith commented, "We don't know our neighbors. Well, we know them to speak to them, but we don't socialize with them. That's part of the reason I didn't like it out here at first." She mentioned that they had problems with several neighbors who allowed their dogs to run free on the Penner's land, scaring Andrew when he was outside playing. Faith was not favorably impressed with the people who lived in the area. "I always thought—well, I didn't think they were redneck, but they were very backwoods. Not that they're any lower than me, it's just that they're different than what I grew up around." Todd added, "I think that it's just education. I mean, I was a redneck before I went to college. I drove a pickup and made a lot of noise." Faith, however, protested, arguing that there was a difference between adolescent male behavior, like Todd's, and some of the oldtimers around here "who are all snaggle-toothed."

Despite the growing number of newcomers, Faith continued to hold that the Dacula area was dominated by these oldtimers. "Just take the city council," she illustrated. "They won't vote to get central water or sewer out here because there is someone on the council who owns a well-digging firm. He'd lose money." Though I could not confirm Faith's claim, her remark highlighted an antagonism with the local leaders who, in her view, steadfastly refused to provide services, such as central sewer and water and garbage pickup, that would make living in the area more convenient. Todd was also opposed to Dacula's proposal to annex their area. Referring to pending legislation, requiring municipalities to provide a specified number of public services in order to maintain their charter, he said, "They get this bill going in the legislature and what do you know they come alive." Despite their opposition to annexation, neither Todd nor Faith contacted Dacula City Council members to express their opinion. Todd believed that the council would never get its act together to successfully annex the area. "They have to fight the County Commission, and my money's with the Commission." In the end, the Dacula City Council was unsuccessful in annexing the area.

The influx of residential development to the area improved the commercial offerings in Faith's estimate. When they first moved to the Dacula area, she recalled, "There wasn't even an Ingles [a regional grocery chain]. We used to go to the other side of Lawrenceville to go grocery shopping." Their perception of the lack of local resources meant that the Penners traveled some distance in fitting together their routine of shopping. Faith did not have a single grocery store that she regularly frequented; instead she usually picked up a few things when she was out. "As long as it's a Kroger, an Ingles, or an A & P, I'm happy," she remarked. On most weekends the couple shopped together at Harry's Farmers Market—a warehouse near the Gwinnett Mall known for its ready-to-eat meals and exotic produce. Todd had his shirts and suits cleaned near his work. Faith often picked up videos at the Blockbusters near Gwinnett Place Mall where she went regularly to shop for herself and the kids. If she needed a gift she was likely to stop at Parisian—a department store in the Mall, because they offered free gift-wrapping.

The Penners purchased their home, life, and car insurance through a firm near Todd's office in Corporate Square at the intersection of a major Atlanta street and I-85. They filled prescriptions at a chain drugstore near their day-care center in Duluth because, as Todd said, "we just started doing it one day when we had to get something for Andrew." The day-care center, The Child's Place, was run by a Church of God congregation in Duluth and was recommended to the Penners by Faith's former coworker. They were very satisfied with the care at the center and laughed about the "fundamentalist" songs, such as one action chorus about stomping on Satan, that Andrew sometimes came home singing. The couple allowed Andrew to participate in a children's cantata, entitled "Bullfrogs and Butterflies," at the church. During one interview when Faith mentioned that name, Andrew began singing, flying throughout the room like a desperate butterfly and hopping on the couch.

Todd Penner could think of no business that the family did in Dacula. "What's there?" he asked rhetorically. Faith, however, reminded him that they sometimes use the drive-through window at the Dairy Queen. But on the whole, these newcomers did not perceive Dacula as a commercial center. "To this day if I need something I go to Lawrenceville or the Mall. I don't even go that direction. It seems like we're not over there except for church," said Faith.

The Penners were also involved in few voluntary associations—local or otherwise. Faith characterized her husband as "not a joiner." "Todd's out of town a lot. When he's out of town, it's every night out to dinner with somebody. So when he gets home he doesn't want to go out to dinner. He's been doing that all week," she commented. Though he had not attended meetings in years, Todd was a member of the Lawrenceville Lions Club because his father wanted him to join when

Todd managed the rental property. "Once in a while in the summer we'll go pick up some barbecue at their fundraising cookouts," Todd acknowledged. He was, however, an active member of a gym near his work, and he and a colleague from work were on a softball team in Snellville.

Faith, who quit her job in downtown Atlanta when Alisa was born, was involved in a women's tennis league. Her tennis partner from Covington, fifteen miles southeast of Atlanta, and she decided to split the distance and joined a league in Lawrenceville. Faith was also a member of a gym in Duluth near the day-care center—making it convenient to drop off the kids for her workout. Faith admitted that she would like to become involved in additional clubs or voluntary activities; but she said: "I didn't feel like there was anything out here to do. I go to the gym every day. That's really my organization."

Beginning in 1992, Faith attended weekly Grief Relief support group meetings at Hebron Baptist Church. During the second trimester of her pregnancy with Alisa, Faith became so depressed that she could hardly rouse herself from bed. Finally, at Todd's insistence, she went to see her doctor who prescribed an antidepressant and encouraged her to find someone with whom she could work through the grief of her parents' deaths. Faith was disinclined to see a psychiatrist or psychologist. "I knew I wasn't crazy or anything," she insisted. One day at the Ingles grocery store near her home, she saw an announcement for Grief Relief meetings at Hebron and decided to attend. The weekly sessions, which were led by a licensed psychologist, began with prayer and expounded a twelve-step model of dealing with personal loss. Each session included an opportunity to speak about the pain and anger of loss. Faith found that one session in particular at which group members took turns screaming into a pillow that a partner held to be especially therapeutic. "You start out feeling really stupid. But then you feel something let go inside of you. You're not alone."

Having a safe place to talk about her immense grief was, Faith believed, a relief for the couple's marriage as well. She recognized that her depression had been wearing on Todd, who wanted to help but did not know what to do. Since the couple's friends were spread throughout the metropolitan area, in such locations as Stone Mountain and Powder Springs, Faith felt that she could not drop in on a friend for support on a particularly bad day. She complained, "I felt like every time

I wanted to go see some of my friends, I had a haul." Though occasionally Todd and she arranged to meet friends for a sports event or a restaurant in downtown Atlanta, Faith needed more consistent emotional and spiritual support, she said. Grief Relief provided a close-knit group of mostly women who provided consistent support. She also said that she was not pressured to join Hebron Baptist Church after Todd and she attended several times and did not like it. "They seem OK with me just coming for the meetings. I really get a lot out of them; it's when I feel closest to God."

For Faith and Todd Penner the routines that formed their neighborhood spanned the metropolitan region. Though they resided near Dacula, they participated in few local events. Faith, in particular, was very purposive in putting together a routine of belonging, including religious participation, that provided the services she and her family needed. However, in late 1993, as they prepared to leave their home in Dacula because of a promotion offered to Todd that required them to relocate to Memphis, Tennessee, Faith lamented, "Now that we are moving to Memphis, things are finally falling in place. Now that I'm just starting to like it and get kind of involved we're moving."

HOME

The home that they left was listed by a national real estate brokerage as

all the bells and whistles
open, bright and truly better than new, this seven year old-
stucco and stone traditional home is waiting for you! 2 sty
foyer; very open family rm.; beautiful formal areas; 4BR; 2.5BA,
full basement. Take I-85N to Highway 316. You're home.
$179,900

Not mentioned in the "for sale" notice was the free-standing double garage, the front yard with a low split-rail fence, or the backyard with a large wooden swing set, a sandbox, and a small trampoline.

On one Sunday when I visited the couple's home, Andrew's hot-wheels was parked parallel with the red Jeep Cherokee that Faith drove and Todd's gray BMW. The large front entryway of the Penner's home had an antique oak hat stand, a side table, and a wall mirror. From the hall, one had immediate access to the formal dining room with its large cherry dinette set and to the formal living room with its cream carpet and rust sofa and chairs. The center of family activity, however, was at the rear of the house where the large kitchen and family room were. The family room had a big screen television, a chintz sofa, two Queen Anne recliners, and a miniature oak rocking chair. Toys were strewn over the wool hooked rug, and a baby swing sat in the corner. On the wall above the sofa was a framed collection of cross-stitch samplers—made by Faith over the years. On another wall were photos of Andrew and Alisa at different ages.

Faith, who had taken a decorating course in college, had worked hard to make her home a cozy and elegant setting in which they could live comfortably as a family and yet entertain Todd's clients and co-workers. Although she said that she loved their home, she preferred not to be "stuck" there. She needed, she said, to get out during the day after she quit her job in downtown Atlanta to care full-time for their children. "I never wanted to be a housewife," she remarked. "Todd knew that when I married him, but it just made sense for me to be with the kids now." Housekeeping especially was not a priority for her, she said, laughing that if I looked in her Jeep, I would get a better sense of how she kept house.

WORK

On my final visit to the Penner's home before they departed for Memphis, Faith apologized for the boxes that filled the front entryway. Moving day was just a week away. This was the first move that Todd's job as a marketing analyst and engineer had required the family to make. Todd described the promotion that necessitated the family's move to Memphis—his corporate headquarters: "I was an engineer. I had eight states and I was assigned certain locations and anything from an engineering maintenance, capital improvement, or environment standpoint was my responsibility. Now I'm manager in charge of design and engineering. Six engineers work for me. I just administer and take care of their budgets. Requires a lot of travel and p.r."

Faith reported that for most of their married life she had been worried about Todd's work habits. "He works too hard," she said. "He's never home before seven or eight and then it's the weekend in the office sometimes, too." These tendencies especially disturbed her because she characterized Todd's father as a workaholic whose "addiction to work destroyed his family." "I think that a teacher said that he wasn't ever going to make anything of himself. And he has been bound and determined to prove her wrong. But now his sons don't call him, his wife left him—but he's got money. So he's a success, right?" she noted.

Todd, however, insisted that his father's example had cautioned him about the costs of success. He explained, "I'm not going to do this until I'm sixty or something like my dad, but when you are just starting out you have to work hard, play the game." Playing the game meant that Todd traveled at least once a week often staying away for two nights. Todd's traveling was especially difficult for Andrew who resented his father's absence and was often petulant on his return, making family relations very tense the evening of Todd's homecoming. Nonetheless, Todd maintained that he was well compensated for the additional stresses that he and his family had to absorb. Asked his salary, he said obliquely, "Well, it's not six figures, but it's not so far from that."

For Faith and Todd, the measure of success for themselves and their family had been a point of contention. Several years ago at a seminar organized by Todd's company, the couple took individual and joint value clarification tests designed to help them understand their personal priorities. On the individual tests, Faith had scored high on family and financial security, whereas she said, "Todd's were totally different, like self-improvement." On the joint test, the couple scored high on competitiveness and compassion—which the session organizers said was not uncommon, but which the Penners found unintelligible. Despite the assurances that their divergent values were not necessarily a bad omen, the discrepancy in their scores was a nagging concern for Faith.

Faith anticipated that in several years she, too, would return to work. "It's going to be my turn for a while," she said. She hoped that Todd would then take more responsibility for housekeeping and the childcare. After their move, Faith wanted to finish her undergraduate degree in accounting, in which she lacked only a few credits. "Even though I've got experience, when you've been out of the job market for several years that piece of paper is important," she asserted. The couple's move to Memphis would make it possible, she hoped, to complete her degree.

The Penner's productive routines required that the family accept mobility and extensive traveling as a condition of advancement and financial security. Faith's decision to stay home with their children in the short-run was a compromise to allow Todd to make career moves that would have been more difficult if the couple had shared childrearing responsibility equitably. Todd described his relationship with Andrew and Alisa as close. He regularly read to them and prepared them for bed. But his work pressures made it difficult for him to spend extensive time with them. Faith noted that though she wanted to be with the children, the decision had not been an easy one. There were times when she wished she were back at work in downtown Atlanta. The couple's compromise involved part-time day care for Andrew and Alisa, which permitted Faith more time on her own. It further entailed an agreement that when Alisa was two years old it would be Faith's turn to return to work, and Todd would then assume more childrearing responsibility. Nonetheless, Faith was skeptical that the transition would be an easy one "when push comes to shove," she said.

CHURCH

The couple's difficulty in balancing family and work had made Reverend Luther Dawson's baptismal prayer for Todd especially apropos, as far as Faith was concerned. They had decided to join Hinton Memorial UMC partially in response to their perceived need for assistance in teaching their children about values. Faith reported, "I said 'Now, Todd, how are our kids going to learn about the Bible and values? 'Well, I'll teach them,' he said. But I said, 'What are you doing to teach them?' His point was that he didn't feel like you had to go to church to be spiritual, and I agree with him. But we were doing nothing for Andrew and Alisa to give them a foundation. He was too busy. When you have the responsibility of your own kids it all comes full circle and you want to instill that [faith] in your kids."

Faith, who had been reared in the Baptist church, believed that foundation was especially important. She said, "Up until I was about eighteen years old, we went three times a week. Sunday, Sunday, and Wednesday. If that foundation is there you will eventually come back." During her teen years, Faith ceased attendance, finding the strictures of attendance too difficult. She felt that Baptists were "too extreme" because of their emphasis on being saved and attending church so often. "I think what's important is that you believe in God," she said. She explained that she believed that it was not as important where— meaning the denominational affiliation—one went, but that one went somewhere. She explained, "My sister became a Presbyterian over the last year. Her husband is a Catholic. But she's really interested in religion. Like Jehovah's Witnesses came to meet her, and I think she's met with them three times, trying to find out what they really believe. So I'm learning a little bit about the Jehovah's Witnesses from her. Maybe she'll try that if it helps her."

Though Todd also held the opinion that going to church was good for a family, he was not fond of religious people. Faith recalled that getting Todd to attend any church was difficult in the beginning because of his views that too many religious people were just hypocritical and because his parents had not set a model of church attendance for their sons. She said, "I was raised in the church pretty much and Todd really wasn't. His parents were, but they never went to church and really never taught him things." Todd attributed his parent's lack of church participation to their childhood experiences. "Both my parents when they were growing up were Baptist. My mother's father was a farmer, and they had six kids. They went every Sunday and Wednesday. My father was the same way. It wasn't an option. So they told me that they weren't going to make us go to church. Most of the people I knew who went to church were a bunch of hypocrites." Faith interrupted, "But I can't ever recall when your parents went to church. I never saw them set an example." Todd responded, "Well, we said grace at the table. There were people that I knew at school, who said that if you don't go to church, you go to hell. On the other side, they did a lot of things that were not Christian or whatever. More than I ever thought about doing."

Initially Faith began to attend Sunday morning religious services in the area on her own with Andrew. Finally, she persuaded Todd to attend Hebron Baptist with her. The experience was, she said, a dismal failure. Todd hated the congregation's large size and felt that services were too orchestrated. The altar call made him particularly uncomfortable. "He'd just stand up there and beg until he got the right number of people down there crying," Todd said, referring to Reverend Bryant Quinn. Several months after their experience at Hebron, Faith convinced Todd to accompany her to Hinton Memorial. She explained how she made her decision to visit the church. "So I saw these two little old quaint churches. One that had been out here—Brooks—was no longer a Methodist church. I've never seen a church change denomination, but that's now something like New Life Baptist, I believe. And I noticed that they've got a fence up around the cemetery where all the Methodists are buried, and it's a national historic site, so they can't do anything with it. So then we were left with one quaint, little, old church, so we tried here. And the people at Hinton are very friendly, and they make you feel welcome."

Todd was much more favorably impressed by the service at Hinton Memorial UMC. "It was just good, solid common sense," he said. "I like it being small. Sitting in Luther's Methodism class, I found that I believed that, too." The couple became regular attenders about six months before Alisa's birth. Faith said, "Once we got out and going we both enjoyed it. When I didn't go I felt like I was missing something. It took me a while to get Todd interested in going all the time. Now he's primarily the one who's interested."

Todd explained his change of heart. "They just teach—I know it's not popular—family values. I praise former Vice President Quayle for getting up there and not being afraid to say that we need more of that. I think if some more of our leaders were that way, we might have a better country. You're supposed to be ashamed, you're not supposed to mention that you believe in those old-fashioned things, like taking care of your family and working hard. We'll go down just like the Roman Empire did. It's coming, unless we change ourselves. Anything goes today, and if you don't believe that you're a real queer duck, you know?" Todd was quick to identify that his views were not like those held by fundamentalist Christians, but that he wanted the church to teach the traditional moral codes. Asked what he felt he was affirming in his baptism, Todd replied: "I believe in a God—nobody's any better than anybody else. It's just like let's just call it even and get on with life. Everything in moderation."[11]

These were also the values that he hopes Alisa and Andrew garnered from their attendance at Vacation Bible School, Sunday school, and United Methodist Tots. Todd explained, "I hope that they learn about God—that there is a Supreme Being—whatever you want to call it. They may grow up to call it Allah, for all I know. If Andrew grows up to be atheistic, I don't care. He truly tries to believe but he just can't; I think God is compassionate enough to understand that. I would rather have him say that than be a hypocrite. I want him to know right from wrong. He's got to be fair and decent. Take care of his family first." Todd and Faith's concern about instilling values in their children prompted their return to church. But they reported that Sunday morning attendance was good for them as well. Faith believed that it made the couple less selfish in their interactions with one another and more patient with the children.

They were, however, somewhat distressed at the level of participation that some members at Hinton expected. "They put us on a committee—I think nurture—right after we started coming. I called up Luther and said that we would not do it," said Faith. Faith and Todd attended worship services most Sundays, bringing their children early for Sunday school. Faith and the children were occasionally present for Wednesday night suppers, and Faith often brought Andrew to children's events. Sometimes, the couple was called upon to serve as impromptu ushers. The ability to choose their own degree of involvement in the congregation without being sanctioned by other members for their choices (despite some pressure for greater participation) was an important factor in their ongoing connection with Hinton.

As they prepared for their move to Memphis, they expressed their concern about finding religious services that would meet their needs. Faith said, "I hope that I can find another group like Grief Relief if I need it and someplace where the kids are taken care of by people who have religious values." Todd also remarked: "I don't care about the denomination, but we need to find a church that's good—small and solid." Faith Penner's choice to attend Grief Relief meetings at Hebron Baptist Church, the couple's decision to place their children in The Child's Place, and their attendance at Hinton Memorial created a multilayered pattern of religious involvement, structured by their perceived needs and less by geographical locality.

In their relations to home, family, church, work, and organizations, Faith and Todd Penner developed routines of belonging that reinforced the norms of choice and achievement. They had a highly diffused system of relationships and organizational ties that spanned the metropolitan Atlanta region. The opportunity for advancement resulted in their

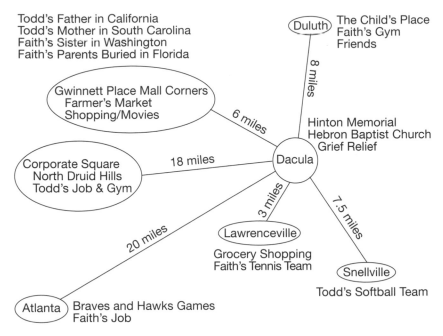

Todd's Father in California
Todd's Mother in South Carolina
Faith's Sister in Washington
Faith's Parents Buried in Florida

Duluth   The Child's Place
          Faith's Gym
          Friends

Gwinnett Place Mall Corners
Farmer's Market
Shopping/Movies

6 miles

8 miles

Hinton Memorial
Hebron Baptist Church
Grief Relief

Corporate Square
North Druid Hills
Todd's Job & Gym

18 miles   Dacula

3 miles

7.5 miles

20 miles

Lawrenceville

Grocery Shopping
Faith's Tennis Team

Snellville

Todd's Softball Team

Atlanta   Braves and Hawks Games
           Faith's Job

Figure 5.2 Routines of Belonging for Todd and Faith Penner

decision to relocate to another burgeoning Sunbelt city. Their concern was less the particular place in which they resided and more the type of place that offered peaceful surroundings and rural appeal as well as relatively easy access to the offerings of the urban area. The consumption routines were determined according to convenience, selection, and timesaving, rather than by the geographical confines of the Dacula community, as the figure below illustrates.

Their productive routines followed the dictates of advancement through mobility. Religious participation helped to compensate for the spatial diffusion of friends and family. The couple's religious participation was extensive but also diffused. Though loyalty to a single neighborhood church was not their primary focus, the Penners were, nonetheless, committed to maintaining religious influences in their lives. The configuration of religious organizations was altered according to their current judgment on what specific influences they needed in their lives.

Conclusion

The routines of belonging of oldtimers and newcomers at Hinton Memorial UMC diverge just as they do for those in the Dacula area generally. As we have seen, this divergence was related in part to generational and educational effects as well as to geographical diffusion and the organizing norms of these routines. For oldtimers, such as Vernon and Marie England, Dacula was the context in which they sought to fashion a decent life based on commitment and cohesion. The town's basic features more or less supplied their needs. For newcomers, such as Todd and Faith Penner, the metropolitan region with its multiple edge cities and exurbs was the context for their lives. Their routines were organized by the norms of achievement and choice and structured by time and clusters of malls, office developments, and entertainment complexes that have risen where major highways cross and converge. Their lives were governed by complex patterns of multidirectional travel that largely bypassed old small towns. For many newcomers, the very concepts of "center" and "periphery" were obsolete in the construction of their routines. Newcomers, through the configuration of their routines of belonging, have recast, if not obliterated, the well-demarcated lines within the metropolis employed by most oldtimers. These different patterns meant that oldtimers and newcomers often had different perceptions of Dacula and the changes occurring there. Thus they often resulted in divergent strategies for responding to events of conflict in the community, as will be explored in chapter 6.

The decentralized networking of newcomers was also carried over into religious participation. Newcomers sought to balance community with diversity and flexibility of services through multilayered religious participation. Mobility and choice were taken-for-granted features of their religious life, as they are within their productive, consumer, and household routines. The multilayered and diffused religious participation of newcomers created organizational dilemmas for some congregations in this changing community. Some religious organizations, such as Hebron Baptist Church, responded by offering specialized services, such as the Grief Relief group, that allowed area newcomers to participate in the generalist congregation at different levels. Though the Penners were invited to join the church, their decision not to do so did not mean that other services were cut off. Other congregations, such as Hinton Memorial UMC, grappled with the meaning of these multiple religious ties. Some long-time members, such as Marie England, perceived the multiple commitments of newcomers as a lack of loyalty to Hinton. This perception sometimes created hard feelings as some oldtimers believed that the religious organization, for whose survival they had sacrificed, was held in low esteem by the newcomers who simply "shopped around" for the most trendy programming. Other oldtimers, however, disagreed. They reasoned that if these newcomers were getting some of what they needed elsewhere, but kept coming to Hinton for some things, then the congregation did not lose members just because they were unable to offer specific services. For their part, newcomers, such as Faith Penner, were sometimes put off by the participation demands upheld by some oldtimers whose routines were more localized and overlapping. Unlike oldtimers who saw committee meetings as opportunities for socializing, Faith saw attendance at such meetings as a drain on her limited personal and family time.[12]

Are exurbanites and others in the process of reinventing the congregation perceiving it as a catalog rather than a single community? In local congregations, especially in exurban locations like Dacula, the meaning of membership, commitment, and loyalty is being renegotiated. In practical terms what happens is fine-grained information transfer as individuals carry ways of doing things from one congregation to another. However, whether this action results in a higher level of organizational adaptation within the ecology is far from clear. It is possible that these multilayered patterns of belonging could create much stronger ties of cooperation and mutualism among local organizations. However, it is also plausible that these multilayered ties may create greater boundedness among organizations as they seek to differentiate from one another.

Congregations are working to balance (1) families' needs for specialized religious services and fluid denominational affiliations with (2) congregational needs for a stable base of resources and participation. Congregations (just as these particular locales) are in the process of constant upheaval and reinvention, decentralizing and thus distributing their prized functions among numerous religious organizations (and over whole metropolitan regions). In so doing, congregations are often facilitating the diffused religious routines that mirror the diffused household, consumer, and productive routines of many newcomers.

Chapter 6	Fighting the Good Fight

*An Ecological Perspective
on Local Conflict*

Reprinted, by permission, from Glenn Matlock, 29 January 1994
© Gwinnett Post Tribune

T HE ASSERTION THAT A "culture war" has been occurring in the United States has fascinated scholars, the popular press, and, to a lesser extent, the American public. Pundits, politicians, and some social scientists have adopted the view that the battle lines between the right and left or conservatives and liberals have been drawn in the American body politic and increasingly in particular places, like Dacula, Georgia. Hyperbole aside, the "culture wars" metaphor of two diametrically opposed parties does seem to depict specific issues within national public debate and religious life (see DiMaggio, Evans, and Bryson 1996).[1] However, it appears that this model does not represent the reality within local communities, even when such hotly contested debates as abortion are considered (cf. Becker 1998, 1999; Ginsburg 1989).

Obviously ideological debates do occur at the local level (cf. Slater 1989; Demerath and Williams 1992; Becker, et al., 1993). Nonetheless, local conflicts are more likely to be about local educational, transportation, environmental, recreational, crime, or development issues. Since sociospatial change is a constant in the American landscape, coalitions interested in the choices that must be made over the direction and effects of change are often at the root of conflict. These conflicts involve specific constituencies, have historically and geographically situated contexts, and are generally quite limited in scope. Alliances arise not primarily in response to broad cultural polarization but in the face of multiple overlapping racial, class, religious, and community interests concerned with the quality of life locally. Sometimes these local interests coincide with the values and objectives of one set of moral entrepreneurs (Becker 1982), special purpose groups (Wuthnow 1988), or political parties and sometimes with another.

Religious organizations when they are implicated in controversies are as likely to be involved in the seemingly more pedestrian issues of localized change as with "hot button" social issues that represent American social cleavages (see Becker 1999). While sometimes these tensions can be recast into conflicts between broad cultural poles—conservative versus liberal or progressive versus orthodox—to do so would impose an alien order.[2] In this chapter, three conflicts in Dacula are recounted. Debates over the use of a church cemetery, the proposal for the expansion of the Gwinnett County–Briscoe Field Airport, and local sentiment related to the statewide controversy over changing the Georgia flag (which includes the Confederate Battle flag) demonstrate the cultural and social fissures and alliances in this rapidly changing community. Within a changing religious ecology, conflict often highlights the emergence of new organizational actors, the fit between organizational processes and community restructuring, and cultural ramifications of specialist or generalist organizational identities.

In everyday life, people have relatively fluid alliances and eclectic views that can coalesce around a host of issues. Local knowledge (Geertz

1983:6) helps people formulate their ideas and actions, especially in the face of rapid change. This local knowledge is "local not just as to place, time, class, and variety of issue, but as to accent—vernacular characterizations of what happens connected to vernacular imaginings of what can happen" (Geertz 1983:215). In settings, such as Dacula, where local imaginations are confronting new realities, creation and conversion of local coalitions and narratives often occur in local religious organizations where people tell one another their "takes" on the local changes. They sharpen their stories in the telling and cast them in imagery that evokes the norms and values at stake. The stories related below highlight the range of particular goods that people view as being at risk in the midst of this rapidly changing community, and show how people's responses draw on a new array of organizational resources, connections, and skills within their ecologies.

The Demanding Presence of the Past: Pleasant Hill Cemetery

In 1993, as members of the Hinton Memorial UMC congregation positioned themselves to reach out to exurban newcomers, whom they had begrudgingly come to believe represented Dacula's future, they were also forced to deal with unresolved tensions of the past. Pleasant Hill Cemetery, which is located adjacent to the Gwinnett Progress Center, became a center of controversy for the congregation and the community. The cemetery, arguably the ceremonial center of Dacula for many longtime residents, was at the nexus of conflicting interests, values, and goals.[3]

The cemetery, located approximately two miles west of Dacula on Fence Road, is on the site where the congregation was first established. Dr. Samuel Freeman, who also donated the land on which Hinton Memorial sat, had bequeathed that land for the church and the cemetery in 1837.[4] Freeman had donated the land in town to the church with the proviso that the Pleasant Hill Cemetery keep its original name. Gwinnett historian James Flanigan (1959:233) writes: "The cemetery at the old location is still being used. . . . A rock wall was erected around the cemetery and is kept in good condition by the families whose loved ones are buried there." However though some still imagined that the cemetery was in "good condition" and that someone was taking care of matters, by the late 1960s, the old church at the cemetery had collapsed, and the rock wall was disintegrating.

The congregation, which had relied on descendants of the dearly departed to care for the graveyard, was required to develop a cemetery fund to pay for upkeep. They began by asking families to donate to the trust fund for cemetery maintenance, and several local long-time residents and congregational members assumed responsibility for the cemetery. The *ad hoc* group informally authorized burials and saw to it that the cemetery was mowed periodically. Finally, in the late 1960s, the congregation established a cemetery committee composed of church and Dacula leaders to oversee the grounds and the trust fund. The original committee, included members of the Hinton family (the congregation's namesake), Vernon England, Miss Irene Abbott, and Adam Wages, who was the self-appointed caretaker. The committee met informally for about a decade, usually during the regular cemetery workdays.

In the 1990s, however, as they aged, the cemetery committee found caring for the grounds more onerous. The Pleasant Hill Cemetery was allowed to fall into disrepair with the church taking only minimal care of it. Adam Wages, now in his seventies, had, however, continued to mow the grass at least once a month. His family had long lived adjacent to the cemetery and buried their dead there. Wages also claimed that his great-great grandfather had given additional land to supplement Dr. Freeman's bequest. His more extensive labor in maintaining the cemetery and his family's history had increased his sense of proprietary oversight, and he eventually became the sole person handling the donations to the cemetery trust fund. Wages, whose family had been members of the Hinton congregation, left Hinton Memorial UMC not long after the Hintons' leave-taking in the late 1970s. He eventually moved his membership to Ebenezer Baptist Church in the aftermath of the church's schism in 1990. In the hurly-burly of the schism and the congregation's struggle to survive, members did little to maintain or provide oversight for the cemetery.

Not until 1993 did Hinton members again increase direct involvement in the care of Pleasant Hill Cemetery. Then an open debate emerged between several community residents, led by Adam Wages and members of Hinton Memorial's namesake family, and the congregation regarding the ownership of the cemetery. The controversy was sparked by several factors. First, several Hinton Memorial UMC members noticed obituary announcements in local newspapers for individuals unknown to them who were said to be buried in Pleasant Hill. These members, including Liza Mayeux and Miss Irene Abbott, became concerned that unattached newcomers were burying their dead in the cemetery, usurping sites that ought to belong to long-time church members. Secondly, the expansion of the Gwinnett Progress Center had resulted in the discovery of several unmarked burial sites. The Progress Center developers had sought permission from Adam Wages to reinter the remains in the Pleasant Hill Cemetery. Several Hinton congregants became irate that Wages had granted permission without seeking the church's approval. Finally, the development of the supermarket distribution center adjacent to the cemetery opened the possibility that Pleasant Hill could be expanded and raised questions of legal ownership. The distribution center's owners were willing to donate several partial acres abutting the cemetery to the legal owners in exchange for their assurance that they would not fight the company's efforts to gain approval from the Gwinnett County commissioners to straighten a road nearby. The proposal, however, was complicated by the congregation's difficulty in proving legal ownership. Since much of the congregation's early business was conducted informally, many records were lost through the years and no definitive title existed.

These multiple factors coalesced to create conflict within the congregation and the community over the cemetery. The conflict escalated in stages until in 1993, the congregation was served with notice of an impending suit to be brought by Wages and several Hinton family members over the ownership of the cemetery. The chain of events leading up to that notice began in 1992 when Liza Mayeux raised the matter of the cemetery. At a Trustees Committee meeting, Mayeux mentioned that she had seen another obituary of someone not from the church buried in the Pleasant Hill Cemetery. She wanted to know if people were getting permission to bury their dead there or were just doing it. Billy Sue Hammond, the Trustees Committee chair, sighed and said that the question of who could authorize burial had been a problem for the last ten years and that the church had not yet done anything about it. Gerhard had refused to have the issue raised during his tenure because he believed it would sidetrack the congregation from what he saw as their central purpose—reaching out to area newcomers. Long-time congregants had also been reluctant to raise the issue because "no one has wanted to get in a fight with Adam and the Hintons again," Hammond admitted. Wages, she claimed, was the only one who knew what was going on with the cemetery trust fund and was the one who authorized burials (including these unknown newcomers).

Nowell Altoona, citing his responsibility for budget oversight in the Gwinnett County School system, argued that it was "just bad practice" and "irrational" to be the ones to whom the cemetery was entrusted and yet not to know anything about the trust fund. Though Miss Abbott agreed, she insisted that Wages and the Hintons would be offended if they started snooping around. Whatever they did, she urged, would have to be framed in terms of wanting to help and relieve some responsibility.

As discussion returned to the obituaries, Billy Sue Hammond admitted that she did not have a problem with people—even newcomers—being buried at the cemetery if they had some connection with the church. But she thought these unknown newcomers were using it because they did not want to pay $500 for a burial plot at places like Memorial Acres, a commercial cemetery off Interstate 85. "Well, I can see why they wouldn't want to pay that kind of money," said Miss Abbott. "And you don't know who you'd be buried next to." Nowell Altoona argued that unless the congregation set some firm guidelines, "they would be responsible for burying all the people in the area." Failing such action, he added, the cemetery would soon be filled, and there would not be places for the people who really belonged there—those who had contributed to the church for years.

Billy Sue Hammond agreed that the only way to handle the situation was to appoint a cemetery committee as subcommittee of the Trustees Committee. She asked if they thought Vernon England would serve again. Reverend Dawson and Miss Abbott said no (emphatically). Dawson responded that it was too messy. He said that he had talked with Vernon about it and that Vernon had said he "knew the people buried there and he wasn't going to fight over their bodies." Billy Sue asked Miss Abbott if she would serve. She vigorously declined as well. Reverend Dawson urged that they get some younger people who did not know the history to serve. By the end of the meeting, the trustees had appointed Altoona as the chair of the cemetery committee and agreed to ask Linda Lyle and Lewis Norman, both congregational newcomers, to fill the other seats.

Within weeks, the cemetery subcommittee drafted a letter to Adam Wages asking him to report on the status of the trust fund and enclosed a copy of a letter that was sent to all area funeral directors, detailing the newly instituted policies regarding authorization of burial.[5] The letter was not well received by Wages who called Reverend Dawson to complain of its "matter-of-fact" tone. Wages also contacted a lawyer to contest the congregation's ownership claims and to establish his family's ownership of the cemetery. Wages contended that property "swapping" at the time the church moved from Pleasant Hill to the present location meant that both property lines and ownership were uncertain. Wages claimed that his "great-great grandpappy" gave land for the cemetery. The Trustees Committee received in response to the subcommittee's letter one that was written by an attorney. The letter stated that the church had no rights to ownership and that the original property reverted to its original owners—the heirs of "great-great grandpappy" Wages—when the church moved.

Meanwhile, the Gwinnett Progress Center developers were moving forward in their efforts to excavate and reinter remains that were holding up the building of a subdivision. The Progress Center was threatened with a suit brought by the Gwinnett Historical Society unless they committed to reinter the remains in three individual burial sites and to place a historical marker at the new location. However, the cemetery committee at Hinton Memorial objected to allocating three burial sites, arguing that since space was at a premium in the cemetery, a single site would have to suffice.[6] As Miss Abbott stated, "All they've got is a box with some bones with a little bit of dirt. Why can't they bury it in one?" The Gwinnett Historical Society, however, was intransigent and moved forward in their plans to sue the Progress Center unless three gravesites were designated. In order to facilitate the allocation of three sites at the Pleasant Hill Cemetery, the Progress Center negotiated with developers of the supermarket distribution center, urging them to donate land abutting the cemetery. These developers were willing to do so, but needed proof of the congregation's ownership in order to receive tax credit and also wanted the church's cooperation in their efforts to straighten the nearby road.

As the number of involved parties grew, the cemetery conflict also grew. Within the congregation, emergency meetings of the trustees were regularly held, and a congregational meeting was called to address the situation. Alfred DeVries bemoaned the conflict, "We all know that it is going to cause a big rift in the community and maybe in the church." However, it became evident in these meetings that a rift had long existed between some church members and Adam Wages and the Hintons. The parties had nursed hard feelings since before the Hinton's leave-taking during Reverend Janelle Shea's tenure. This cemetery situation was not creating anything new; it was simply resurrecting conflict that many in the congregation and community hoped was long buried. The strategies of many oldtimers, who preferred to ignore the problem, had served to delay the conflict.

Newcomers to the congregation urged resolution of the issue once and for all. Liza Mayeux, Linda Lyle, and Lewis Norman argued for hiring a lawyer to file a lawsuit against Wages and the Hintons. In a three-hour administrative committee meeting, congregants debated the merits of legal action. The debate was both theological and practical. Alfred DeVries, whose teenage son was buried in the Pleasant Hill Cemetery, contended, the "Bible says that we shouldn't solve our troubles in a court of law." Norman concurred that under normal circumstances he, too, would be opposed to legal action. But, he countered, "we're dealing here with Christians who are threatening us with a law suit and this fight's been going on for decades." DeVries wondered aloud, "Do two wrongs make a right?" "No," offered Mayeux, "but one wrong—one 'looong' wrong—doesn't make a right either."

Billy Sue Hammond argued that they needed to move quickly to resolve the issue of ownership if they wanted the additional land to be donated to the church. "We're dealing here with the time-tables of developers. They want a resolution." She said to DeVries, "Your son's buried up there, and if we don't act pretty soon there isn't going to be enough room for you to be buried beside him." That reasoning persuaded DeVries who agreed to vote in favor of hiring a lawyer. Miss Abbott, however, remained determined in her opposition to legal action. It was,

she argued, "no way to treat good people." Lyle countered that this was
not a question of good and bad people, rather it was a matter of property and business dealings. In the end, Abbott reluctantly agreed to ab-
stain from voting since she was still opposed. "It might as well be
unanimous," she said. The long evening ended with a unanimous vote
to hire legal counsel and sue Wages and the Hintons.

The notes from my field journal of that meeting highlight the tension that permeated the room: "I kept trying to look nonchalant all
evening. But I'd chewed my nails down by 10:00 [p.m.]. At one point,
Miss Abbott looked at me and said, 'We probably shouldn't be saying
any of this in front of you who are writing a book.' I knew that I wasn't
particularly welcome, but no one asked me to leave."

The Pleasant Hill Cemetery controversy highlighted buried tensions
in this changing community. It revealed that in many ways the oldtimers' Dacula was a "community by inertia," that lingered relatively
effortlessly by virtue of proximity and absence of movement. What the
sense of community lacked in internal coherence, it compensated for
in affective commitment and secrecy.[7] The past had, however, left the
congregation and community with a living matrix of constraints and
possibilities within which to work in the present. Hinton newcomers
were again faced with long-standing community fissures with which
oldtimers had refused to deal. The roots of this conflict were in the historic tensions between the congregation's leadership elites and the rank
and file. As one congregant stated, "It seems like the long hand of Freeman and the Hintons is still swatting at us from the grave."

The resolution to this conflict was a long time in coming. Finally,
in 1996, Fence Road was straightened, graves were allocated, historic
markers were erected, Pleasant Hill Cemetery was expanded, and the
hard feelings among the parties began to subside. Both sides had served
legal papers. But in the end, compromise prevailed, as Hinton Memorial agreed to include a community member, for then Wages, on the
cemetery oversight committee.

In this rapidly changing exurb—operating on the timeclocks of
developers—the taken-for-granted commonsense patterns of doing
things and assumed social meanings were disrupted. The feud (as un-
pleasant as many oldtimers felt that it was) was a familiar local cultural
pattern. By replaying those battles in a time of rapid change, commu-

nity oldtimers were, in part, attempting to reinforce an old social order and meanings that were passing from the scene. The familiar social cleavages in the community were, however, becoming less salient as the area exurbanized. Multiple new players, including powerful economic organizations and newly politicized local interest groups, were now also implicated. And these new players reframed the import and connotations of the familiar cleavages. These groups had interests that had little to do with the community's history of antipathies and feuds. Likewise most newcomers at Hinton Memorial UMC had little concern about the history of conflict; instead they wanted to see the situation resolved so as not to drain the congregation's already scarce financial resources and volunteer labor.

In this case, newcomers were not privy to intimate details of the history of antipathy and their organizational routines were more diffused. Therefore, they were less involved with the local players. They could be agents for bringing an end to long-standing feuds and to help oldtimers shape a new local social order. These personal, deeply rooted conflicts were often devastating when local groups needed to mobilize to negotiate relations with new organizations and bureaucratic forces. Coser (1991) explains that within social groups in which networks and role sets are interarticulated, "fights are personal regardless of whether or not people team up with one another to give vent to their sense of justice" (72). Thus Coser notes that these hostilities and conflicts can be especially vehement.[8] In Dacula, some in the community had been unable to overcome long-standing antipathies in order to organize response to the cemetery conflict. In this situation, the resources of newcomers—including a relative distance from the personal battles over the cemetery—provided their means of inclusion. Oldtimers noted that in this new situation newcomers offered something that was valuable to them. Even though some oldtimers were hesitant to incorporate newcomers fully in the leadership of the church, they realized that they benefited from their new perspectives and lack of old baggage.

The Pleasant Hill Cemetery conflict also represented tensions between local community growth and local community preservation coalitions. Growth controversies have been a staple of urban deconcentration. These controversies arise from the recognition that rapid growth turns small towns into edge cities and exurban areas in a way that is socially transforming. In this controversy, the battles over the Pleasant Hill Cemetery necessitated that the congregation deal with the demanding presence of the past. The conflict was a manifestation of the fundamental social process of shaping a particular place. In this, as in many locality-based conflicts, religious organizations provided an important staging ground for reframing the meaning of the local feuds in the face of considerable local change.

Competing Communities: Gwinnett County–Briscoe Field Airport

Airport Fly Away
The people in the general area of Lawrenceville, including those in the Dacula area, raised their voices against enlarging Briscoe Field to handle passenger service. The whole area had sort of a town meeting atmosphere. This was a fine hour of democratic action.

The representatives of our republic kind of government got the loud and clear message. Our people can be proud of their response to this issue. The response also serves notice on elected officials that the electorate ain't dead yet.

That announcement printed in the Hinton Memorial UMC "All around Town" in March 1994 signaled the end of a controversy in the congregation and the community. The proposed expansion of the Gwinnett County–Briscoe Field Airport to create a new regional airport was met by members of Hinton Memorial UMC with immediate grassroots action. As Sarah Coser said, "There was a rumble you could hear all the way to the statehouse. This was one place that was not going to be railroaded. That rumble was the sound of people putting on the brakes." The issue united many newcomers and oldtimers in a common effort to redefine their relationship with the metropolitan region and to protect what they perceived as their superior quality of life. At the center of the antigrowth faction was Hinton Memorial UMC. Hebron Baptist, however, saw the airport and growth generally as an opportunity for expanding their mission throughout northeast metropolitan Atlanta. In their definitions of how the controversy should be connected to fundamental values of Christian community, these two congregations within the ecology differed significantly.

The airport controversy began in 1991 when the Gwinnett County Airport Authority began studying the feasibility of commuter air service at Briscoe Field. Response to the report fell along lines of economic interest: more than 250 local homeowners, mostly oldtimers, were opposed. Local boosters and large landholders saw the potential advantage of offering commercial service to accommodate local corporations whose employees wished to avoid traveling across Atlanta to Hartsfield International.[9] Before the panel made much headway, however, an economic recession set in and the issue was dropped. In 1993 and 1994, when the proposal to expand the airport was revived, the grassroots opposition was different. In addition to local homeowners, opposition came from local civic organizations, including Hinton Memorial UMC, which reframed the proposal as an assault on Dacula's quality of life.

At Hinton Memorial UMC, the airport controversy again placed the congregation at the center of the community. Congregational oldtimers involved in this most recent battle recalled a time prior to the 1970s when the Hinton Memorial UMC was the most prestigious church in the community with a say in almost everything that occurred in the area. In recent years, Hebron Baptist, however, had usurped Hinton's position as the "high-status congregation," according to many local observers, and Hinton congregants had developed a niche identity as the area's legacy church. Hinton Memorial, which had defined itself in opposition to the encroachment of urban sprawl, was a natural site for the development of airport opposition. Hinton Memorial congregants, who had read and enjoyed the adventures of Bogan and Grunt's big adventure to Atlanta serialized in the "All around Town," continued to uphold the view of Atlanta as exotic and "other." During this local transformation, Dacula residents could call upon the resources of the church to bolster their image of small-town life. Congregants at Hinton Memorial UMC helped to shape the discussion of this issue as about the burdens of metropolitan deconcentration and about an attack by big government on local residents.

The organizing efforts at Hinton Memorial were extensive. I first learned of them when I received a call from Carol Hatch, a Hinton newcomer whom I had met only briefly. "Nancy," she asked, "do you know any state representatives or appointed officials you can call?" No, I had to admit I did not. "What's going on?" I asked. Carol went on to tell me the news of the proposed airport. "We have to stop it or we'll be just like Union City," she said, referring to the town south of Atlanta near Hartsfield International Airport. Union City was in the airport flight path and an exodus of middle-class families had depressed the town's economy and hastened white flight in the area. Carol made it clear to me that the congregation's survival and Dacula's quality of life were at stake in this issue. "Call anybody you know and tell them to stop the airport expansion," she pleaded. Carol had also organized a petition drive, called all the members in the church directory, and was working her way through the congregation's visitors cards.

The Sunday after the airport proposal was announced publicly, the announcement time during the Hinton Memorial UMC worship service was filled with discussion of the organizing efforts to stop the airport expansion. Celia Dent, a congregational newcomer who worked as a graphic designer for a state environmental agency, had designed posters announcing a public forum to be held at the church. The poster copied a media campaign by a local television station that urged listeners to "Stop the Violence" and included an outstretched palm. "Stop the Airport"—printed in red ink—read the poster, with a black outstretched hand below. By equating the airport development with crime, organizers touched one of the community's hottest buttons and capitalized on the free-floating anxieties of many local residents about increased crime.

Hinton Memorial oldtimers, who had opposed the Reverend Luther Dawson's mixing of religion and politics in his sermonic condemnations of the state lottery, now joined efforts with newcomers to distribute posters and invite local residents to a forum. "This is different," argued Alfred DeVries when I pointed out the seeming inconsistency, "this isn't about opinions, it's about our homes." On issues of the maintenance of local quality of life, oldtimers and newcomers suspended their opposition to mixing politics and religion. Religious involvement in issues of direct local impact was seen in the congregation as acceptable, in contrast to participation in larger supposedly ideological debates, such as abortion and the lottery.

The forum, held on a Wednesday night, was attended by a near-capacity crowd at Hinton Memorial. When I pulled into the parking lot, individuals were standing around in clusters outside smoking and talking. The lot was filled with more Jeep Cherokees and minivans than were usually present for a Sunday service. Inside Nowell Altoona played Broadway show tunes on the piano as people milled about. Several persons in the audience and on the platform wore sweatshirts with an airplane overlaid with the universal Ø sign. As the meeting got underway, Reverend Luther Dawson opened with a prayer for mutual understanding and peaceableness. Celia Dent began the forum by asking those in attendance about what they thought this battle was about. Several opponents to the proposal argued that this was not simply a NIMBY (Not In My Back Yard) opposition. Rather local residents were organizing because they were tired of having changes "shoved down our throats," by Atlanta and Gwinnett County officials, as one individual shouted. "It's time we take control of the growth," said someone in the audience. "Our way or no way!" Heads nodded in support of the proposition that local residents have a greater say in the growth that they contended had been occurring unimpeded in the community.

Only one Hinton congregant stood during the meeting to support the airport expansion. Todd Penner, whose job necessitated extensive travel, spoke in favor of the airport expansion. "I know that it's not popular, but I think there are a lot of people like me around here who could use some relief from that hour drive to the airport and another half-hour finding a parking place," stated Penner. "There's no denying it now. Dacula's a part of metro Atlanta, and we've got to take the bad with the good." "But what's the good?" a man in a sweatsuit asked. "We get more traffic, more crime, more taxes. When are we going to start getting to the good stuff?" For those hostile to the airport expansion, this controversy tapped a reservoir of mistrust in government and a belief that officials too often imposed their dictatorial programs on an unwilling electorate. Also tapped in this controversy were the longstanding antipathies between Atlanta and the Gwinnett suburbs— antipathies which had been exposed in the 1971 and 1990 rejection of MARTA (the metro area public transit) within the county.

The airport controversy highlighted the changed relationship of northeast Gwinnett County with the Atlanta metropolitan area, and plumbed the depths of some local residents' fears about the seeming obliteration of the well-demarcated lines that set this small town off from the metropolitan Atlanta region. The physical isolation of Dacula was presumed to nurture community, personal involvement in local concerns, and social control of deviance, whereas inclusion in the metropolitan community was presumed to result in deviance, especially crime, the breakdown of community, the rise of impersonal behaviors, and the loss of deep involvement with others.

Exurbanization, however, created one type of community locally as some newcomers and oldtimers joined forces to stop the airport. The power of definition of the community was no longer in the hands of local governments, such as the Dacula City Council. The things that really mattered to local folks were increasingly being decided in metropolitan-wide discussions—to which newcomers often had greater access because of their network ties and professional resources. To continue not to participate in those discussions meant that Dacula would have little voice. Thus grassroots organizing, in this instance begun by newcomers, aimed to find common ground among oldtimers and newcomers in order to develop a strategy for opposing changes in their locale about which they had little say. Opponents to the planned expansion of the Gwinnett County–Briscoe Field Airport were able to stop the development. That the residents won their battle was not, however, a sign that they continued to be a modest parochial enclave preserving the past, but rather it revealed that this coalition of oldtimers and newcomers made them a potent political force whose fears about alterations in their quality of life could not be ignored.

The involvement of Hinton Memorial UMC in this controversy highlighted the role of local religious institutions in shaping debates about quality of life locally. Demerath and Williams (1992) found in their study of Springfield, Massachusetts, evidence of religious "organizational secularization"—that is, the tendency to "lose sight of basic objectives while allowing means to become ends in their own right. Because of the otherworldly nature of many religious objectives, churches are especially vulnerable to such this-worldly stress" (291–292). Their contention is that organizations are increasingly pressed to tell, or translate, their religious story in terms of nonreligious concerns. In this translation, they argue, much of the religious content is lost, therefore, diminishing the power of religion (see also Ammerman 1993b). However, the opposite seems to be the case in the example offered here. Local religious organizations had long been influential in shaping the quality of life in Dacula. In this new circumstance of exurbanization, their role in shaping the debate about local quality of life attested to their influence even within a religious organizational ecology with contested status hierarchies.

At Hebron Baptist Church the airport controversy was interpreted quite differently. For many locals, Hebron was a prime illustration of what was happening to their community. Too much growth, too fast. Hebron's leaders had benefited from the population influx and anticipated that more opportunity for growth in the area would further advance the church's mission and in so doing spread the gospel. As Hinton Memorial's "All around Town" was signaling success in stopping uncontrolled growth and airport expansion, Hebron's March, 1994 newsletter, "Vision," was soliciting Neighborhood Watchmen with the following appeal. "Just take a short drive from our church in any direction and you will begin to notice something new. Where there use to be woods, pastures, and fields, now there are subdivisions being built. Statistics show that 55 percent of Gwinnett County residents were not born in Georgia. These newcomers need new friends, a new church that can help them grow spiritually, and Jesus. Hebron can give them all three!" Neighborhood Watchmen were evangelistic teams who also helped newcomers feel safe in their new surroundings, by keeping an eye out for crime. Reducing risk of violence, or at least its associated anxiety, when combined with a friendly handshake could, Hebron leaders surmised, provide the new type of "welcome wagon" that exurbanites craved.

Reverend Bryant Quinn regularly preached about the benefits of community growth as he encouraged congregants to be active in their recruitment to Hebron. "God has brought us a new harvest," he enthused as he spoke about homes and strip malls popping up across the area. On the airport expansion, in particular, Quinn spoke about the "necessity for changing old ways." No wonder that Hinton members increasingly saw Hebron as one of a range of big organizations arrayed against them. Thus while some newcomers were engaged in their anxious struggle with the county over the sprawl, in which they inevitably participated, others viewed the exurban spaces as full of new neighbors

who could bring renewal to congregations and the local community. It
was the calling of Christian congregations, argued many Hebron members, to prepare for change, because the good news must go out to all
who are welcomed into the Kingdom of God.

Hebron Baptist's comfortable relationship with the Gwinnett
County police, for whom the church provided chaplains, as well as the
megachurch's enlarged constituency gave the church a local political
voice. While the church provided no particular aid to the progrowth
factions within the community, Quinn's relative silence on such an important local issue and his general expansive view of Dacula's exurbanization comforted some local officials who saw the future in the
subdivisions that Quinn eyed for evangelism.

Although the airport controversy was resolved with the cessation
of Gwinnett County's plans to expand the airport, the antigrowth and
progrowth forces would soon spar over the development project called
"the Mall of Georgia" to be built north of Dacula. In this skirmish,
progrowth factions won the day. Opened in 1999, the mall was designed
to "recall simpler days," as the public relations materials suggest. Calling the mall a "village," designers modeled it on a town square with
freestanding shops. Unlike the all-under-one-roof mall, the "village" will
allow open-air shopping and conviviality around a central plaza, foun-
tain, and bandstand. Architect Jeffry Wierenga noted that what he seeking was "a small-town Georgia feel." Hebron Baptist and other religious
groups have been pressing the developers to create space for congregations in their new Main Street of the South.

Symbolic Representation: The Georgia Flag

As particular places, such as Dacula, Georgia, accumulate political
power, questions about the nature and meaning of the exurban South's
growth are also raised. Pundits have argued that the 1994 Republican
"revolution" occurred in no small degree because of the increased power
of the South, and in particular southern exurbs, such as Dacula. A *New
York Times* article, 19 December 1994, articulated this view: "While the
1990 census found that most Americans live in the suburbs, last month's
election demonstrated a ramification of that phenomenon: suburban
voters—particularly those in the South—now hold the key to political

power." The political clout of these new exurban locations has also not been lost on politicians currying their favor—as their victory in the airport controversy also demonstrated.

Gwinnett County had received much less attention from the national media regarding the political developments in the South than other metropolitan counties, particularly Cobb County—north of Atlanta.[10] But local, state, and national politicians had not failed to attest to their fellow feeling with Gwinnett residents. Former Speaker of the House Newt Gingrich believed he represented them when he was quoted in a 1 August 1994 *New York Times* article: "These people want safety, and they believe big cities have failed and are controlled by people who are incapable of delivering goods and services. What they find there is a sort of Norman Rockwell world. . . . The values that would have been *The Saturday Evening Post* of the mid-50's are the values of most of these people now." He also believed that he was doing their bidding by turning more control over what happens locally to local governments. Many members of Hinton Memorial UMC agreed that democratic liberalism had led to too much bureaucracy, draining their savings through taxes, limiting their opportunities to find better jobs locally, and establishing an elite ruling culture in Congress. They also believed that, on the whole, government had become antagonistic to the traditional values of their religious and family lives. Though they were careful to distinguish their views from those of fundamentalists, many Hinton oldtimers and newcomers had suspicions that their way of life was passing from the American scene.

During an adult Sunday school class at Hinton Memorial in 1992, congregants discussed religion and politics. The class, which usually began in the church kitchen around a cup of coffee, often provided a forum where congregants vented about current issues. On the Sunday before the national presidential election, class members bemoaned the state of politics. Alvin Wilford argued that there was really no longer any choice within national politics. "If Bill Clinton and Manuel Noriega were the only candidates," he posed to the class, "who would you vote for?" When Alvin said jokingly that Noriega was not running, Nelson Hammond interjected, "maybe that's too bad." Nelson Hammond concurred that national elections were primarily about choices between two evils. Margie Golick commented that she just wanted to write in on the ballot "None of the above, start over." This discussion of the dismal state of national politics led to an analysis of the "better days" when as Nelson Hammond said, "my friend Governor Lester Maddox didn't compromise about moral issues."[11]

The relationship between the current political mistrust expressed by many newcomers and oldtimers at Hinton Memorial and their adherence to the traditions of the "Old South" was a complicated one. During my time in Dacula, I often heard residents express a longing for the political certainty of a distant past. Yet congregants were also somewhat cynical about politicians' use of their nostalgia. The controversy over the Georgia State flag highlighted some of the frustrations and suspicions of these exurban voters.

The flag controversy had deep roots in the culture of the South (cf. Cobb 1991). The current Georgia flag was redesigned in 1956 by the State Legislature to incorporate the St. Andrew's cross of the Confederate battle flag to show, argued flag opponents, contempt for the wave of desegregation rulings beginning to come from Federal courts. Governor Zell Miller put changing the flag at the top of his legislative agenda in 1993, but withdrew his proposal after the measure provoked controversy in the legislature and appeared doomed. In July 1994, Holiday Inn Worldwide disclosed that it had asked its Georgia hotels, as an act of racial sensitivity, not to fly the flag. In 1993 and 1994, a Republican gubernatorial candidate used the issue of the Georgia flag as a wedge point in state politics. He used the song "Dixie" in campaign ads as part of a promotion to keep the flag flying. Another 1996 Republican candidate continued the themes in advertising in select counties, including Gwinnett.

Most congregants at Hinton Memorial UMC were much less directly involved in the controversy over the Georgia State flag than they were in both the cemetery and the airport conflicts, though the controversy was regularly discussed in the adult and senior citizen Sunday school classes. John Kass, a local schoolteacher, found the entire matter frustrating. He was not for changing the flag, but he was not like the "snot-chewing bigots" shown on television, he complained. In 1995, Lewis Norman, another congregational newcomer, detected cynical manipulation of public sentiment behind the controversy. "It started out with the Indians and the Braves," he argued. "Now it's this before the Olympics." Norman was referring to protests by Native Americans during the Atlanta Braves pennant race. The activists opposed the symbolism of the tomahawk chop and the team's stereotypical mascot.

Newcomer Faith Penner saw the use of the issue by 1994 Republican gubernatorial candidate tastelessly obvious. But she also thought civil rights groups were after "nothing more than free publicity and the opportunity to stir up some controversy right before a major event." The local media, she also complained, sought a sensational story. "They keep showing these people out here or in Forsyth County--like Daughters of the Confederacy—who are against changing the flag," she argued. "And they act like it's their fault. They're not the ones to blame. It's the ones behind the cameras who want to find somebody to blame for this." Others in the Sunday school classes believed, as Nelson Hammond said, "I feel like our values and traditions are totally under siege." Billy Sue Hammond concurred, "Respect for the flag is just something passed down in our family. It's not politically correct, but I'm proud to be Southern. Take the flag away and you take an important part of our past. We don't want to give up the past."

For most Hinton Memorial UMC congregants, the flag issue was simply not important enough to prompt them to move beyond airing their complaints in the safe space of the church's fellowship hall. However, others in the congregation and in Dacula were more active in their support of the flag as an important symbol. During the height of the flag controversy, state flags showed up unexpectedly around Dacula. Waters Odds and Ends in Dacula, where they sold yard ornaments, began advertising "Georgia Flags For Sale" on the sign in front of the compound. In the name of preservation of culture and heritage, several Hinton oldtimers, including Marie England and the Confederate Dames, became actively engaged in opposing change to the Georgia State flag. Marie argued that they did not want to offend anyone, but that the flag was about all that was left of the South.

For many congregants at Hinton Memorial, the controversy over the Georgia State flag highlighted both the extent to which they believed that their traditional heritage—whether or not they were from the South—was under siege and the feelings that politicians and the dominant media were cynically using their commitments and values for deceptive and self-serving purposes. Most felt that they were easy targets of parody and misrepresentation, whereby much of what they believed in was lampooned, impugned, and put down. As one congregant said to me after a Sunday school class during which she expressed her opposition to changing the flag, "Now, I suppose you will write that we're all racists."

The Georgia flag continues to be a wedge issue in political debates in the state. Former Governor Zell Miller, one of Georgia's most popular politicians, lost considerable political support during his effort to change the Georgia flag. He soon took a more acquiescent tone, urging that the flag should remain. In 1997, the Eleventh Circuit Court of the United States dismissed a lawsuit arguing that the Georgia flag violated the constitutional rights of free speech and equal protection of black citizens. Just as the controversy was at a fever pitch in February 1997, New York's Republican governor, George Pataki, mandated removal of the Georgia flag from the New York Capitol building, arguing that the confederate flag was offensive. Georgia legislators reacted with the anticipated counteraction of removing the New York flag from the Georgia Capitol. Antics not withstanding, there has been little movement on altering the flag. In 1999, it remained atop the Georgia Capitol and was flying high at the Dacula Memorial Day parade. The New York flag has also been quietly returned to its former location. The props are back in place but little of the underlying controversy has been resolved.

Conclusion

The changes that have been occurring in Dacula emphasize one reality about our national demography: many Americans prefer living in deconcentrated settlement spaces—suburbs and exurbs. By 1990 almost half of all Americans called these locations home. But whereas earlier waves of suburbanization created bedroom communities, today's deconcentration often occurs in rings around edge cities. As urban deconcentration occurs, more and more small towns, such as Dacula are drawn into the metropolitan orbit. Analysis of the resulting redefinition of these communities and of the attempts of these communities to alter the social practices and ideals of small-town life provides an important window on contemporary political, cultural, and religious tensions.

The analysis of this redefinition and response presented here highlights several important findings. First, resistance versus accommodation to urban restructuring was the basis of one type of local conflict. Some newcomers and oldtimers in small towns, now exurbs, such as Dacula, viewed themselves in an adversarial relationship with the city. Both culturally and politically, the city is perceived as the seat of power, mandating and representing the local changes. For most Dacula residents, however, Gwinnett County had become the seat of city authority. Individuals saw their particular place as under siege from "big" power entities, whether government or private developers. Given the limits of time and information, some locals relied on the assumption that their interests did not coincide with the interests of "the powers that be" in the metro Atlanta region.

Yet increasingly as the individuals who reside in the exurban locale are connected to Atlanta's economic, social, and political life, challenges were expressed about whether local interests contrasted so dramatically with metropolitan-wide interests. For example, Todd Penner highlighted assumptions of interrelationship, assumptions not widely shared by newcomers and oldtimers for whom preservation of their sense of cultural distance from Atlanta overrode other interests. With continued population inflow, however, those individuals who favor accommodation over resistance to various economic, organizational, and cultural forms of metropolitan incorporation will likely increase numerically and in their local power. For example, while the behemoth Hebron remained silent on the local contest about the airport, Quinn and congregational leaders were generally in the camp of the progrowth factions within the locale. For now and into the foreseeable future, divergent interpretations of local interests and goals will create tensions about the relationship between this former small town and the metropolitan region.

Second, maintenance of tradition versus appreciation for tolerance shaped another axis of local conflict. Dacula residents often realized that politicians shrewdly manipulated their desire for local traditions that defined them in opposition to metro Atlanta and their longing for a sense of historical connection. For some this realization created a moral quandary; they wanted both to maintain their traditions and to be seen as broad-minded. Oldtimers were more likely to state that tradition, as defined by the particular symbols they valued, was worth maintaining even in the face of public perceptions of intolerance. Newcomers were often more likely to direct the allegation of intolerance toward those who raised protests regarding these symbolic issues. Initially, newcomers often defined the conflicts as frivolous, simply serving the interests of those cultural groups, for example, African Americans and Native Americans, who were seeking broader public recognition. They often additionally contended that these special group interests were based in intolerance—a failure to "live and let live." By defining as intolerant those who sought to alter perceived traditional cultural symbols, newcomers who discussed the conflict over the Georgia flag were able to maintain that their support for these symbols was, in fact, in support of tolerance, cultural survival, and diversity.

Third, religious organizations varied in the types of conflicts that were salient to them as well as in their responses to the various conflicts. Congregations, such as Hinton Memorial UMC, which developed culturally specialist identities, were likely to engage in conflicts that defined them as locally partisan. Congregations, such as Hebron Baptist, which was self-defined as serving the northeast metro Atlanta area, were much less likely to become involved in specifically local conflicts. Their organizational generalism necessitated a greater tolerance on a range of local interests. However, Hebron was more likely to become involved in debates and conflicts that were not restricted to local issues, for example, providing support for anti-abortion groups within the metro area. However, even silence thundered when the congregation was the size of Hebron. By providing no aid and comfort to the antigrowth groups, Hebron defined the interests of local Christians as becoming "watchmen" for anxious newcomers, rather than preservationists of small-town culture.

Congregations whose responsibility it was, according to many local residents, to vouchsafe their quality of life often shaped their responses in relation to what they perceived as the relevant environment as well as in relation to divergent organizational and cultural identities. Furthermore, religious organizations, in particular, devised strategies for redefining the nature of the community and they redefined the appropriate roles of religious groups as they were shaped by the alterations in the organizational ecology. Here specialist versus generalist organizational and cultural approaches helped to determine the conflicts that were engaged.

Finally, within congregations the resources for dealing with long-standing conflicts within the community were altered by the arrival of new neighbors. While sometimes conflicts arose because of the different perspectives and resources that newcomers brought, at times newcomers also assisted oldtimers in resolving ancient conflicts based in longstanding feuds. In the case of the cemetery battle, new players, by moving beyond long-standing personal animosities, were able to resolve a conflict that had been brewing for years.

Conflict within a changing community underscores the fluid and multiple norms (or logics) used by various parties. Culturally localist perspectives were at loggerheads with views that took for granted Dacula's incorporation into the metropolitan region. In other instances, traditional symbols, even those that emerged in times of racial tension and bigotry, were reframed to become signs of supposed tolerance and cultural survival. In order to understand cultural tensions in local communities, scholars cannot afford to bring assumptions that suggest that "culture wars" divide communities along ideological battle lines. Rather, we must attend more to the local framing of conflicts.

Chapter 7

Concluding Remarks

LIONEL HALL predicted that he was attending one of the last of his favorite Gwinnett County events—the annual county fair. Hall, who moved to the area in 1991, laughingly commented that he was the area's new representative resident—white, thirty-two years old, married, with a mortgage on a three-bedroom home, and 1.3 kids (his wife was beginning her second trimester). Wandering around the livestock exhibit at the 1993 fair, Hall said that he did not expect to see the prize sheep, cows, and hogs in another five years. "Well, look around you. How many of these people do you think are sending their kids to 4–H? Pretty soon this will be just another kinda country fair for city folk." "Like you?" I asked. "Like me," Hall admitted wistfully.

Arnie Falls, whose family has had a farm near Dacula for three generations, looked out his window at bulldozers. When we spoke in 1995, he had sold half a section to developers who were clearing land for a subdivision, to be named "Falls Paddock." Arnie commented that he had taken a bit of criticism (though usually not to his face) about his decision to sell the parcel. "To tell you the truth, I probably agree with them [the critics], to an extent." He went on to explain why he did not feel entirely at ease with his decision. Arnie's ancestors had come to the area to farm; he felt some responsibility to keep that up. "But there's no money in cattle and alfalfa; now from these subdivisions, you can keep yourself in coffee."

In the concluding remarks of this book, I focus on three levels of analysis that were vital for giving accounts of the change. Individual narratives focused primarily on how personal lives have changed since the exurban development began. Likewise, individuals in these changed environments have divergent ways of organizing their lives in relationship to organizations. Exploring these diverse patterns of commitment also allows us to see how constituents of local organizations helped to shape organizational response. Organizations, either launched in response to alterations in the environment or responding to these transformations, provide another level of analysis. In this work, I have focused on an ecological view of organizational change, rather than giving congregational accounts of the change in only a single congregation. Depth in accounts of both interorganizational relations and of intraorganizational processes is necessary to interpret the effects of change within this exurbanizing community. Likewise, these organizations' framing of change shapes how they respond to both newcomers and oldtimers in the community. Finally, the cultural level of analysis helps us examine new patterns of life that alter how and where people connect with one another in the settlement spaces of exurbia. While increasingly politicians and city planners decry the effects of urban "sprawl" on the urban landscape, nonetheless greater understanding of the cultural values and connections that currently exist in these deconcentrated areas may provide a perspective on how the diverse groups of individuals who find themselves in exurbia may come together to respond to quality of life issues and provide clues to how religious interests may be involved in framing issues and mobilizing people in the process.

Narrating Accountings of Urban and Religious Restructuring

In places like Dacula, cultural transformation has been underway—often at a speed that seems dizzying to local residents. Both newcomers and oldtimers are seeking new ways of life in relatively low-density exurbs. Whether residents are pushed toward exurbs or drawn there is the topic of much academic debate. As I was in the field developing my own theories about what was happening, I quickly realized that locals had their own detailed and thoughtful accounts. Dacula residents analyzed urban deconcentration variously. Alfred DeVries surmised that Dacula's alteration was being driven by the "big government" of Gwinnett County and the "big money" of incoming developers. Billy Sue Hammond named the driving agents as well-financed developers and individual homeowners. As a real estate agent, she credited homebuyers as creating the ideals, such as fenced-in yards and two-car garages in subdivisions with swimming and tennis facilities, which developers took as blueprints for building. Bethany Alley, a local newcomer whose children attended Dacula schools, identified the educational infrastructure as the motor of change. "People with families don't move where the schools are messed up, unless they can afford private school. Most of us are out here because the schools are good." Others noted that with working families came greater demand for service sector businesses, such as restaurants, dry cleaners, day-care centers, and fitness centers. These new businesses, in turn, need employees, and so the cycle continues. These new service organizations now exist alongside long-standing firms. With urban restructuring, the relations among organizations within the locality are reconfigured. Local residents expressed diverse perspectives, drawing on their personal experiences and interests, in accounting for the changes wrought by urban restructuring.

Dacula has, indeed, changed from a rural small town on the distant outreaches of Atlanta to an exurb fully in the grip of the city's expansion. In 1999, Highway 316 was regularly on morning traffic reports' list of most congested roads, and the problem of gridlock increasingly occupied Gwinnett County officials. In Dacula, as in numerous locales across the nation and the globe, the patterns of urban deconcentration have created new conditions for everyday life. My efforts have not been to give the definitive account of the sources of urban restructuring. Perhaps the diverse theories of Dacula residents provide the necessary multiple points of view. Economic, cultural, infrastructural, and individual factors interact. However, when examined within local environments, the existence of altered and innovative organizations provided a practical, observable embodiment of the local effects of urban restructuring.

Also, individuals developed complex negotiations about how and where they participated in these organizations. Individuals' relations with religious organizations, in particular, exemplified this complexity.

A fruitful approach for understanding this complexity requires looking at the interorganizational and interpersonal networks to see how relations shape religious identity and options. For example, Rachel Patterson, the twenty-three-year-old daughter of the bivocational pastor of Dacula Church of God, followed me out of church on Sunday morning in 1995. She wondered if I had been to Ebenezer Baptist Church yet. "You really should go there some Sunday evening. I've been participating in their Tuesday morning women's group." She went on to describe the Praise Keepers group that had formed as local women supported their husbands' participation in the Promise Keepers movement of evangelical men. "Doesn't it bother your father that you're attending another church?" "Not at all," she quipped. "He knows that we're too small to have a special group like that." Rachel assured me that her father was just happy that she and her husband had found some support for their often-rocky marriage.

Organizations that result from religious and social movements, such as Promise Keepers, allow some congregants to maintain loyalty to their local congregation, while also obtaining specialized support that many small congregations cannot offer. Whether a devised strategy or not, these organizations are willing to tolerate multilayered religious involvement in order to sustain commitment in the face of changing individual needs. Faith Penner, also, found that her limited participation at Hebron Baptist where she was involved in a grief support group, enabled her to continue loyalty to Hinton Memorial UMC, where such systems of concentrated support, were not offered. Likewise, individuals who participated in political groups that were an expression of their religious beliefs often did so in addition to their congregational loyalty. Thus individuals at the local level have developed more complex patterns of religious loyalty, which may be dispersed among a variety of religious groups. Their religious commitment is not lower overall, though it may appear that loyalty to any single institution has diminished.

In fact, this tension about the meaning of commitment often came up in association with the religious proselytizing and community canvasing done by some religious groups. For many locals, it was not clear what the purpose of this activity was. For example, during my 1993 interview with her, Liza Mayeux, a Hinton Memorial UMC member and full-time homemaker, expressed her offense at Hebron Baptist's regular visitation programs. "They've visited us. Three times. Knowing—I point blank told him I was going to Hinton Methodist Church. I was teaching Sunday school. . . . 'We were just in the area and thought we'd come by.' Why were they pushing? Lord, they've got more than they can handle, obviously. We call them 'Hebronites.' I mean, that's a pretty good word for them. Some of the people in this subdivision who are unchurched lock their doors and turn out their lights when they see [the Hebron visitation group] coming. Or they've got a watch out in the subdivision. They'll start calling each other. 'It's Tuesday night. They're hoofing it on the street again.'" Mayeux perceived that Hebron Baptist was involved in a well-known practice of "sheep stealing," that is, attracting church members from other churches. Clearly, most Hebron volunteers, who weekly made their way through Dacula's neighborhoods, would not have been adverse to this outcome.

But Mayeux missed another subtler message that Hebron members communicated. Often, they highlighted the programs and spiritual support that the congregation provided, apart from worship, and invited newcomers to find a way to participate that "met their needs." Hebron evangelists believed that they were building community by encouraging a multiplicity of ties to other families, friends and institutions. Shelby Clarke, a young Hebron visitation coordinator, said, "We are simply trying to let people know what we have to offer and encourage them to get involved. Maybe we can help with the after-school program, the LifeSkills seminars, or with the day care. We don't really care how they get in, we just want to see God bless them somehow through Hebron." By accommodating and, to some extent, encouraging the multilayered religious belonging that characterized the experience of the faithful, such as Rachel Patterson and Faith Penner, these religious organizations were supporting the creation of new organizational connections and promoting the development of specialist and generalist organizations within the religious ecology. This change in patterns of participation is also reflected in the contested meaning of commitment to congregations.

As an increasing number of people have a multilayered pattern of religious belonging, religious organizations can either accept or discourage this pattern. Among Hebron adherents and leaders, there was tacit acceptance of these multiple ties. However, the acceptance was only extended so far, that is, within the broadly defined evangelical subculture. For example, Hebron leaders discouraged participation in exercise or relaxation classes based on Eastern religious ideas or practices. Other congregations, such as Hinton UMC and First Baptist–Dacula, have interpreted these multiple ties as a lack of loyalty to their congregation, instead of viewing them as important for the exchange of information among organizations.

However, it does not necessarily follow that organizations that create strict boundaries are the best adapters to environmental change. While they clearly create strong, dense, and uniform subcultures that are cohesive, they may fail to promote ties that allow for the incorporation of new information and that mobilize resources in the environment. By becoming cliques, with highly interarticulated relations, they foreshorten their own adaptive capabilities. Patterns of multiple ties link individuals and resources within and across organizations and localities. Religious organizations have interests both in enabling and constraining these influences on their communal life.

By focusing on the linkages created by individuals within religious organizations, this study moves away from the emphasis on the entrepencurial leader as the primary agent of adaptation. The interweaving of participants' routines of religious belonging can produce significant alteration in local congregations. When leadership fails or is unable to envision strategies of action that respond to alterations in their environment, congregants may respond by drawing on knowledge and resources devised from participation within other religious groups as well as other types of organizations. Thus the composition and strategies of each group are influenced both by the population of organizations and by members' relation to the other organizations within the ecology.

Organizing Urban and Religious Change: Restructuring Ecologies

The shifting variety of organizations provides a marker of change.[1] Country stores are replaced with antique shops. Filling stations are supplanted by complexes with fast food, gas, and groceries. Locals and newcomers alike note the changing complex of cultural, religious, and commercial organizations. Many organizations that have long existed in this exurban environment are simply incapable of adapting to new populations. One insight that researchers of religious organizations can gain from the organizational ecology approach is that adaptation to new environmental circumstances is often impossible (Ammerman 1997a, 346–347). Thus organizational replacement occurs as new organizations that are suited to survive under new conditions enter the ecology.

The problem in the case of urban restructuring is that some of the families who have relocated to exurbs did so, in part, because they were seeking the very types of organizations that have trouble adapting to their presence. Many newcomers wanted a simpler lifestyle that the small town seemed to offer, but they also demanded the conveniences necessary for life in the faster lane. It was the pace at which organizational demise and replacement happened that often created anxiety and nostalgia among locals. Just as some mused about how they had been moved closer to Atlanta, oldtimers and newcomers alike often spoke about how time simply seemed to be speeding up or that they felt disoriented in their own community. This impression of discontinuity can create edginess among some locals, who then are ripe for mobilization in opposition to change or conversely succumb to the assurance offered by some organizations that are maintaining continuity with the past, whether that is symbolized in the Georgia flag or a small-town Georgia "village" cum mall.

For scholars of religion who are interested in mapping religious change, greater attention must be paid to the changed shape of urban life and the altered patterns of interaction among organizations and individuals that these restructurings have engendered. Localities matter because they are the sites of shared history and of relations of interdependence on economic, governmental, educational, religious, and cultural patterns. The resources and development patterns of localities contribute to the innovative and cooperative organizational strategies devised there.[2]

As researchers, we must attend to local community ecologies. And when we do, we must attend not simply to the birth and death of organizations, but also to how the speed at which organizational change happens and the extent to which one cultural response to transformation is talk of the loss of simplicity or personal autonomy, and concern about moral certainty. Organizations that address these common moral sentiments are likely to find both organizational and cultural fit in rapidly changing environments. The form that this cultural response takes may vary organizationally. On the one hand, the megachurch Hebron Baptist provided a new organizational format with a discourse that assured members of moral certainty and "family values," even as it promoted the area's demographic transformation. Hinton Memorial UMC, on the other hand, maintained its former organizational form but specialized in a cultural style that was vehemently antigrowth and localist.

Urban restructuring has resulted in once "closed" religious ecologies becoming increasingly open, as newcomers expand the available membership base, as denominations shift resources to take advantage of growing exurban locales, and as religious leaders find opportunities to plant new congregations. However, these exurban spaces also can fill up quickly making success in new religious plantings more challenging. As was the case with Felding Chapel and Perimeter Ministries, some congregations cannot survive in a fast-changing urban environment.

Those that do survive are related to one another and other organizations within the contexts in which they are embedded. Their culture as well as their organizational type should be understood as functions of their local relations. The shifts in the organizational environment resulting from organizational foundings, such as the creation of Trinity Christian Fellowship, and from the changes in organizational form, for example Hebron Baptist's alteration from country congregation to megachurch, alter significantly the relationship among organizations.

As seen in chapter 3, status rivalry is one outcome of this new population of organizations. The tensions over status are particularly strong in religious groups because different religious groups have divergent self-adopted missions. Thus it is difficult for both insiders and outsiders to judge whether a congregation is successful as long as it is keeping its doors open. At the local level where religious organizations coexist within space, new status relations, sometimes tenuous, are formed as religious restructuring occurs. Early innovators may set a particular standard of what constitutes successful adaptation; however, not all organizations follow that standard, even when they have the leadership, and the financial and cultural resources to do so. Nonetheless, a new standard-setter on the local scene destabilizes the extant status order among congregations. The result is often status rivalry in which the primary good sought is not necessarily members and financial resources from a common pool, but rather local prestige and sense of power. During times of rapid change in the local context, multiple standards for allocating status are likely to coexist, creating tensions among groups and sometimes blocking organizational cooperation. In Dacula, for example, some congregations, such as Hinton Memorial UMC, were losing their appeal as the community's middlest of the middle-class congregations as denominational affiliation became less vital in individuals' choice of worshiping community. At the same time, others were gaining status based on sundry criteria, such as the scope of their programming, their pastor's reputation as spokesperson for a political special-purpose group, or local media coverage of congregational events.

However, even when status rivalry and new status markers were in play, congregations were not only in competition with one another. Often they promoted the multilayered religious participation that is increasingly common in places such as exurbia. Additionally, even when competition is a viable response, congregations often combine forces both overtly and inadvertently. When they work together to care for children seeking recreational facilities, or allow the multilayered religious participation discussed earlier, religious organizations within an ecology often consider how their actions or failure to act will affect not only themselves and other churches, but also the community in which they are located.

While pastors, layleaders, and bystanders celebrated the Dacula's increased religious offerings, congregations and religious groups also worried about local religious health, or bemoaned the tolerance or intolerance of other religious groups. Eventually though the conversation usually centered on the perceived or actual relations with particular local congregations and religious groups. The local religious ecology was not only the unit that was being restructured, but also often the agent to accomplish the restructuring. Particular places are the sites where proximity both shapes shared religious meanings and necessitates divergent organizational forms and cultural approaches. Congregations developed specialist and generalist approaches in response to alterations within their population of organizations. Specialist congregations identified an underserved group, an atypical organizational form, or a specialized identity and focused on it. Like Trinity Christian Fellowship, they sometimes developed organizational strategies that sent out groups to establish new congregations in other localities rather than seeking to enlarge its own local following. Another specialist approach was to appeal to a common yearning among both oldtimers and newcomers, bridging the demographic distinctions by the creation of a collective tradition, as did Hinton Memorial UMC. One generalist congregation exhibited broad appeal by becoming a tremendously complex and large organization that encompassed many specialized subgroups. This megachurch was an early innovator, and other organizations sometimes sought to emulate this pattern. Other congregations attempted to merge divergent cultural styles within their worship and programming. This attempt at adaptation, however, was seldom successful in appealing to these variant populations. Still other congregations, such as Felding Chapel and Perimeter Ministries, became dormant or died because of their unwillingness or inability to change either their culture or their organizational form to fit within an altered and denser ecology.

Within the market competition model, religious groups and their leaders are interpreted as seeking to optimize their success by developing organizational styles and religious systems that are the most efficient in attracting and holding members. Those groups that accomplish this flourish; others decline numerically and their cultural power wanes. Some that are so out of step with the change happening within their environment may even close their doors. While this notion of the "survival of the fittest" may be one lesson that comes from viewing the relations among religious organizations locally, it is not the only one to be drawn. Additionally, while some scholars focus on only one congregation as inevitably responsible for the religious life of the community, an ecological approach highlights the interactions among organizations and the divergent visions they hold for the community's future well-being. Thus rather than seeking to designate the best organizational type for surviving under circumstances of change or emphasizing only one type of civic religion, this study has focused on the alterations in the entire ecology and the dense network of religious interchange, as is necessary, in order to understand the dynamics of religious restructuring.

A framework that emphasizes religious ecologies not only addresses how religious organizations approach current circumstances of rapid change, but also underscores the need to generate resources for responding to unpredictable future changes in the environment. As was evident in the case of Hinton Memorial UMC, change kept coming even after the congregation had developed an initial response. In the hiring of Reverend Gerhard who was supposed to draw the area's newcomers, Hinton Memorial UMC was adapting to the changes in the environment. However, the schism resulted in still more changes ahead and a different approach to change was fashioned with the arrival of Reverend Dawson.

Thus any organization must not only address the immediate changes that demand alterations in the organizational form or cultural style, but it also must recognize that change will continue to come, demanding more and different responses. Those organizations that maximize their efficiency in response to early change may be poorly equipped to address future alterations in the environment and in the organizational ecology. What succeeds in the midst of present change may not result in "winning" ways with the next wave of change. Thus organizational and cultural variations and mutations form a range of ecological responses. Groups develop generalist or specialist organizational and/or cultural responses. Not all organizations are optimizers under the current circumstances of social change. Rather some may conserve organizational and cultural forms that may offer future resources.

By focusing on the religious organizational ecology, we gain perspective on the diversity and vitality of organizational forms and cultures within any population of organizations. An ecological perspective allows us to see the need for maintaining a variety in the "gene pool" for the evolution of adaptations to yet unforeseen changes in the environment. By simultaneously following divergent patterns of change, organizations preserve the possibility that they or future organizations will be able to respond to a broader range of unanticipated coming changes. Local knowledge, culture, and networks give shape to organizations that have greater flexibility; and within ecologies this diversity enables adaptability among the population of organizations.

Also during periods of rapid environmental change, both new religious groups and new forms of organization emerge. Ecologically speaking, one hazard under these conditions is an overabundance of religious organizations. These particular places attract individuals and organizations with religious entrepreneurial vigor. Denominations demand growth from established congregations, or announce the establishment of rival groups with greater access to denominational resources. Charismatic leaders supply religiously energizing worship to newcomers and form congregations. Congregations split, creating nascent religious organizations. In a rapidly changing environment, the fertile ground can sometimes cause too much organizational proliferation. This situation results in an increased jeopardy for new groups. More of them may fail as the ecology becomes increasingly crowded and the struggle for survival more intense.

Within communities, congregations continue the work of serving the faithful, framing issues of concern to locals, and tending the traditions that they have been handed. Increasingly we must turn our attention to these particular places in order to account for religious restructuring in the United States. Religious life in all its local detail reveals the shape of things to come.

The Shape of Things to Come

The community connections and sense of place that drew many exurban newcomers to Dacula and places like it around the United States are increasingly strained by the migration to ever more distant exurbs. Interstates and town-to-market roads bear more traffic than they were designed to handle. Traffic and congestion were often identified as the biggest concern by both Dacula's oldtimers and newcomers. The particular place that they moved to when they carefully selected Dacula was becoming more like other once rural locales where now malls and traffic reign. The schools that had once promised sylvan playgrounds for their children filled their open spaces with trailers to accommodate the crowds. Dacula's residents worried that the developers who planned for bigger malls and transportation hubs would eventually win and their quality of life would decline.

Dacula is, indeed, the picture of what is come. Exurban spaces are filling up as political leaders in metropolitan regions puzzle over how to respond to the environmental impact of nearly unimpeded growth. Exurbia is on the minds of more politicians as they mandate green space and roll back development in order to protect farmland around urban centers. Economic expansion has created a residential and commercial reality that may not be sustainable during times of belt-tightening. Urban deconcentration will likely be unable to continue unabated.

For those scholars interested in the fate of religious organizations in the exurban future, the response is already becoming apparent. Religious groups will continue to go where the people are, planting congregations and buttressing the ideals of community life that families want when they move to these particular places. Some congregational cultures will preserve and protect the local legacy for those who seek a sense of enduring community ties, while other religious groups will innovate to attract individuals whose loose civic ties allow them to find new patterns of engagement (cf. Wuthnow 1998). Congregations will explore new ways of reaching out to their communities as they continue to be locations for preserving local quality of life—however diversely that is defined. Though exurbia may now be getting the attention from political leaders it has long needed, religious communities are already firmly planted there and will continue to adapt.

Appendix   Interview Schedule

INITIALLY INTERVIEW SUBJECTS were selected by virtue of their knowledge of the workings and history of the community or religious organizations. These key informants became the basis for much of the oral history of Dacula and various congregations. After general historical frameworks for the exurb and congregations were in place, I began more formal interviewing. I sought representative samples from the identified populations within the locality and congregations, for example, age-related, gender-related, newcomer/ oldtimer, active/marginal. Interviews of oldtimers and newcomers provided a strong and relatively deep data base for comparison. Using follow-up interviews, I explored the links among individuals and organizations more directly.

The interview schedule below was adapted for different circumstances. For secular leaders and general local informants, the informal interviews included questions related primarily to changes within the community. For members and leaders within congregations, all sections of the interview schedule were used.

Individual Interview Schedule
PRELIMINARIES
Inform the individual about the circumstances of the study and receive permission to tape-record interview. All interviews will be confidential. If I plan to quote from an interview using an individual's name, I will seek permission first. Your church's name and location will be used in the final documents from the study.

COMMUNITY CHANGES
How long have you lived in the Dacula area?
Tell me about your earliest memories of Dacula.
What do you think have been the most significant changes through your

years in the area? How do you think people in the community have
responded to those changes?

What problems do you think that the youth in Dacula and the surrounding area face?

PERSONAL

Walk me through a typical week for you. Where do you go and what do
you do?

What do you do for a living?

Where were you educated?

Would you tell me about your own life history? What have been the important events?

Who are your five closest friends? How do you know them?

How do you make big decisions? Use specific example.

RELIGIOUS BELONGING

What religious groups are you involved in?

What do you like best about these groups? Why?

What do you like least? Why?

When do you feel closest to God?

If you are a member (or leader) of a congregation, how do you feel you fit
into the congregation?

How would you describe the congregation to someone you wanted to invite?

What difference does attending (this church) make in your family life?

What are the important things that you think the church should teach children?

Have you ever gone to someone in a church or a pastor for help of any
kind?

How have you helped people from the church?

What do you see as the issues that your church needs to be addressing
today?

CONGREGATIONAL HISTORY AND CHANGES

How long have you been attending the church?

Tell me why you first decided to come to (this church)? Was there a specific event or person that was instrumental in your coming to the congregation?

What had you heard about the congregation before you began to attend?

What do you think have been the important events in your church's history?

How do new people find out about the history at (this church)? How important is it that they know the history?

What sort of people like it best at (this church)?

What do you wish could be changed at (this church)?

What do you see as the key issues facing (this church) now and in the next five years?

What difference do you think the changes around Dacula have meant for (this church)?

What other churches do you know about in the area? What are you opinions of them?

ORGANIZATIONAL DYNAMICS

What do you think are the important things going on at the church?

What do you think should be preached about? Do you think sermons should address politics, family, money, relationships, jobs? Are there any topics that you think it would be best if they were never or seldom spoke about from the pulpit?

In a typical week, how many hours are you involved at the church? Has that gone up or down in the past five years? What programs are you involved in?

Do you think you are more or less involved than the average person at (this church)?

Are you a member of (this church)? If so, why did you join? Or why haven't you joined?

How many people from your family have attended (this church)? Who? Are they still attending? If not, why did they stop attending?

Has the church ever asked you to help a person or organization in the community not associated with (this church)?

Who are the important people in the church's life? Who do you think are the most influential people in the church? Why?

Who at your church best represents the real nature of the church? Why?

Who do you think are potential leaders? Why?

What kind of person is the best sort of pastor for this church?

What have been the significant disagreements about church policy that you can recall?

For Hinton Memorial members only: What happened to cause the split in 1990? What were the things that led up to it? How did it affect your life? What has been the aftermath?

Have you ever had a membership drive at this church? If so, when? What
sorts of things did the church try?

Is there anything else that I haven't asked about that you think I should
know?

Notes

Chapter 1 Changing Places

1. Here, as throughout, names of individuals have been changed and some distinguishing characteristics have been altered.
2. Dacula is the actual name of the community in Gwinnett County, Georgia.
3. Flynt (1994) also provides a detailed history of a small-town congregation, Mt. Hebron (Baptist) Church in Leeds, Alabama, which became incorporated into metropolitan Birmingham during the 1970s. This careful history does not, however, substantially address Mt. Hebron's relations with other congregations in the locale.
4. Bell's masterly *Childerley* (1994) details the dynamics of exurban change in an English village. In particular, Bell explores the shift in the moral order of the community as pastoralism replaces social class as the community's moral foundation. His discussion of an exurb is, however, distinct from this in that he identifies a locale where significant rural life continues to exist.
5. The coinage of labels for these new decentralized formations has been something of an academic growth industry. Fishman (1990) notes that "the new city's construction has been so rapid and so unforeseen that we lack even a commonly accepted name for what we have created" (12). Though Vance (1964) had already developed the view of the "non-centric" city. Gottdiener and Kephart (1991) characterize these formations as "deconcentrated" and "polynucleated." Fishman (1987) identifies them as "techno-city" and "techno-burb." Baldassare (1986) names them "transformed suburbs." Kling, Olin, and Poster (1991) have coined the term, "postsuburban region" for the phenomenon. Other terms that are circulated include "outer cities" and "new urban villages." Watson and Gibson (1995) simply dub the entire urban complex "postmodern." I use "edge city" and "exurb"—the terms of Garreau (1991) and Spectorsky (1957), respectively. Geographers and planners employ these terms most regularly (cf. Nelson 1988; Achs 1992; Hamblen 1992; Trefil 1994). For a discussion of the history of these terms, see Sharpe and Wallock (1994).
6. Spectorsky (1957) was the first to call the fringes of an exclusive residential area outside of the New York City metropolitan region area "exurbs"—from which workers commuted to jobs located generally in the central business district. Spectorsky contended that exurbanites shared an attraction to a curious mix of "high tech" and rustic charm that was present in this location. Profiling the exurbanite, he wrote: "[y]our true exurbanite is gadget happy. He is never so delighted as when he is combining his love for old things and his fascination with new ones" (39). Fava (1975), however, argued exurbanization

differs from earlier deconcentration movements. Many exurban residents have been born and bred in the suburbs, rather than having decentralized from the center city. Their moves are from suburb to suburb to exurb, and they thus have little direct life experience with high-density living and central city problems. Contemporary critics of this pattern of urban expansion include Hannerz 1980; Kowinski 1985; Whyte 1988; Davis 1990; Stanback 1991; Kunster 1993.

7. Currently the term "exurb" is likely to show up in newspaper articles about "urban sprawl." These accounts demonstrate that although exurbanites may be drawn to small-town settings distant from the urban hustle, they are as likely as first- and second-tier suburbanites to live in planned subdivisions. According to a 23 October 1994 *Atlanta Journal and Constitution* article, the move to the exurbs in the metro Atlanta region has been led by real estate developers. "Agents say cheaper land prices in outlying counties are luring builders, who translate their savings into more house for the money. Buyers who would rather face a long commute each day than a big mortgage payment each month are following builders further out to new subdivisions." These commutes are now as likely to be to edge cities as to the Atlanta's central business district in downtown. In an article entitled "Outward Bound," published in the *Atlanta Journal and Constitution*, 2 October 1994, Richard Greer reported that for the first time more housing sales dollars were spent in exurbs than in urban neighborhoods.

8. The report developed by researchers at Dun and Bradstreet examined the growth of the nation's counties with at least 100,000 inhabitants: Gwinnett County, according to these findings, had experienced the fastest rate of population growth (50.4 percent) anywhere in the nation in the preceding five years. This report was picked up in national print media (namely, *American Demographics*, *The New York Times*, *Time Magazine*, and *The Wall Street Journal*) bringing the county to national attention.

9. In 1991, Gwinnett County had 372,500 residents; that total rose to 493,889 by 1996 (Selig Center for Growth, Terry College of Business, University of Georgia, based on data from U.S. Department of Commerce, Bureau of the Census, and Bureau of Economic Analysis).

10. Selig Center for Economic Growth, Terry College of Business, University of Georgia, based on data from Georgia Department of Labor, Labor Information Systems.

11. Giddens (1991) contends that three dynamic processes create the character of high modernity: separation of time and space; disembedding mechanisms; and institutional reflexivity. Giddens views the dissolution of traditional norms and values as well as the breaking up and decentralization of traditional expertise as the central trait of "detraditionalization." Tradition, in this context, can be said to be a way of orienting oneself with regard to the past that does not conserve the past, but rather reconstructs it. This tension between what some regard as the past and what that past will mean in new contexts revitalizes the past in Giddens' view. Over time, the old and new is what creates the collective memory (see also Hobsbawm 1983). This process was clearly present in Dacula.

12. Describing the process of exurbanization in a long-established New England village—Old Harbor—Dobriner (1963) addressed the phenomenon of small towns merging with sprawling American metropolitan regions. His description and evaluation perpetuates the nostalgic image of the small town as the last good *gemeinschaftlich* haven. He evaluates the process of exurbanization: "For

suburbanites, Old Harbor is another commodity; it is a product that can be rationally consumed; it is a means by which they hope to achieve a complex series of personal goals. For the villagers, on the other hand, Old Harbor is not a means to anything; it is an end in itself" (136). Although some small town residents share this view of usurpation, a much more complicated mix of sentiments was found in Dacula. Sometimes long-time residents saw opportunities as well as loss in the sociospatial changes in the small town (cf. Warner 1988).

13. Routines of belonging is my term for "mental maps"—a concept discussed by Fishman (1990) as household, consumption, and production network maps of families.

14. As a part of qualitative research, conceptualizing and exploring available interpretive models extends throughout the entire course of the research project. Thus, I often worked with several sensitizing theories to provide alternative interpretations of my findings. Thus, elsewhere I have employed particular insights of a market competition model, see Eiesland (1997). However, in the end I came to agree with Neitz and Mueser (1997) who also question the relative usefulness of market competitions and rational choice models for inductively attuned research in religion.

15. For other critiques of the rational choice model, see also Warner 1997; Ammerman 1997b.

16. Fligstein (1991) and Brint and Karabel (1991) both attend to national-level analysis. In exploring religious organizations, Liebman, Sutton, and Wuthnow (1988) also attend to national-level denominational dynamics. Singh, Tucker, and Meinhard (1991) explore metropolitan-wide ecological dynamics through quantitative analysis. Barnett and Carroll (1987) do focus on a specific community ecology, though religious organizations are not addressed.

17. The distinction between specialist and generalist organizations relates to their niche width (Freeman and Hannan 1983, 103–116). Generalist organizations depend upon a wider range of environmental resources—for example, space, money, and people—for survival. Specialist organizations survive utilizing a more narrow range of environmental resources (cf. Barnett and Carroll 1987).

18. For an affirmation of the case study format, see Burawoy (1991), Orum and Feagin (1991), and Warner (1991).

19. The zip code for the Dacula area is 30211. In 1990, the total population in the zip-code area was 7,349.

Chapter 2 *"The Way It Looks from Here"*

1. Though the body of literature on the suburbs has expanded apace with the phenomena it investigates, the scholarly analysis of the suburbs has for decades tended to treat the phenomena as a unitary category. Furthermore, these interpretations of suburbia have frequently reflected America's love/hate relationship with the suburbs. Prior to the 1920s, most intellectuals lauded the growth of suburbs as reasonable withdrawal from the congested and dangerous life of the cramped city. But a sea change was evident in the early 1920s when Mumford pronounced the suburbs as a whole, "those vast acres of nondescript monotony that, call them West Philadelphia or Long Island City or what you will, are but the anonymous districts of Coketown" (1924:185–186). For nearly four decades to follow, studies of the suburbs were largely commentaries on the general themes of homogeneity and conformism (cf. McConaghy 1993).

Whyte (1956), for example, identifies the "suburban problem" as transience; since the organization family lacks roots, they substitute a rampant "togetherness" that penalizes diversity and abuses privacy. Whyte also was among the first to popularize the term "sprawl" for suburban development. These popular notions have been and continue to be a powerful image of the suburbs. Yet this conception of the "generic suburb" tends to downplay the significant variations in types of suburbs, exurbs, and edge cities and to mask regional variations in patterns of urban deconcentration.

This image of the generic suburb populated by conformist consumers began to be countered within the nascent subdiscipline of the sociology of suburbs in the early 1960s. The work of Bennett Berger, *Working-Class Suburb* (1960), highlighted the diversity among types of suburbanites. He wrote: "In spite of the string of symbolic epithets that identifies suburbia as the citadel of standardization and vulgarization and conformity, suburbia is testimony to the fact that Americans are living better than ever before" (102). These more nuanced studies (see, for example, Donaldson 1969; Fischer 1982; Jackson 1985; Baumgartner 1988; Stilgoe 1988; Kelly 1989; and Marsh 1990) provide a much richer picture of suburban life that accounts, in part, for their massive appeal to Americans, as well as for persistent racial segregation, economic and careerist stresses on the suburban family, and the ecological damage from auto-driven lifestyles. The specific study of exurbs and edge cities began most prolifically with the critique and scholarly elaboration of Garreau's *Edge City* (1991).

2. For a detailed history of Gwinnett County, see Flanigan (1943 & 1959), Bartley (1990), and Worthy (1994). Attention is given to Gwinnett County's recent history in Hartshorn (1976), Stone (1989), Hepburn (1992), and Ebner (1994).

3. Previous names for the town included Freemantown and Chincapin Grove.

4. Some of my informants argued that this period of commuting "in" to Atlanta or inner-tier suburbs for industrial jobs was the beginning of Dacula's exurban life. Alfred DeVries certainly saw this as the beginning of the end for Dacula's commercial district. Hise (1993), whose analysis of Los Angeles shows how industrial employment led the march to the urban periphery, supports Alfred's views.

5. In 1950, the national proportion of total employment for manufacturing was 26 percent with the next largest sector, retailing and construction, at 22.6 percent. In the 1980s, while the proportion of workers in retailing and construction remained virtually unchanged, employment in manufacturing declined to 22 percent (Gottdiener 1994).

6. Between 1945 and 1975, the Sunbelt doubled its population. The scholarly consensus among sociologists and historians defines the Sunbelt as thirteen southern states—Alabama, Arizona, Arkansas, Florida, Georgia, Louisiana, Mississippi, New Mexico, North Carolina, Oklahoma, South Carolina, Tennessee, and Texas—plus parts of two western states: California (southern counties below San Luis Obispo) and southern Nevada (Las Vegas, SMSA) (see Bernard and Rice 1983).

7. As Abbott (1987) writes: "The great Atlanta building boom of the sixties and early seventies focused national attention on the central business district, but the suburbs were the real beneficiaries" (189). The population of Atlanta grew by 2 percent from 1960 to 1970 and actually declined slightly from 1970 to 1975, whereas the suburban ring doubled during that same fifteen years.

8. Dacula's population had nearly doubled between 1990 (1,577) and 1994.

9. Between 1990 and 1997 the annual rate of increase in the population for

Dacula's zip code was 7 percent—among the highest in Gwinnett County (see CACI Marketing Systems 1998:62–C).

10. In an April 1991 *Georgia Trend* article, an urban planner commented, "Atlanta is a city of small towns, but the huge proportion of the people live in unincorporated areas."

11. Data for census tracts 506.01 and 506.02 (1990) and 506 (1980), U.S. Bureau of the Census Population and Housing, 1980 and 1990. This area was also designated Planning Area #6 by the Gwinnett County Department of Planning.

12. According to the Gwinnett County Police Department and Metro Atlanta Crime Commission, rate of major crimes per ten thousand residents in 1992 was 269.59 for Dacula (census tract 506.02); for Gwinnett County the total was 494.60; for the five-county metro Atlanta area the rate was 846.25. The violent crime rates per ten thousand residents were 13.48, 22.60, and 110.96 for Dacula, Gwinnett County, and the metro area, respectively.

13. According to 1990 census data for census tract 506.02, 47.55 percent of households contained children. For Gwinnett County, 44.17 percent of households contained children, and 36.63 percent of households had children in the five county metro area. In the Dacula area, 7.88 percent of the residents were sixty-five or older, compared to 4.75 percent in Gwinnett and 7.66 in the metro Atlanta region. Twenty-six percent of residents in the Dacula area were born outside of Georgia, whereas 54.96 percent in Gwinnett County and 48.96 percent in the Atlanta region were not native Georgians (U.S. Bureau of the Census, 1990; *Census of Population and Housing: Georgia*).

14. The scores for Dacula students compared more favorably in middle and high school than in elementary school. Performance of third graders in Dacula was 3.90, Gwinnett County 4.17, and metro Atlanta 3.91. Fifth graders in Dacula scored 6.60, whereas Gwinnett county and metro Atlanta students scored 6.70 and 6.22. Eighth graders at Dacula (10.50) fared better than their Gwinnett (10.48) and metro Atlanta (9.58) fellow middle schoolers (Georgia Department of Education 1994).

15. Individuals with demographic profiles similar to Dacula residents' were also slightly more likely to be a members of a fraternal order, to go freshwater fishing, and to buy country music albums than those resembling residents of Gwinnett County or the United States. These data came from a market comparison survey conducted by Mediamark Research Inc. (1991–1992).

16. Based on market comparison surveys conducted by Mediamark Research Inc. (1991–1992) for individuals with demographic profiles similar to local residents.

17. The percentage of Dacula residents who play golf was 11.10, for Gwinnett residents 12.40, and for U.S. residents as a whole 10.00. Local residents were as likely to drink domestic beer as the U.S. population (12.80 percent) and slightly more likely to do so than Gwinnett County residents (12.67 percent). Gwinnett citizens as a whole were more likely to own an American car at 41.72 percent of car owners owning a domestic make, compared to 38.80 percent of Dacula area residents and 36.60 percent of U.S. car owners (Mediamark Research 1991–1992).

18. According to a June 1994 *American Demographics* article, "Alone in the Car," 84 percent of Gwinnett County residents drove to work alone. Reasons given for preference to drive alone is high-paying jobs, flexible work hours, and poor public transit.

19. The new name was endorsed by the state legislature in 1995, and new highway signs went up within weeks.

20. Garreau (1991:427) classified the Gwinnett Place Mall Corners as an emerging edge city. In the years since Garreau's study, growth in the area and perceptions of local inhabitants have developed so that designation of the area as an edge city is now warranted.

21. Fishman (1987) described these deconcentrated urban settlements as a "new city," which is, "a peripheral zone, perhaps as large as a county, that has emerged as a viable social and economic unit. Spread out along its highway growth corridors are shopping malls, industrial parks, campuslike office complexes, hospitals, schools and a full range of housing types. Its residents look to their immediate surroundings rather than to the city for their jobs and other needs; and its industries find not only the employees they need, but also specialized services" (184). The features of these "new cities" included growth corridors rather than downtowns, low-density development, and complex patterns of multidirectional travel that largely bypass the old city centers and make "center" and "periphery" distinctions obsolete.

22. According to a special report, published in the *Atlanta Journal and Constitution*, 13 November 1994, using data from analysis of 1993 police incident reports for metro jurisdictions and Metro Atlanta Crime Commission statistics.

23. In addition to the ceding of much governmental power of small towns to the county, "shadow governments" have arisen throughout the county (Teaford 1997; Garreau 1991). These shadow governments, such as homeowners' associations and business alliances, are privately owned or quasi-public institutions that have accrued considerable power and influence in shaping the patterns of life and growth in the area. Garreau highlights the way in which these "shadow governments" perform functions usually carried out by governmental entities, such as assessing mandatory fees, setting rules and regulations, and limited police power (1991:187). For further discussion of the role of these organizations in the shaping of edge city and exurban environments, see McDowell (1990).

24. This first wave of newcomers was composed of "elective parochials," as described by Warner (1988).

25. Goldfield (1991) highlights the slow recognition of the urban quality of the South. Often when Southern history or culture is addressed, the focus is on the rural, making the urban South seem to be an anomaly to be explained.

Chapter 3 *A Place to Be Religious*

1. The congregations of Dacula constitute an organizational ecology. Although no formal ministerial or congregational association existed among them, there were numerous informal relations and ties, including conducting common Thanksgiving and Fourth of July services, devising collective processes for serving indigent families, and appointing members to Dacula Elementary's educational advisory council. In addition, when a crisis occurred within the community, many religious organizations cooperated to raise funds or awareness—for example, when Church of Christ on Auburn Road burned in 1996. A diverse range of congregations took offerings to assist with the rebuilding.

2. This cannot be asserted unequivocally since we do not have records of early churches that closed soon after founding.

3. Though it is beyond the scope of this work to review the extensive literature on religion in the suburbs—which has often included, though not differentiated, exurbs—the scholarly treatment of religion in the suburbs has histori-

cally, like much of the general suburban literature, been heavily overlaid with evaluative judgments rather than careful analysis of organizational forms and practices (Hudnut-Beumler 1994; cf. Bailey and McElvaney 1970). Winter (1961) posed the "dilemma of metropolitan Protestantism" as the superficiality of suburban churches (35), the loss of meaningful religious community (37), and the moral tragedy of white flight and the abandonment of the inner city (47). Schroeder, et al. (1974) identify privatization as the distinctive feature of suburban religious life and finds there a scarcity of "authentic religion," that is, religion that "always fosters a vision of the inclusiveness of the whole, a sense of common good, and a concern for the well-being of all humankind" (122–123). Hudnut-Beumler designates this literature the "Suburban Jeremiad." In recent years, the jeremiad has taken on new overtones of environmentalism, and criticism of sprawl has come to the fore.

4. This expansion of what religious leaders and groups defined as their ecology accounted for my inclusion of religious organizations that were outside of the Dacula zip code; but these groups were perceived to be related to Dacula—either because of history or because of deliberate outreach done in the locality.

5. Baptist bodies included Southern Baptist, Negro Baptists, Primitive Baptists, and Colored Primitive Baptists. Methodist groups included the Methodist Episcopal Church, Methodist Episcopal Church–South, and African Methodist Episcopal Zion Church. Presbyterians constituted 2.1 percent of the church-going population. Others, including Pentecostals, accounted for 1.1 percent of the total.

6. Catholics represented 14.2 percent of the religious adherents in the county. All other groups reported adherents of 5 percent and below the county's total (Bradley, et al. 1992:101). Trend data for Gwinnett County show that rates of religious participation dipped slightly from the 1970s but have gone up dramatically since the 1980s. In 1971, 46.1 percent of the total population were church adherents, compared to 46.2 for the state as a whole (Johnson et al. 1974:42, 46). In 1980, the rate was 33.7 percent of the total population as church adherents, compared to 47.8 for the state as a whole (Quinn et al. 1982:67, 72). The number of religious organizations increased from eighty-eight in 1971 to 122 in 1980. Religious membership for Gwinnett County reported by Bradley et al. (1992) was 43.9 percent of the total population, compared to 57.6 percent for Georgia as a whole. Gwinnett's rate of religious participation is comparable to, though somewhat lower than, that reported in the seven-county Atlanta metropolitan region.

7. Research conducted by WEFA Group, National Decision Systems, reported by Gayle White in 29 December 1998 *Atlanta Journal and Constitution*, E2. The projections are based on comparison of religious organizational expansion compared to growth in other sectors within the county, calibrated on national patterns.

8. Young married couples with children are more likely to join religious organizations and attend religious services than are young adults who are childless and unmarried (Carroll and Roozen 1975; Roozen, McKinney, and Thompson 1990; Stolzenberg, Blair-Loy, and Waite 1995). Chaves (1991) suggests that religion in the United States is primarily a family-oriented undertaking, noting that church attendance is highest for those living in conventional families.

9. For attention to the specific effects of a megachurch on a religious ecology, see Eiesland 1997.

10. Vaughan (1993) and Thumma (1996) confer megachurch status at two thou-

sand members; Schaller (1992) places the numerical cutoff at one thousand. Still others (R. Olson 1988) place the limit as low as eight hundred. One quandary in defining and designating megachurches is dealing with Catholic parishes. These congregations differ considerably from the current picture of megachurches but some, nonetheless, fit criteria of size and theological conservatism. Yet they are not typically included in counts of megachurches (Thumma 1993; 1996).

11. In addition to the newsletter that was distributed free, the congregation offered cassette tapes of the weekly sermons for a nominal fee and low-cost videotapes of special services, including cantatas and religious plays, which kept nominal members attached to the church.

12. The weekly "Vision" contained a short commentary by Quinn (concluded with "I Love You, Bryant"); a schedule of weekly events at the church; requests for workers and resources; prayer needs; miscellaneous announcements; notice of new members by name, separated by those who were baptized and those who transferred membership; and personal notes, including thanks to workers, notice of weddings, births, and deaths. Quinn's commentaries focused largely on events happening in the congregation or in the Dacula community, such as the success of the Dacula High School football team. Occasionally events in the Atlanta metropolitan area warranted mentioning, such as the 1994 Billy Graham Crusade. From 1992 to 1993, the newsletter distributed before national elections in November contained no mention of politics.

13. Therapeutic personalism combines focus on expressivism—allowing members to express themselves and discover new insights in group interaction—and medical and therapeutic models which highlight self-awareness, healing, and the realization of deeper life goals (cf. Bellah et al. 1985; Wuthnow 1994b).

14. Schor (1991) highlights these stresses. Half of all employed mothers reported that working outside of the home caused either "a lot" or an "extreme" level of stress. This stress has placed tremendous burdens on marriages. Two-earner couples have less time together, which researchers have found reduces the happiness and satisfaction of a marriage. Stress-related diseases have skyrocketed, especially among women. Karesek and Theorel (1990:166) note that worker compensation claims related to stress tripled during just the first half of the 1980s. See also Hochschild and Machung (1989).

15. The gendered norms in this congregation take for granted that most women work outside the home as a financial and personal necessity. However, the norms also reinforce traditional views such as the belief that men ought to provide for and protect women, that women should appear feminine, and that men should be the "head" of the household (Stacey 1990:133–135; Ammerman 1987:134–146). On the whole these gender norms do not differ significantly from those held by Southerners in general, according to a "Southern Life" poll reported in the _Atlanta Journal and Constitution_, 3 July 1994. Fifty-three percent of Southern men agreed with the statement, "Women who don't care about their appearance are not very feminine," compared to 41 percent non-Southern; whereas 52 percent of Southern women agreed with the statement compared to 40 percent non-Southern women. More Southern than non-Southern men and women agreed with the statement "Most men think they're better than women."

16. Minimizing denominational ties increased the entrepreneurial quality of the congregation. Hadaway (1993) notes that the Southern Baptist Convention,

more than some other mainstream conservative denominations, has many entrepreneurial churches that are only "peripherally 'denominational'" (353). Many of these congregations are megachurches that see themselves as benefiting the denomination more than the other way around.

17. A sample of thirty newsletters from 1993 and 1994 revealed that the average number of baptisms per week was 8.9, and the average number of membership transfers per week was 9.1. The average number of baptisms in each of the three Sunday morning services was three. In 1994 the church reported 530 converts.

18. This generalization is based on mulitlayered participation at Hebron. A study conducted at Hebron in 1994 compared worship service attendance with the total number of individuals involved in Sunday schools, support groups, etc. It indicates that approximately 37 percent of participants in worship services do not participate in other church activities. Furthermore, church leaders estimate that approximately 10 percent of participants in church-sponsored support groups are not participants in worship services because of membership in other churches (cf. Faith Penner discussed in chapter 5). Thus the structures for assuring personal religious accountability within the church for a significant subpopulation of Hebron worship participants was relatively low when compared with the high commitment rhetoric.

19. Hinton Memorial's history is addressed in detail in chapter 4.

20. Roof (1993), in his study of religious patterns among baby boomers, contends that a high degree of interfaith marriage and blended families has resulted in the decline of denominationalism. He predicts that this trend will only intensify. He writes: "Denominational boundaries within Protestantism will likely erode further, as increasing numbers of Americans grow up knowing very little about their religious heritages" (249). Others also note the prevalence of religious voluntarism (cf. Roof and McKinney 1987; Hammond 1992; Warner 1993). In a study of five Baptist congregations, D. Olson (1989) notes another disincentive to religious participation among seekers. He demonstrates that churches with the highest numbers of church friends per attenders have either stable or declining membership. He argues that this finding is due to a saturation of people's friendship networks, so that new attenders tend to find the congregation cliquish and do not persist in attending.

21. When asked, several congregants could not identify what these acronyms signified. One commented, "I don't know, but it seems about right to name a youth group RIOT, don't you think?"

22. Trinity Fellowship of Churches is similar to, though smaller than, such groups as Vineyard Christian Fellowship and Calvary Chapel. See Miller (1997) for a discussion of the organizational liaisons of these groups.

23. This strategy includes developing smaller, dependent congregations which utilize the resources, including office personnel of the "mother" congregation until they are mature enough to stand on their own.

24. Although it is beyond the scope of this work, it could be argued that contrary to Miller (1993; 1997) who detects in these megachurches a postmodern organizational form, these very large congregations exhibit a significant modernist influence in their valorization of bigness and centralization. More plausibly, congregations that adopt deliberate "mothering" strategies, for instance, may exhibit a postmodern organizational shift toward smallness and decentralization (Clegg 1990). For a careful discussion of the pros and cons of

identifying organizations as modern or postmodern, see Hassard and Parker (1993).

25. "Family" in this context has strong ideological underpinnings, not unrelated to the contemporary debates about "family values," including such notions as normalcy, heterosexuality, and social stability. Family is understood as a "traditional" or "conventional" two-parent nuclear family. This definition of family does not, however, identify the variety of kinship stories present in this congregation. To explore contemporary debates about the evolution of "family" and its contemporary religious meanings and contexts, see Stacey (1990).

26. It is worth noting, as a sideline, that actors in these spiritual dramas are just as likely to be male as female. Men and women are expected to nurture "newborn" Christians. This equalitarian imagery does not, however, translate into equal power-sharing within the congregation. Although women serve extensively on the Program Staff, none are represented on the Pastor's Committee, the local governing body.

27. Patterns of male-dominated authority in conservative religious groups are discussed at length in Ammerman (1987), Tipton (1982), Stacey (1990), and Davidman (1991). These works highlight the symbolic relationship among God as Father, the pastor/rabbi as Father, and the father of the family. At First Baptist–Dacula, this symbolic relationship was reinforced by the church as a "family business."

28. I am not yet persuaded by Thumma (1996) who argues that though "very large churches have been around since the beginning of Christianity" (404), megachurches are a "recent social phenomenon" offering a unique pattern of organization, programmatic ministries, and membership relations (405). I do, however, agree that megachurches are relatively new to the localities in which they are currently thriving, that is, Sunbelt suburban and exurban locations (409).

29. In merging congregations, special purpose groups, and support groups, this type highlights the commonality of these groups when viewed locally. This view differs from Wuthnow (1994a) who argues that "different kinds of religious organizations operate in different ways—need different resources from their host environments, set different goals, have different internal and external constraints, and accomplish some tasks more easily than others" (6). Wuthnow goes on to contend that congregations have a public presence, that is they are institutions of a particularly recognizable sort, that does not characterize the other organizational types (43–45). Furthermore, congregations have a corporate identity, in part, because of their legal recognition and their endurance over time. In contrast to this view, I contend that congregations, support groups, and special purpose groups are organizationally similar at the local level. These groups make similar demands on the loyalty, finances, and time of members. They tend to have task-oriented division of labor and fluid leadership patterns. They generally have face-to-face meetings at least monthly. Furthermore, at the local level, these groups do have a public presence through, for example, announcements in the local newspaper and newsletters distributed to a wider public. Finally, it is worth noting that these groups' presence is more often perceived as a social movement and a decline within established organizations—representing the existence of "subaltern counter publics" (Fraser 1990)—than as a centralized institutional force with bureaucratic legitimation.

Chapter 4   New Neighbors

1. Geertz (1983) identifies the importance of maintaining loyalty to the local. "To the ethnographer, sorting through the machinery of distant ideas, the shapes of knowledge are always ineluctably local, indivisible from their instruments and encasements. One may veil this fact with ecumenical rhetoric or blur it with strenuous theory, but one cannot really make it go away" (4).

2. The survey referred to in this and subsequent references to Hinton Memorial was administered by the author under the auspices of the Congregations in Changing Communities project, directed by Nancy Ammerman. Thirty-eight people completed the survey, accounting for approximately 76 percent of average Sunday attendance.

3. Neville (1987) describes such homecoming pilgrimages. She contends that they provide a sense of changeless place in the midst of the increasingly urban New South and a time of face-to-face relations in a culture of mediated and technologically diffused relations. Pilgrimages help shape an alternation between rural and urban, community and structure, and kin-based society and individualized society. They are different from our everyday life, often recalling an earlier time of unity and immediacy.

4. The matter of the cemetery is discussed at length in chapter 6.

5. Doctrinal emphases in the Holiness movement in the Methodist Church included healing, Christian perfection, eschatology, and local organizational autonomy. Several congregants at Hinton recall being less concerned about the theological perspectives of Martins than his preaching about hell and his "ranting" during sermons.

6. From 1910 to 1994, the congregation had forty-four pastors who had an average length of tenure of one year and ten months. The modal length of pastoral leadership at the church was one year or less, and only five ministers lasted four years or longer.

7. Dudley (1983), Evans and Evans (1983), and LeFevre (1975) write of the inverse situation: conflict which emerges from declining membership and efforts begun to stem the exodus.

8. Hadden (1969) and Wood (1981) emphasize clergy/laity conflict as the basis for much of church conflict. They argue that the clergy and laity have two different stands on social activism and different levels of resources to institute their policies. The underlying assumption is that the clergy is more cosmopolitan and educated—hence more liberal—than the congregation. In this situation, such analysis does not fit. Here the opposite was true.

9. Clark (1993) highlights the role of hymn-singing in transmitting the religious identity of a group. Her comments are apropos of the changes at Hinton Memorial: "a denomination ignores its musical tradition, past and present, to its peril. Not only are its roots in the past severed but also its ability to refashion those roots in contemporary religious terms is diminished" (115).

10. For a careful discussion of the relations of denominational structures in this schism, see Eiesland 1999.

11. As boundaries separating denominations have blurred and as denominations have diversified internally, congregations and denominations have lost clarity about doctrinal identity and distinctiveness. Carroll and Roof (1993) highlight how organizational changes within and across denominations and the rapid rate of change have resulted in "identity crises" for denominations and congregations (cf. Wuthnow 1988). When this occurs, denominational affiliations

no longer "fit people into the local community while providing reference to the larger society" (Swatos 1981:223) in the same way that they had done, and the status-conferring role of individual's religious membership is altered. Additionally, they no longer serve as a coherent "community of memory" in quite the same way (Bellah, et al. 1985).

12. Harrison and Maniha (1978) highlight the importance of bureaucratic organization (polity) in analyzing the impact of the charismatic/Neo-Pentecostal movement. An important factor in the growth of charismatic groups and in their management was found to be the power of the parent organization—denomination or regional governing body—to enforce its wishes. They contend that the governance and power of the Catholic church allowed its structures to absorb and diffuse the Neo-Pentecostals; whereas the Episcopal church was less able to prevent Neo-Pentecostal dissent and factionalizing. The United Methodist Church has an episcopal polity.

13. The issue of apportionment—the per capita funds owed to the conference by each church in the United Methodist connectional system—is particularly controversial at Hinton, especially among younger members who see the denomination as a drain on their local budget.

14. Since apportionment dues are based, in part, on the number of members, Hinton had a financial incentive for purging the membership roll.

15. Weber's distinction between tradition or patrimonial organization and bureaucracy illuminates this dynamic. Traditional groups differentiate not on the basis of skills and tasks but with regard to special, irreplaceable relationships (1968:638–639). Bureaucratic organizations are rationalized so as to fit correlate skills and tasks efficiently and so as to meet ultimate values (1968:85–86).

16. Ammerman (1997c), reporting on the prevalence of such individuals in the Congregations in Changing Communities project, argues that "'meaning' for Golden Rule Christians consists not in cognitive or ideological structures, not in answers to life's great questions, but in practices that cohere in something the person can call a 'good life'" (202).

17. One exception to this pattern was the return of an elderly woman who had accompanied her daughter and grandchildren to Trinity. She had been absent from Hinton Memorial UMC for several years when she returned to the church in 1993. Her return was met with considerable ambivalence in the senior Sunday school class. Ms. Abbott did not speak directly to her for several weeks. In the end, this elderly woman attended Hinton Memorial sporadically for a year and returned to Trinity in late 1994.

18. Stacey (1990) highlights the pervasive use of "traditional" families to refer to modern nuclear families. She contends that the invocation of "tradition" emphasizes the archetypal character of a specific kinship relationship (7). Davidman (1991) highlights the invocation of tradition as opposition to group-specific diagnoses of the most pernicious aspects, often related to gender roles and morality codes, of modernity.

19. The newsletter also includes a women's page with recipes and a children's page, as well as a column by the pastor and several pages of advertisements. The newsletter does not, however, give Hinton an exceptionally high profile, and it lists all churches in the Dacula, Hog Mountain, and Harbins areas. Hinton Memorial began a newsletter for church members in 1979; gradually the focus of the publication changed, shifting under Dawson toward the community and expanding its circulation to include all Dacula residents. The newsletter was

first published under the name "Dacula Dateline," changing its name and beginning citywide distribution in 1984. In a 23 June 1988, *Gwinnett Daily News* article, then editor Caroline Barr commented, "It has become a line of communication in the community, and I'm finding that more people are reading it. I feel good because we're being of service to the community." Under Gerhard, the newsletter evolved into an evangelistic tool. After his departure, the congregational organ returned to its earlier format as community crier, and even enhanced its localist character.

20. Bellah and associates (1985) highlight the importance of "tradition and commitment" in communities of memory, which are constructed in part by a common narrative. They write: "Communities, in the sense we are using the term, have a history—in an important sense they are constituted by their past—and for this reason we can speak of a real community as a 'community of memory,' one that does not forget its past. In order not to forget its past, a community is involved in retelling its story, its constitutive narrative" (153). Warner (1988), Waters (1990), and Davidman (1991) highlight the role of election or choice in the construction and extension of such narratives.

21. In that, the church did not differ considerably from groups chronicled by numerous scholars of religion whose ethnographic studies have highlighted the contemporary resurgence and vitality of religious particularism, usually based on ideological and/or ritual conservatism (cf. Ammerman 1987; Neitz 1987; Warner 1988; Kaufman 1991; Davidman 1991). Theorists have also commented on the rise of religious particularism. Robertson (1990; 1991a; 1991b; 1992) highlights the broad implications and relations of particularistic groups in the global environment of universal/particular cultural polarity. He contends that this polarity is worked out through reciprocal processes of the "universalization of the particular and the particularization of the universal." That is, although the world is becoming "one" place, this "oneness" is spawning a heightened realization of our "manyness" as reactionary groups place a greater stake in their particular identities. Hence, oneness and manyness exist dialectically in tension. As we become more aware of our cultural and institutional interconnectedness so that our traditional racial, religious, ethnic, and national identities become relativized, we become more inclined to engage in, what Robertson calls, a generalized "search for fundamentals" (1991b). Robertson (1990) contends that searching for fundamentals is seen in the nostalgic search for a local identity, history, and community.

22. Reed (1986) observes that a localistic orientation—"an attachment to their place and their people"—is one of the cultural characteristics that continues to make Southerners distinctive in the larger nation (33). Reed notes that in the South there is a "symbiotic relation" between regional culture and local institutions.

23. Gottdiener (1985) describes these evolving coalitions as "growth networks." The idea of networks captures, according to Gottdiener, the way alliances can form around a host of issues associated with development, often splitting classes into factions. These growth networks also highlight the diversity of people who may coalesce around common interests, often only temporarily. For example, many community groups may have their own interests, which are manifest in local politics. They join in coalitions to push for some version of growth while opposing other coalitions that have their own vision of the future.

24. The question of assimilation and the maintenance of a distinctively Southern culture has been debated quite extensively. Though Arsenault (1990) does not

pronounce the death of Southern regionalism, he contends that technological advances, especially air conditioning, and the press acclimate newcomers and contribute to a dramatic decline in regional distinctiveness. He notes, "As long as air conditioning, abetted by immigration, urbanization, and broad technological change, continues to make inroads, the South's distinctive character will continue to diminish, never to rise again" (199). Other scholars have maintained that a cultural distinctiveness persists in Southern cities. Southern metropolitan areas have, according to Goldfield and Rabinowitz, remained "Southern" in many ways while participating in the modernizing economic boom (1990). Likewise Miller and Pozetta (1988) assert: "The new urban South, by its diversity alone, challenges the simpler South, but as southerners adapt to the new urban worlds growing up in their midst, they likely will discover that in their very diversity of culture, interest, and power those cities have ample room for southern ways as well. To some extent, they always have" (15). Yet these scholars do adequately identify the processes whereby Southernness is maintained and reconfigured in the process of suburbanization, in particular. Shibley (1996) has argued for the existence of a distinctive Southern style of religiousity, but likewise fails to deal with the dramatic urbanization of the traditional South.

25. The necessity of teaching particularity has been emphasized by Ammerman (1987).

26. Waters (1990) researched "symbolic ethnicity" in two suburbs, one in California and the other in Philadelphia; Ammerman notes that the neighborhood in which the fundamentalist congregation in her study is located "could be a suburban neighborhood anywhere" (1987:25–26). Stacey's study of new evangelicals (1990) also takes place in suburban Silicon Valley.

27. Wilkenson (1988) writes: "Suburbia itself may have become less communal . . . [one] sees a mass of over-equipped houses and yards which have become small, private islands. Front porch society, where everyone met everyone, has been closed down by domestic technology: the automobile, electronic entertainment, and air conditioning. Families vanish indoors (or into their backyards) or whisk themselves away on wheels" (43).

28. Cox's appointment to the church was orchestrated by Reverend Janelle Shea who was at the time superintendent in the area in which Cox served. Shea's assistance had been sought by Billy Sue and Nelson Hammond who hoped that she would advocate for her former charge at closed-door conference meetings.

Chapter 5   *Making Faith*

1. I am not claiming that these families are strictly representative of oldtimers and newcomers. Rather the stories of these family units highlight general patterns—diverse as the specifics are. The stories presented here about the routines of Vernon and Marie England and Todd and Faith Penner are cultural representations of the transformations that have accompanied and, to a large extent, comprised the organizational alteration in this exurban location.

2. Household networks represent the places that are part of family or personal life, such as day-care centers, schools, churches or synagogues, community centers, parks, and homes of friends or playmates. According to Fishman (1990), household networks of residents under the condition of urban deconcentration are generally more localized than are the consumption and production networks—which are generally wider than the traditional urban neighborhood

or the small town. The network of consumption is comprised of the retail centers of malls, supermarkets, specialty stores, restaurants, health clubs, and convention centers. This network is often widely scattered. The network of production includes the locations of employment for all members of the family, as well as the suppliers for those enterprises. Fishman's discussion of network maps is intimately related to Fischer's (1982) analysis of localized and dispersed networks. I combine these notions to describe "routines of belonging" as habitual organizational and individual interactions.

3. A sizable literature exists on network analysis and on the relations among small towns or rural areas and metropolitan locations (cf. Vidich and Bensman 1958; Haga and Folse 1971). These works largely use types of network analysis and mental mapping to discover where the inhabitants of a location shop, worship, bank, visit, etc. The limitation of simply plotting interactions is that it does not highlight sufficiently the meaning that inhabitants make of their network and maps. My focus is on both the maps and networks and on the perceptions of oldtimers and newcomers of intercommunity relations.

4. Jackson (1985) notes that the first wave of suburbanization occurred between 1815 and 1875, when the first railroad suburbs were developed. However, large-scale suburbanization did not occur until 1945. He argues that these postwar suburbs shared five common characteristics, including peripheral location, low density, architectural similarity, easy availability, and economic and racial homogeneity (238–241). He writes: "the creation of good, inexpensive suburban housing on an unprecedented scale was a unique achievement in the world" (245).

5. Bellah et al. (1985) write: "While mobile professionals in the Unites States do indeed engage themselves in complicated networks of intimate relationships, these networks are often not tied to a particular place. One may maintain close friendships with a host of people scattered all across the country" (186). More likely, however, is the diffusion of intimates primarily within a single metropolitan area with its deconcentrated pattern of edge cities and exurbs. Thus one's household, consumption, and productive networks are isomorphically related.

6. Wuthnow (1988) argues that the increased organizational pluralism brought about by the growth of special purpose groups, specialized ministries, coalitions, home fellowship and support groups did not take the place of membership in denominationally affiliated congregations (120–121). However, they did, I argue, alter the meaning and context for congregational membership, allowing for multilayered religious participation in which church membership is not necessarily privileged.

7. The "melting pot" view of religion corresponded to the view of the assimilation of immigrants over several generations (Glazer and Moynihan 1963; Gordon 1964; Sowell 1981; Lieberson and Waters 1988). Over time, the melting pot theory suggested, free market economy and the institution of democratic politics, both of which allowed for active participation and public life, would result in the melting of immigrant enclaves. The theory was based, argue Lieberson (1980), Morawska (1990), and Takaki (1993), on the view of the United States as a land of unlimited opportunity and mobility. Many scholars have challenged this assumption in the melting pot theory. They contend that while individual attributes, such as personal ambition and responsible living, are important for success, institutional impediments also exist which prevent immigrants from realizing their full potential.

8. Roof (1993) detects in this multilayered participation a postmodern turn—a "mixing of codes." He writes about the boomer generation: "Members of this generation have few inhibitions about multiple associations with vastly different groups. . . . Even more common is the phenomenon of picking and choosing beliefs from a variety of sources, which results in the 'multilayered spirituality' found within organized religion" (201).

9. The Lodge, in addition to sponsoring community betterment campaigns, also provided a focal point for anti-integrationist sentiment in the area, according to some long-time Dacula residents. The conflict in the South during the 1950s did not bypass Dacula. Though Marie and Vernon's life was primarily concerned with the pressures and necessities of their daily lives, especially as their young family continued to grow, the emotional and social turmoil related to racial change was not absent from their lives.

10. Baumgartner (1988) argues that the conflict resolution styles of suburban life correspond to moral minimalism, whereby conflicts are resolved through a combination of nonconfrontation and informal social pressure. This example suggests that while nonconfrontation may be typical of suburbs, as is Baumgartner's claim, it is certainly common in other geographical locations and among other populations. Greenhouse (1986) highlights the processes of conflict within a congregation, which she notes in reference to the Baptist church she studied "where neither avoidance or confrontation is feasible, a structural alternative to disputing is brotherhood" (117). Greenhouse notes that brotherhood allows for explanation of offensive behavior within the communal definitions or makes a virtue of ignoring it.

11. Ammerman (1997c) notes that this type of Golden Rule Christianity, described by Todd Penner, includes both tolerance and desire for caring relationships within religious communities.

12. Roof (1993) writes about this phenomenon: "They [baby boomers] want good programs, inspired worship, and meaningful ways of serving their faith. But what does the church offer? All too often, as [one baby boomer pastor] said, 'We stick them on a committee.' Churches and other religious institutions expect them to 'fit in' to existing programs and structures. Consequently, returning boomers often experience a gap between what they are looking for and what is offered to them by organized religion" (184). Though Roof sees this experience as a sign of the lack in many congregations of "any sensitivity to their deeper concerns, or a structure designed to help people to grow spiritually," an equally plausible explanation is that many religious organizations continue to take for granted overlapping networks.

Chapter 6   *Fighting the Good Fight*

1. Clearly some do not take it to be hyperbole. See, for example, Hunter's *Before the Shooting Begins* (1994). Such rhetorical flourish is, in my view, not only unwarranted, but also imprudent. Though it is beyond the scope of this work to do so, one could contend that these debates are kept alive, in part, by continued publication of works arguing that public discourse has ceased or has become inherently uncivil.

2. Various dichotomous theses of contemporary cultural "wars" or bipolar conflicts exist. I will not detail those arguments here. Perhaps the best known and most popularized version of the cultural duality is Hunter's explicit "culture wars" thesis. Hunter (1991) argues that this "war" is about the power to de-

fine reality. He writes: "the power to define reality is not an abstract power. Indeed, as we have seen, nothing less is at stake than a sense of justice and fair play, an assurance that life is as it should be, indeed nothing less is at stake than a way of life. And because the conflict ultimately involves a struggle for power, a variety of other tangible factors are invariably involved, including money (a great deal of it), reputation, livelihood, and a considerable array of other resources" (52–53).

The conflict is over competing visions of the American life, defined by, Hunter argues, two opposing camps, "orthodox" and "progressive." He distinguishes the camps on the issue of moral or cultural authority. The orthodox side adheres to "an external, definable, and transcendent authority" while the progressive side follows "the prevailing assumptions of contemporary life" (1991:44–45). Hunter finds evidence of this polarization across a range of cultural fields, including family, art, education, law, and politics. However, repeatedly in offering evidence of a bifurcated public, Hunter appeals not to everyday folks and local settings, but to reports and stances by such organizations as the National Congregational Council (177), the National Organization of Women (181), Citizens for Excellence in Education (197), and the American Civil Liberties Union (268). What Hunter demonstrates is that special purpose groups have a bipolar conception of American culture. In this he adds little to Wuthnow (1988) who wrote: "like weeds in the sidewalk, the growth of [special purpose] groups may have widened the cracks that only a few decades ago consisted of nothing more than hairline seams" (130). Wuthnow has further contended that evidence of a cultural divide in American culture has depended on media and interest-group accounts. Wuthnow (1988) also traces contemporary religious battles to earlier modernist and fundamentalist tensions (though he also argues that new elements have emerged) and detects two distinct civil religions, one favored by religious conservatives and the other by religious liberals.

3. Cemetery battles were relatively common in Gwinnett County, as they are in many exurban locations (cf. Garreau 1991). In 1991, an article in the "Gwinnett Extra" of the *Atlanta Journal and Constitution*, 3 March, reported that a Gwinnett County jury ordered a Norcross church to pay more than $300,000 to a family whose relatives' graves were bulldozed for a construction project. The controversy over the case resulted in the passage of the Georgia Cemetery Law, which stipulated a five-step process to identify and plan for the preservation or mitigation of a cemetery within a proposed project. In 1992, an article in the *Atlanta Journal and Constitution*, 17 May, reported that extensive grave robbing was occurring in Gwinnett County. Native American burial mounds were particularly vulnerable.

4. Prior to this time, individual burial sites were extremely common in the area, as in much of the country. Butler (1990) notes: "In both urban and rural settings, sanctified graveyards sharply limited the use of individual burial sites, a practice that had been common earlier and, in the southern colonies of the eighteenth century, was a legacy of seventeenth century institutional lethargy" (271). See also Stilgoe (1982:218–241).

5. The letter to the funeral directors stated that Pleasant Hill was a private cemetery operated by the trustees of Hinton Memorial UMC and that burials were restricted and a fee was charged for the "purpose of assuring the perpetual care and maintenance of this historic cemetery." It also noted that the fee payable to the trustees committee must be made prior to interment.

6. Oldtimers at Hinton Memorial queried why the Gwinnett Historical Society insisted on reinterment at Pleasant Hill Cemetery. Reasons given by the Society were several. Pleasant Hill was the closest cemetery to the original site, and it was also the only nearby cemetery that continued to allow burial. The cemetery at Hebron Baptist Church had been closed for several years and was now often used for overflow parking at the megachurch.

7. Getting oldtimers at Hinton Memorial to talk about controversies that existed in the congregation before the 1990 schism was extremely difficult. Although I felt well accepted within the congregation on the whole, I was clearly not to be trusted with the details of those family secrets.

8. Granovetter (1982; 1973) highlights as well how these strong local ties can be ineffective in the contemporary world. He analyzed the contradiction between the closeness of relationships in the Italian community of Boston's West End and the fact that this community was not strong enough to organize against the urban renewal that eventually destroyed it.

9. Garreau (1991) cites the upgrading of satellite airports to operate at commercial capacity as a sure sign of edge city development.

10. Cobb County gained national attention in 1993 when county commissioners passed resolutions highlighting the county's adherence to "family values" and opposition to the "homosexual lifestyle." Commissioners also revoked financial support for a local theater which presented a play with a gay character.

11. According to Grantham (1994), "Lester Maddox had won the governorship in 1966 with a racist and reactionary campaign" (291).

Chapter 7   *Concluding Remarks*

1. Hannan and Freeman (1989) argue that change within population of organizations is best studied by investigating how environmental factors relate to the rate at which new organizations are created, the rate at which existing organizations die, and the rate at which organizations alter their forms. For a helpful overview of recent work in organizational ecology see Singh and Lumsden (1990).

2. Scholars are attending to organizational factors among congregations and other religious groups at the local level. After this text was substantially completed, *Sacred Companies: Organizational Aspects of Religion and Religious Aspects of Organizations* (1998) was released. *Sacred Companies* contains numerous articles that will provide important information for scholars seeking to develop research programs on local community and religious organizational ecologies.

Bibliography

Abbott, Carl. 1990. "New West, New South, New Region: The Discovery of the Sunbelt." Pp. 7–24 in Raymond A. Mohl, ed. *Searching for the Sunbelt: Historical Perspectives on a Region.* Knoxville: University of Tennessee Press.

———. 1987. *The New Urban America: Growth and Politics in Sunbelt Cities.* Chapel Hill: University of North Carolina Press.

Abbott, Phillip. 1987. *Seeking Many Inventions: The Idea of Community in America.* Knoxville: University of Tennessee Press.

Achs, Nicole. 1992. "Exurbia." *American City and County* 107 (7):64–66, 68.

Ammerman, Nancy T. 1997a. *Congregation and Community.* New Brunswick, N.J.: Rutgers University Press.

———. 1997b. "Religious Choice and Religious Vitality." Pp. 119–132 in Lawrence A. Young, ed. *Rational Choice Theory and Religion: Summary and Assessment.* New York: Routledge.

———. 1997c. "Golden Rule Christianity: Lived Religion in the American Mainstream." Pp. 196–216 in David D. Hall, ed. *Lived Religion in America: Toward a History of Practice.* Princeton, N.J.: Princeton University Press.

———. 1994a. "Denominations: Who and What are We Studying?" Pp. 111–133 in R. Bruce Mullin and Russell Richey, eds. *Reimagining Denominationalism: Interpretative Essays.* New York: Oxford University Press.

———. 1994b. "Telling Congregational Stories." The 1993 H. Paul Douglass Lecture, *Review of Religious Research* 35:289–301.

———. 1993a. "SBC Moderates and the Making of a Postmodern Denomination." *The Christian Century* September 22–29, 1993: 896–899.

———. 1993b. Review of *A Bridging of Faiths: Religion and Politics in a New England City. Society* 31 (1):91–93.

———. 1990. *Baptist Battles: Social Change and Religious Conflict in the Southern Baptist Convention.* New Brunswick, N.J.: Rutgers University Press.

———. 1987. *Bible Believers: Fundamentalists in the Modern World.* New Brunswick, N.J.: Rutgers University Press.

Arsenault, Raymond. 1990. "The Air Conditioner and Southern Culture." Pp. 176–211 in Raymond A. Mohl, ed. *Searching for the Sunbelt: Historical Perspectives on a Region.* Knoxville: University of Tennessee Press.

Atlanta Regional Commission. 1994. *Annual Report.* Atlanta, Georgia.

"A United Methodist Evangelist Talks About His Church." 1986. *Good News* 20 (September/October):34–35.

Ayers, Edward L. 1992. *The Promise of the New South: Life after Reconstruction.* New York: Oxford University Press.

Bailey, Wilfred M., and William K. McElvaney. 1970. *Christ's Suburban Body*. Nashville: Abingdon Press.

Baldassare, Mark. 1986. *Trouble in Paradise: The Suburban Transformation of America*. New York: Columbia University Press.

Barlett, Peggy. 1993. *American Dreams, Rural Realities: Family Farms in Crisis*. Chapel Hill: University of North Carolina Press.

Barnett, W.P., and G.R. Carroll. 1987. "Competition and Mutualism among Early Telephone Companies." *Administrative Science Quarterly* 32(3):400–421.

Barthes, Roland. 1986. "Semiology and the Urban." Pp. 87–98 in Mark Gottdiener and Alexandros Lagopoulos, eds. *The City and the Sign*. New York: Columbia University Press.

Bartley, Numan V. 1990. *The Creation of Modern Georgia*. Revised ed. Athens: University of Georgia Press.

Baumgartner, M.P. 1988. *The Moral Order of a Suburb*. New York: Oxford University Press.

Becker, Howard S. 1982. *Art Worlds*. Berkeley: University of California Press.

Becker, Penny E. 1999. *Congregations in Conflict: Cultural Models of Local Religious Life*. New York: Cambridge University Press.

———. 1998. "Congregational Models and Conflict: A Study of How Institutions Shape Organizational Process." Pp. 231–255 in N.J. Demerath, III, Peter Dobkin Hall, Terry Schmitt, and Rhys H. Williams. *Sacred Companies: Organizational Aspects of Religion and Religious Aspects of Organizations*. New York: Oxford University Press.

Becker, Penny E., Stephen J. Ellingson, Richard W. Flory, Wendy Griswold, Fred Kniss, and Timothy Nelson. 1993. "Straining at the Tie That Binds: Congregational Conflict in the 1980s." *Review of Religious Research* 34(3):193–209.

Bell, Michael Mayerfeld. 1994. *Childerley: Nature and Morality in a Country Village*. Chicago: University of Chicago Press.

Bellah, Robert N., Richard Madsen, William Sullivan, Ann Swidler, and Steven M. Tipton. 1991. *The Good Society*. New York: Alfred A. Knopf.

———. 1985. *Habits of the Heart: Individualism and Commitment in American Life*. New York: Harper and Row, Perennial Library

Berger, Bennett. 1971. *Looking for America: Essays on Youth, Suburbia, and Other American Obsessions*. Englewood Cliffs, N.J.: Prentice-Hall.

———. 1960. *Working-Class Suburb: A Study of Auto Workers in Suburbia*. Berkeley: University of California Press.

Bernard, Richard M., and Bradley R. Rice. 1983. *Sunbelt Cities: Politics and Growth Since World War II*. Austin: University of Texas Press.

Berry, Brian, and John D. Kasarda. 1977. *Contemporary Urban Ecology*. New York: Macmillan.

Bradley, Martin B., Norman M. Green, Jr., Dale Jones, Mac Lynn, and Lou McNeil. 1992. *Churches and Church Membership in the United States, 1990*. Atlanta: Glenmary Research Center.

Brint, Steven, and Jerome Karabel. 1991. "Institutional Origins and Transformations: The Case of American Community Colleges." Pp. 337–360 in Walter W. Powell and Paul J. DiMaggio, eds. *The New Institutionalism in Organizational Analysis*. Chicago: University of Chicago Press.

Brittain, Jack, and Douglas Wholey. 1988. "Competition and Coexistence in Organizational Communities: Population Dynamics in Electronic Components Manufacturing." Pp. 195–222 in Glenn R. Carroll, ed. *Ecological Models of Organizations*. Cambridge, Mass.: Ballinger.

Bullard, Robert D., and Joe R. Feagin. 1991. "Racism and the City." in Mark Gottdiener and Chris G. Pickvance, eds. *Urban Life in Transition*. Newbury Park, Calif.: Sage.

Burawoy, Michael. 1991. "The Extended Case Method." Pp. 271–287 in Michael Burawoy, et al. *Ethnography Unbound: Power and Resistance in the Modern Metropolis*. Berkeley: University of California Press.

Butler, Jon. 1990. *Awash in a Sea of Faith: Christianizing the American People*. Cambridge: Harvard University Press.

CACI Marketing Systems. 1998. *The Sourcebook of Zip Code Demographics*. 12th ed. Arlington, Va.: CACI Marketing Systems.

Carroll, Jackson, and Wade Clark Roof, eds. 1993. "Introduction." in Jackson Carroll and Wade Clark Roof, eds. *Beyond Establishment: Protestant Identity in a Post-Protestant Age*. Louisville, Ky.: Westminster/John Knox Press.

Carroll, Jackson, and David A. Roozen. 1975. *Religious Participation in American Society: An Analysis of Social and Religious Trends and Their Interaction*. Hartford, Conn.: Hartford Seminary Foundation.

Chaves, Mark. 1993. "Denominations as Dual Structures: An Organizational Analysis." *Sociology of Religion* (2):147–169.

———. 1991. "Family Structure and Protestant Church Attendance: The Sociological Basis of Cohort and Age Effects." *Journal for the Scientific Study of Religion* 39:329–340.

Clark, Linda J. 1993. "'Songs My Mother Taught Me': Hymns as Transmitters of Faith." Pp. 99–115 in Jackson Carroll and Wade Clark Roof, eds. *Beyond Establishment: Protestant Identity in a Post-Protestant Age*. Louisville, Ky.: Westminster/John Knox Press.

Clark, Willam A.V., and Marianne Kuijpers-Linde. 1994. "Commuting in Restructuring Urban Regions." *Urban Studies* 31:465–483.

Clegg, Stewart. 1990. *Modern Organizations: Organization Studies in the Postmodern World*. London: Sage.

Clifford, James. 1988. *The Predicament of Culture: Twentieth Century Ethnography, Literature and Art*. Cambridge: Harvard University Press.

Coalter, M.J., J.M. Mulder, and L.B. Weeks, eds. 1990. *The Mainstream Protestant "Decline": The Presbyterian Pattern*. Louisville, Ky.: Westminster/John Knox.

Cobb, James C. 1991. "Tomorrow Seems Like Yesterday: The South's Future in the Nation and the World." Pp. 217–237 in Joe P. Dunn and Howard L. Preston, eds. *The Future South: A Historical Perspective for the Twenty-first Century*. Urbana: University of Illinois Press.

Codrescu, Andrei, and David Graham. 1993. *Road Scholar: Coast to Coast Late in the Century*. New York: Hyperion.

Connerton, Paul. 1989. *How Societies Remember*. Cambridge: Cambridge University Press.

Coser, Rose L. 1991. *In Defense of Modernity: Role Complexity and Individual Autonomy*. Stanford, Calif.: Stanford University Press.

Cowdrey, Albert E. 1983. *This Land, This South: An Environmental History*. Lexington: University Press of Kentucky.

Davidman, Lynn. 1991. *Tradition in a Rootless World: Women Turn to Orthodox Judaism*. Berkeley: University of California Press.

Davis, Mike. 1990. *City of Quartz: Excavating the Future in Los Angeles*. New York: Verso.

Demerath, III, N. J., Peter Dobkin Hall, Terry Schmitt, and Rhys H. Williams. 1998. *Sacred Companies: Organizational Aspects of Religion and Religious Aspects of Organizations*. New York: Oxford University Press.

Demerath, III, N.J., and Rhys H. Williams. 1992. *A Bridging of Faiths: Religion and Politics in a New England City*. Princeton, N.J.: Princeton University Press.

DiMaggio, Paul. 1998. "The Relevance of Organization Theory to the Study of Religion." Pp. 7–23 in N.J. Demerath, III, Peter Dobkins Hall, Terry Schmidt, and Rhys H. Williams, eds. *Sacred Companies: Organizational Aspects of Religion and Religious Aspects of Organizations*. New York: Oxford University Press.

DiMaggio, Paul, John Evans, and Bethany Bryson. 1996. "Have Americans' Social Attitudes Become More Polarized?" *American Journal of Sociology* 102:890–955.

DiMaggio, Paul J., and Walter W. Powell. 1991. "The Iron Cage Revisited: Institutional Isomorphism and Collective Rationality in Organization Fields." Pp. 63–82 in Walter W. Powell and Paul J. DiMaggio, eds. *The New Institutionalism in Organizational Analysis*. Chicago: University of Chicago Press.

Dobriner, William N. 1963. *Class in Suburbia*. Englewood Cliffs, N.J.: Prentice-Hall.

Donaldson, Scott. 1969. *The Suburban Myth*. New York: Columbia University Press.

Dudley, Carl S., ed. 1983. *Building Effective Ministry*. Nashville: Abingdon Press.

Ebner, Michael. 1994. "Defining Its Place in the Metropolis: Gwinnett County, 1945–1990." Unpublished paper presented at the annual meetings of the Organization of American Historians, Atlanta, Georgia.

Eiesland, Nancy L. 1997. "Contending with a Giant: The Impact of a Megachurch on Exurban Religious Institutions." Pp. 191–220 in Penny Edgell Becker and Nancy L. Eiesland, eds. *Contemporary American Religion: An Ethnographic Reader*. Walnut Creek, Calif.: AltaMira Press.

———. 1999. "Irreconcilable Differences: Conflict, Schism, and Religious Restructuring in a United Methodist Church." In Edith Blumhofer, Russell Spittler, and Grant Wacker, eds. *Pentecostal Currents in American Protestantism*. Chicago: University of Illinois Press.

Eiesland, Nancy L., and R. Stephen Warner. 1998. "Ecology: Seeing the Congregation in Context." Pp. 40–77 in Nancy T. Ammerman, Jackson Carroll, Carl Dudley, and William McKinney, eds. *Studying Congregations*. Nashville: Abingdon Press.

Emirbayer, Mustafa, and Jeff Goodwin. 1994. "Network Analysis, Culture, and the Problem of Agency." *American Journal of Sociology* 99 (6):1411–1454.

Evans, Alice F., and Robert A. Evans. 1983. "A Church in Transition." Pp. 3–31 in Carl S. Dudley, ed. *Building Effective Ministry*. Nashville: Abingdon.

Fava, Sylvia. 1975. "Beyond Suburbia." *Annals of the American Academy of Political and Social Science* 422:10–24.

Feagin, Joe. 1983. *The Urban Real Estate Game*. Englewood Cliffs, N.J.: Prentice-Hall.

Fetterman, David. 1989. *Ethnography Step by Step*. Newbury Park, Calif.: Sage.

Finke, Roger, and Rodney Stark. 1992. *The Churching of America, 1776–1990: Winners and Losers in Our Religious Economy*. New Brunswick, N.J.: Rutgers University Press.

Finke, Roger. 1989. "Demographics of Religious Participation: An Ecological Approach, 1850–1980." *Journal for the Scientific Study of Religion* (29):45–58.

Fischer, Claude S. 1991. "Ambivalent Communities: How Americans Understand Their Localities." Pp. 79–90 in Alan Wolf, ed. *America at Century's End*. Berkeley: University of California Press.

———. 1982. *To Dwell among Friends: Personal Networks in Town and City*. Chicago: University of Chicago Press.

Fishman, Robert. 1990. "Megalopolis Unbound." *Wilson Quarterly* (winter):25–45

———. 1987. *Bourgeois Utopias: The Rise and Fall of Suburbia.* New York: Basic Books.

Flanigan, James C. 1943. *History of Gwinnett County Georgia, 1881–1943.* Vol. 1. Hapeville, Ga.: Tyler and Company.

———. 1959. *History of Gwinnett County Georgia, 1881–1960.* Vol. 2. Hapeville, Ga.: Longino & Porter, Inc.

Fligstein, Neil. 1991. "The Structural Transformation of American Industry: An Institutional Account of the Causes of Diversification in the Largest Firms, 1919–1979." Pp. 311–336 in Walter W. Powell and Paul J. DiMaggio, eds. *The New Institutionalism in Organizational Analysis.* Chicago: University of Chicago Press.

Flynt, Wayne. 1994. "'A Special Feeling of Closeness': Mt. Hebron Baptist Church, Leeds, Alabama." Pp. 103–158 in James Wind and James Lewis, eds. *American Congregations: New Perspectives in the Study of Congregations.* Vol. 1. Chicago: University of Chicago Press.

Fraser, Nancy. 1990. "Rethinking the Public Sphere: A Contribution to the Critique of Actually Existing Democracy." *Social Text* 25/26:56–80.

Freeman, John, Glenn R. Carroll, and Michael T. Hannan. 1983. "The Liability of Newness: Age Dependence in Organizational Death Rates." *American Sociological Review* 48:692–710.

Freeman, John, and Michael T. Hannan. 1983. "Niche Width and the Dynamics of Organizational Populations." *American Journal of Sociology* 88:1116–1145.

Friedland, Roger, and Robert Alford. 1991. "Bringing Society Back In: Symbols Practices and Institutional Contradictions." Pp. 232–263 in Walter W. Powell and Paul J. DiMaggio, *The Institutionalism in Organizational Analysis.* Chicago: University of Chicago Press.

Gans, Herbert. 1967. *The Levittowners: Ways of Life and Politics in a New Suburban Community.* New York: Pantheon Books.

Garreau, Joel. 1991. *Edge City: Life on the New Frontier.* New York: Doubleday.

Geertz, Clifford. 1983. *Local Knowledge: Further Essays in Interpretive Anthropology.* New York: Basic Books.

Georgia Department of Education. 1994. *Annual Report on Educational Advancement.* State Printing Office.

Giddens, Anthony. 1991. *Modernity and Self-Identity: Self and Society in the Late Modern Age.* Stanford: Stanford University Press.

Ginsburg, Faye D. 1989. *Contested Lives: The Abortion Debate in an American Community.* Berkeley: University of California Press.

Glaser, Barney, and Anselm Strauss. 1967. *The Discovery of Grounded Theory: Strategies for Qualitative Research.* Chicago: Aldine.

Glazer, Nathan, and Patrick Moynihan. 1963. *Beyond the Melting Pot.* Cambridge: MIT Press.

Goldfield, David R. 1991. "The City as Southern History: The Past and the Promise of Tomorrow." Pp. 11–48 in Joe P. Dunn and Howard L. Preston, eds. *The Future South: A Historical Perspective for the Twenty-first Century.* Urbana: University of Illinois Press.

Goldfield, David R., and Howard N. Rabinowitz. 1990. "The Vanishing South." Pp. 224–233 in Raymond A. Mohl, ed. *Searching for the Sunbelt: Historical Perspectives on a Region.* Knoxville: University of Tennessee Press.

Gordon, Milton M. 1964. *Assimilation in American Life: The Role of Race, Religion, and National Origins.* New York: Oxford University Press.

Gottdiener, Mark. 1994. *The New Urban Sociology*. New York: McGraw-Hill.

———. 1985. *The Social Production of Urban Space*. Austin: University of Texas Press.

Gottdiener, Mark, and George Kephart. 1991. "The Multinucleated Metropolitan Region: A Comparative Analysis." In Rob Kling, Spencer Olin, and Mark Poster, eds. *Postsuburban California: The Transformation of Orange County since World War II*. Berkeley: University of California Press.

Granovetter, Mark. 1982. "The Strength of Weak Ties: A Network Theory Revisited." In Peter V. Marsden and Nan Lin, eds. *Social Structure and Network Analysis*. Beverly Hills, Calif.: Sage Publications.

———. 1973. "The Strength of Weak Ties." *American Journal of Sociology* 78:1360–1380.

Grantham, Dewey W.1994. *The South in Modern America: A Region at Odds*. New York: HarperCollins.

Greenhouse, Carol J. 1986. *Praying for Justice: Faith, Order, and Community in an American Town*. Ithaca, N.Y.: Cornell University Press.

Griffith, R. Marie. 1997. *God's Daughters: Evangelical Women and the Power of Submission*. Berkeley: University of California Press.

Gwinnett County Planning and Development Department. 1992. *Gwinnett 2000 Land Use Plan*.

Gwinnett Post-Tribune. 1992–1995

Hadaway, C. Kirk. 1993. "Church Growth in North America: The Character of a Religious Marketplace." Pp. 346–357 in David A. Roozen and C. Kirk Hadaway, eds., *Church and Denominational Growth*. Nashville: Abingdon Press.

Hadaway, C. Kirk, and David A. Roozen. 1993. "Denominational Growth and Decline." Pp. 37–46 in David A. Roozen and C. Kirk Hadaway, eds. *Church and Denominational Growth*. Nashville: Abingdon Press.

Hadden, Jeffrey K. 1969. *The Gathering Storm in the Churches*. Garden City, N.Y.: Doubleday.

Haga, William J., and Clinton L. Folse. 1971. "Trade Patterns and Community Identity." *Rural Sociology* 6:42–51.

Hamblen, Matt. 1992. "Frontierland." *Planning* 58(4):16–21.

Hammond, Phillip E. 1992. *Religion and Personal Autonomy: The Third Disestablishment in America*. Columbia: University of South Carolina Press.

Hannan, Michael T., and John Freeman. 1989. *Organizational Ecology*. Cambridge: Harvard University Press.

———. 1977. "The Population Ecology of Organizations." *American Journal of Sociology* 82:929–964.

Hannerz, Ulf. 1980. *Exploring the City*. New York: Columbia University Press.

Harrison, Michael I., and John K. Maniha. 1978. "Dynamics of Dissenting Movements within Established Organizations: Two Cases and a Theoretical Interpretation." *Journal for the Scientific Study of Religion* 17:207–224.

Hartshorn, Truman A. 1976. *Metropolis in Georgia: Atlanta's Rise as a Major Transaction Center*. Cambridge, Mass.: Ballinger Publishing Company.

Hassard, John, and Martin Parker, eds. 1993. *Postmodernism and Organizations*. Newbury Park, Calif.: Sage Publications.

Hawley, Amos. 1981. *Urban Society: An Ecological Approach*. 2d ed. New York: J. Wiley and Sons.

Heenan, David A. 1991. *The New Corporate Frontier: The Big Move to Small Town USA*. New York: McGraw Hill.

Hepburn, Lawrence R, ed. 1992. *Contemporary Georgia*. 2d ed. Athens, Ga.: Carl Vinson Institute of Government.

Herberg, Will. 1960. *Protestant, Catholic, Jew.* 2d ed. Garden City, N.Y.: Anchor Books.

Hill, R.C., and M. Levenhagen. 1994. "Metaphors and Mental Models: Sensemaking and Sensegiving in Innovative and Entrepreneurial Activities." *Journal of Management 21(6):1057–1074.*

Hise, Greg. 1993. "Home Building and Industrial Decentralization in Los Angeles: The Roots of the Postwar Urban Region." *Journal of Urban History* 19:95–125.

Hobsbawm, Eric J. 1983. "Introduction: Inventing Tradition." Pp. 1–14 in Eric J. Hobsbawm and Terence O. Ranger, eds. *The Invention of Tradition.* Cambridge: Cambridge University Press.

Hochschild, Arlie, and Ann Machung. 1989. *The Second Shift.* New York: Viking Press.

Hoge, Dean R., Benton Johnson, and Donald A. Luidens. 1994. *Vanishing Boundaries: The Religion of Mainline Protestant Baby Boomers.* Louisville, Ky.: Westminster/John Knox Press.

Hoge, Dean R., and David A. Roozen. 1979. "Some Sociological Conclusions about Church Trends." in Dean R. Hoge and David A. Roozen, eds. *Understanding Church Growth and Decline: 1950–1978.* New York: Pilgrim Press.

Hudnut-Beumler, James. 1994. *Looking for God in the Suburbs: The Religion of the American Dream and its Critics, 1945–1965.* New Brunswick, N.J.: Rutgers University Press.

Hunter, James Davison. 1994. *Before the Shooting Begins: Searching for Democracy in America's Culture War.* New York: Free Press.

———. 1991. *Culture Wars: The Struggle to Define America.* New York: Basic Books.

Iannaccone, Laurence R. 1994. "Why Strict Churches are Strong." *American Journal of Sociology* 99:1180–1211.

———. 1991. "The Consequences of Religious Market Structure." *Rationality and Society* 3 (April):156–177.

———. 1990 "Religious Practice: A Human Capital Approach." *Journal for the Scientific Study of Religion* 29(3):297–314.

Jackson, Kenneth. 1985. *Crabgrass Frontier: The Suburbanization of the United States.* New York: Oxford University Press.

Johnson, Douglas, Paul R. Picard, and Bernard Quinn. 1974. *Churches and Church Membership in the United States, 1971.* Washington, D.C.: Glenmary Research Center.

Jorgensen, Danny. 1989. *Participant Observation: A Methodology for Human Studies.* Newbury Park, Calif.: Sage Publications.

Karesek, Robert, and Töres Theorel. 1990. *Healthy Work: Stress Productivity and the Reconstruction of Working Life.* New York: Basic Books.

Kaufman, Debra. 1991. *Rachel's Daughters.* New Brunswick, N.J.: Rutgers University Press.

Kelly, Barbara M., ed. 1989. *Suburbia Re-examined.* New York: Greenwood Press.

Kephart, George. 1991. "Economic Restructuring, Population Redistribution, and Migration in the United States." In Mark Gottdiener and C. G. Pickvance, eds. *Urban Life in Transition.* Newbury Park, Calif.: Sage Publications.

Kling, Rob, Spencer Olin, and Mark Poster. 1991. "The Emergence of Postsuburbia: An Introduction." In Rob Kling, Spencer Olin, and Mark Poster, eds. *Postsuburban California: The Transformation of Orange County since World War II.* Berkeley: University of California Press.

Kowinski, William S. 1985. *The Malling of America.* New York: William Morrow and Company, Inc.

Kunster, James H. 1993. *The Geography of Nowhere: The Rise and Decline of America's Man-Made Landscape.* New York: Simon and Schuster.

LeFevre, Perry D., ed. 1975. *Conflict in a Voluntary Association: A Case Study of a Classic Suburban Church Fight.* Chicago: Exploration Press.

Liebman, Robert C., John R. Sutton, and Robert Wuthnow. 1988. "Exploring the Social Sources of Denominationalism: Schisms in American Protestant Denominations, 1890–1980." *American Sociological Review* 53:343–352.

Lieberson, Stanley. 1980. *A Piece of the Pie: Black and White Immigrants since 1880.* Berkeley: University of California Press.

Lieberson, Stanley, and Mary C. Waters. 1988. *From Many Strands: Ethnic and Racial Groups in Contemporary America.* New York: Russell Sage.

Lynd, Robert S., and Helen Merrell Lynd. 1956. *Middletown: A Study in American Culture.* New York: Harcourt, Brace, Jovanovich.

Lyson, Thomas A. 1989. *Two Sides to the Sunbelt: The Growing Divergence Between the Rural and Urban South.* New York: Praeger.

McConaghy, Lorraine. 1993. "No Ordinary Place: Three Postwar Suburbs and their Critics." Unpublished doctoral dissertation. University of Washington.

McDowell, Bruce. 1990. *The Privatization of Metropolitan America.* Washington, D.C.: U.S. Advisory Commission on Intergovernmental Affairs.

Marler, Penny L., and David A. Roozen. 1993. "From Church Tradition to Consumer Choice: The Gallup Surveys of the Unchurched American." Pp. 253–277 in David A. Roozen and C. Kirk Hadaway, eds. *Church and Denominational Growth.* Nashville, Tenn.: Abingdon Press.

Marsh, Margaret. 1990. *Suburban Lives.* New Brunswick, N.J.: Rutgers University Press.

Mediamark Research. 1991–1992. "Gwinnett." Unpublished report.

Meyer, John W., and W. Richard Scott. 1983. *Organizational Environments: Ritual and Rationality.* Beverly Hills, Calif.: Sage Publications.

Miller, Donald E. 1997. *Reinventing American Protestantism: Christianity in the New Millenium.* Berkeley: University of California Press.

———.1993. "Postmodern Characteristics of Three Rapidly Growing Religious Movements: Calvary Chapel, the Vineyard Christian Fellowship, and Hope Chapel." Unpublished paper, presented at annual meetings of the Society for the Scientific Study of Religion, Raleigh, N.C.

Miller, Randall M., and George E. Pozzeta, eds. 1988. *Shades of the Sunbelt: Essays on Ethnicity, Race and the Urban South.* New York: Greenwood.

Mora, Pat. 1993. *Nepantla: Essays from the Land in the Middle.* Albuquerque: University of New Mexico Press.

Morawska, Ewa. 1990. "The Sociology and Historiography of Immigration." In Virginia Yans-McLaughlin, ed. *Immigration Reconsidered: History, Sociology and Politics.* New York: Oxford University Press.

Mumford, Lewis. 1924. "The Wilderness of Suburbia." *New Republic* 21 (September 7).

Neitz, Mary Jo. 1987. *Charisma and Community.* New Brunswick, N.J.: Transaction Books.

Neitz, Mary Jo, and Peter R. Mueser. 1997. "Economic Man and the Sociology of Religion: A Critique of the Rational Choice Approach." Pp. 105–118 in Lawrence A. Young, ed. *Rational Choice Theory and Religion: Summary and Assessment.* New York: Routledge.

Nelson, Arthur C. 1988. "An Empirical Note on How Regional Urban Containment Policy Influences an Interaction between Greenbelt and Exurban Land Markets." *American Planning Association Journal* 54 (2):178–184.

Neville, Gwen. 1987. *Kinship and Pilgrimage: Rituals of Reunion in American Protestant Culture*. New York: Oxford University Press.

Oldenberg, Ray. 1989. *The Great Good Place*. New York: Paragon Books.

Olson, Daniel V.A. 1993. "Fellowship Ties and the Transmission of Religious Identity." Pp. 32–53 in Jackson Carroll and Wade Clark Roof, eds. *Beyond Establishment: Protestant Identity in a Post-Protestant Age*. Louisville, Ky.: Westminster/John Knox Press.

———. 1989. "Church Friendships: Boon or Barrier to Church Growth?" *Journal for the Scientific Study of Religion* 28(4):432–447.

Olson, Richard. 1988. *The Largest Congregations in the United States: An Empirical Study of Church Growth and Decline*. Ann Arbor, Mich.: University Microfilms.

Orum, Anthony M., and Joe R. Feagin. 1991. "A Tale of Two Case Studies." In Joe Feagin, Anthony Orum, and Gideon Sjoberg, eds. *A Case for the Case Study*. Chapel Hill: University of North Carolina Press.

Park, Robert E., and Ernest W. Burgess. 1969. Revised ed. *Introduction to the Science of Sociology*. Chicago: University of Chicago Press.

Perin, Constance. 1977. *Everything in Its Place: Social Order and Land Use in America*. Princeton, N.J.: Princeton University Press.

Pope, Liston. 1942. *Millhands and Preachers*. New Haven: Yale University Press.

Powter, Susan. 1993. *Stop the Insanity!* New York: Simon and Schuster.

Quinn, Bernard, Herman Anderson, Martin Bradley, Paul Goetting, and Peggy Shriver. 1982. *Churches and Church Membership in the United States, 1980*. Atlanta: Glenmary Research Center.

Reed, John Shelton. 1986. *The Enduring South: Subcultural Persistence in Mass Society*. Chapel Hill: University of North Carolina Press.

Robertson, Roland. 1992. *Globalization: Social Theory and Global Culture*. Newbury Park, Calif.: Sage Publications.

———. 1991a. "The Globalization Paradigm: Thinking Globally." *Religion and Social Order* 1:207–224.

———. 1991b. "Globalization, Modernization & Postmodernization: The Ambiguous Position of Religion." In Roland Robertson and William R. Garrett, eds. *Religion and Global Order*. New York: Paragon House Publishers.

———. 1990. "Mapping the Global Condition: Globalization as the Central Concept." *Theory, Culture & Society* 7:15–30.

Roof, Wade Clark. 1993. *A Generation of Seekers: The Spiritual Journeys of the Baby-Boom Generation*. San Francisco: HarperSanFrancisco.

———. 1978. *Community and Commitment*. New York: Elsevier.

———. 1976. "Traditional Religion in Contemporary Society: A Theory of Local-Cosmopolitan Plausibility." *American Sociological Review* 41(2):195–208.

Roof, Wade Clark, and William McKinney. 1987. *American Mainline Religion*. New Brunswick, N.J.: Rutgers University Press.

Roozen, David A. 1993. "Denominations Grow as Individuals Join Congregations." Pp. 15–35 in David A. Roozen and C. Kirk Hadaway, eds., *Church and Denominational Growth*. Nashville, Tenn.: Abingdon Press.

Roozen, David A., William McKinney, and Jackson Carroll. 1984. *Varieties of Religious Presence: Mission in Public Life*. New York: Pilgrim Press.

Roozen, David A., William McKinney, and Wayne Thompson. 1990. "The Big Chill Generation Warms to Worship." *Review of Religious Research* 31:314–322.

Schaller, Lyle E. 1992. *The Seven-Day-a-Week Church*. Nashville, Tenn.: Abingdon Press.

———. 1990. "Megachurch!" *Christianity Today* (March 5):20–24

Schor, Juliet. 1991. *The Overworked American: The Unexpected Decline of Leisure.* New York: Basic Books.

Schroeder, W. Widick, Victor Obenhaus, Larry A. Jones, and Thomas Sweetser, S. J. 1974. *Suburban Religion: Churches and Synagogues in the American Experience.* Chicago: Center for the Scientific Study of Religion.

Schulman, Bruce J. 1991. *From Cotton Belt to Sunbelt: Federal Policy, Economic Development, and the Transformation of the South, 1938–1980.* New York: Oxford University Press.

Sharpe, William, and Leonard Wallock. 1994. "Bold New City or Built-up 'Burb: Redefining Contemporary Suburbia." *American Quarterly* 46:1–61

Shibley, Mark. 1996. *Resurgent Evangelicalism in the United States: Mapping Cultural Change since 1970.* Columbia: University of South Carolina Press.

Singh, Jitendra, and Charles J. Lumsden. 1990. "Theory and Research in Organizational Ecology." *Annual Review of Sociology* 16:161–199.

Singh, Jitendra, David Tucker, and Agnes Meinhard. 1991. "Institutional Change and Ecological Dynamics." Pp. 390–422 in Walter W. Powell and Paul J. DiMaggio, eds. *The New Institutionalism in Organizational Analysis.* Chicago: University of Chicago Press.

Slater, Nelle G., ed. 1989. *Tensions between Citizenship and Discipleship: A Case Study.* New York: Pilgrim Press.

Smith, David H. 1992. "A Neglected Type of Voluntary Nonprofit Organization: Exploration of the Semiformal, Fluid-Membership Organization" *Nonprofit and Voluntary Sector Quarterly* 21 (3):251–269.

Sowell, Thomas. 1981. *Ethnic America.* New York: Basic Books.

Spectorsky, A. C. 1957. *The Exurbanites.* New York: Berkley.

Stacey, Judith. 1990. *Brave New Families: Stories of Domestic Upheaval in Late Twentieth Century America.* New York: Basic Books.

Stanback, Jr., Thomas M. 1991. *The New Suburbanization: Challenge to the Central City.* Boulder: Westview Press.

Stilgoe, John R. 1988. *Borderland: Origins of the American Suburb, 1820–1939.* New Haven: Yale University Press.

———. 1982. *Common Landscape in America, 1580–1845.* New Haven: Yale University Press.

Stolzenberg, Ross M., Mary Blair-Loy, and Linda J. Waite. 1995. "Religious Participation in Early Adulthood: Age and Family Life Cycle Effects on Church Membership." *American Sociological Review* 60:84–103.

Stone, Clarence N. 1989. *Regime Politics: Governing Atlanta, 1946–1988.* Lawrence: University of Kansas Press.

Strauss, Anselm. 1978. *Negotiations: Varieties, Contexts, Processes, and Social Order.* San Francisco: Jossey-Bass.

Strauss, Anselm, and Juliet Corbin. 1994. "Grounded Theory Methodology: An Overview." Pp. 273–285 in Norman K. Denzin and Yvonne S. Lincoln, eds. *Handbook of Qualitative Research.* Thousand Oaks, Calif.: Sage Publications.

Swatos, William. 1981. "Beyond Denominationalism?: Community and Culture in American Religion." *Journal for the Scientific Study of Religion* 20:217–227.

Swidler, Ann. 1986. "Culture in Action: Symbols and Strategies." *American Sociological Review* 51:273–286.

Takaki, Ronald. 1993. *A Different Mirror: A History of Multicultural America.* Boston: Little, Brown and Company.

Teaford, Jon C. 1993. *The Twentieth-Century American City.* 2d ed. Baltimore: Johns Hopkins University Press.

————. 1997. *Post-Suburbia: Government and Politics in the Edge Cities*. Baltimore: Johns Hopkins University Press.

Thumma, Scott L. 1996. "The Kingdom, the Power, and the Glory: The Megachurch in Modern American Society." Unpublished dissertation. Emory University, Graduate Division of Religion.

————. 1993. "Sketching a Mega-Trend: The Phenomenal Proliferation of Very Large Churches in the United States." Unpublished paper, presented at the annual meeting of the Association for the Sociology of Religion, Miami, Fla.

Tipton, Steven M. 1982. *Getting Saved from the Sixties*. Berkeley: University of California Press.

Tittle, Charles R., and Mark C. Stafford. 1992. "Urban Theory, Urbanism, and Suburban Residence." *Social Forces* 70 (3):725–744.

Trefil, James S. 1994. *A Scientist in the City*. New York: Doubleday.

U.S. Bureau of the Census. 1990. *Social and Economic Characteristics, 1990*. U.S. Printing Office.

————. 1990. *Census of Population and Housing, 1990*. U.S. Printing Office.

————. 1990. *General Population Characteristics: Georgia*. U.S. Printing Office.

————. 1990. *State and Metropolitan Area Data Book, 1991*. U.S. Printing Office.

————. 1986. *State and Metropolitan Area Data Book, 1986*. U.S. Printing Office.

————. 1970. *Census of Population and Housing, 1970*. U.S. Printing Office.

————. 1830–1980. *General Population Characteristics: Georgia*. U.S. Printing Office.

Vance, James E. 1964. *Geography and Urban Evolution in the San Francisco Bay Area*. Berkeley: University of California Press.

VanMaanen, John. 1988. *Tales of the Field: On Writing Ethnography*. Chicago: University of Chicago Press.

Vaughan, John N. 1993. *Megachurches and America's Cities: How Churches Grow*. Grand Rapids, Mich.: Baker Books.

Vidich, Arthur J., and Joseph Bensman. 1958. *Small Town in Mass Society*. Revised ed. Princeton, N. J.: Princeton University Press.

Warner, R. Stephen. 1997. "Convergence Toward the New Paradigm: A Case of Induction." Pp.87–101 in Lawrence Young, ed. *Rational Choice Theory and Religion: Summary and Assessment*. New York: Routledge.

————.1994. "The Place of the Congregation in the Contemporary American Religious Configuration." Pp. 54–99 in James Wind and James Lewis, eds. *American Congregations: New Perspectives in the Study of Congregations*. Vol. 2. Chicago: University of Chicago Press.

————. 1993. "Work in Progress toward a New Paradigm for the Sociological Study of Religion in the United States." *American Journal of Sociology* 98 (5):1044–1093.

————. 1991. "Oenology: The Making of New Wine." In Joe Feagin, Anthony Orum and Gideon Sjoberg, eds. *A Case for the Case Study*. Chapel Hill: University of North Carolina Press.

————. 1988. *New Wine in Old Wineskins: Evangelicals and Liberals in a Small-town Church*. Berkeley: University of California Press.

Waters, Mary C. 1990. *Ethnic Options: Choosing Identities in America*. Berkeley: University of California Press.

Watson, Justin. 1997. *The Christian Coalition: Dreams for Restoration, Demands for Recognition*. New York: St. Martins Press.

Watson, Sophie, and Katherine Gibson, eds. 1995. *Postmodern Cities and Spaces*. Cambridge, Mass.: Blackwell Publishers.

Weber, Max. 1922/1958. *The City*. Don Martindale and Gertrud Neuworth, trans. Glencoe, Ill.: Free Press.

————. 1922/1964. *The Sociology of Religion*. Ephraim Fischoff, trans. Boston: Beacon Press.

————. 1923/1968. *Economy and Society*. Edward A. Schils and Max Rheinstein, trans. Cambridge: Harvard University Press.

Wellman, Barry, and Barry Leighton. 1979. "Networks, Neighborhoods, and Communities: Approaches to the Study of the Community Question." *Urban Affairs Quarterly* 14:363–390.

Whyte, William H. 1988. *City: Rediscovering the Center*. New York: Doubleday.

————. 1956. *The Organization Man*. New York: Simon and Schuster.

Wilkenson, Rupert. 1988. *The Pursuit of American Character*. New York: Harper & Row.

Winter, Gibson. 1961. *The Suburban Captivity of the Churches: An Analysis of Protestant Responsibility in the Expanding Metropolis*. New York: Doubleday.

Wolf, Margery. 1992. *A Thrice Told Tale: Feminism, Postmodernism, and Ethnographic Responsibility*. Stanford, Calif.: Stanford University Press.

Wood, James R. 1981. *Leadership in Voluntary Organizations: The Controversy over Social Action in Protestant Churches*. New Brunswick, N.J.: Rutgers University Press.

Worthy, Marvin N. 1994. *The History of Gwinnett County Georgia, 1818–1993*. Lawrenceville, Ga : Board of Commissioners of Gwinnett County

Wuthnow, Robert. 1998. *Loose Connections: Joining Together in America's Fragmented Communities*. Cambridge: Harvard University Press.

————. 1994a. *Producing the Sacred: An Essay on Public Religion*. Urbana: University of Illinois Press.

————. 1994b. *Sharing the Journey: Support Groups and America's New Quest for Community*. New York: Free Press.

————. 1988. *The Restructuring of American Religion: Society and Faith since World War II*. Princeton, N.J.: University Press.

Wuthnow, Robert, and Kevin Princeton Christiano. 1979. "The Effects of Residential Migration on Church Attendance in the United States." In Robert Wuthnow, ed. *The Religious Dimension: New Directions in Quantitative Research*. New York: Academic Press.

Index

About the Author

Nancy L. Eiesland is assistant professor of sociology of religion at the Candler School of Theology and the Graduate Division of Religion of Emory University in Atlanta. She coedited (with Penny Edgell Becker) *Contemporary American Religion: An Ethnographic Reader* (1997). She has authored numerous articles, chapters, and books on such topics as urban and religious change, gender and religion, and disability studies in religion.